Social Interaction and English Language Teacher Identity

Studies in Social Interaction
Series Editors: Steve Walsh, Paul Seedhouse and Christopher Jenks

Presenting data from a range of social contexts including education, the media, the workplace, and professional development, the *Studies in Social Interaction* series uncovers, among other things, the ways in which tasks are accomplished, identities formed and communities established. Each volume in the series places social interaction at the centre of discussion and presents a clear overview of the work which has been done in a particular context. Books in the series provide examples of how data can be approached and used to uncover social-interaction themes and issues, and explore how research in social interaction can feed into a better understanding of professional practices and develop new research agendas. Through stimulating tasks and accompanying commentaries, readers are engaged and challenged to reflect on particular themes and relate the discussion to their own context.

Series Editors
Steve Walsh is Professor of Applied Linguistics at Newcastle University

Paul Seedhouse is Professor of Educational and Applied Linguistics at Newcastle University

Christopher Jenks is Assistant Professor of English and Intensive English/TESOL Coordinator at the University of South Dakota

Titles available in the series:

Visit the Studies in Social Interaction website at
http://www.euppublishing.com/series/ssint

Social Interaction and English Language Teacher Identity

John Gray and Tom Morton

EDINBURGH
University Press

Edinburgh University Press is one of the leading university presses in the UK. We publish academic books and journals in our selected subject areas across the humanities and social sciences, combining cutting-edge scholarship with high editorial and production values to produce academic works of lasting importance. For more information visit our website: edinburghuniversitypress.com

Edinburgh University Press Ltd
The Tun – Holyrood Road
12(2f) Jackson's Entry
Edinburgh EH8 8PJ

Typeset in 10/12 Minion by
Servis Filmsetting Ltd, Stockport, Cheshire,
and printed and bound in Great Britain

A CIP record for this book is available from the British Library

ISBN 978-0-7486-5610-3 (hardback)
ISBN 978-0-7486-5611-0 (paperback)
ISBN 978-0-7486-5612-7 (webready pdf)
ISBN 978-0-7486-5614-1 (epub)

CONTENTS

ACKNOWLEDGEMENTS

The gestation of this book has been lengthy. We've discussed it for hours in Madrid, in our offices at Birkbeck and the UCL Institute of Education, over coffees in Gordon Square and lunches in Bloomsbury, on WhatsApp and via Skype for at least the last five years. Frustratingly, at various times our work commitments have taken us away from it and on occasion the project seemed to be on the verge of collapse. That didn't happen, thanks in large part to the constant encouragement of Steve Walsh and the patience of Edinburgh University Press – as well as our own belief that there *was* a book to be written on English language teacher identity in which social interaction was foregrounded.

In addition to thanking Steve and Edinburgh University Press, we would also like to thank the numerous friends, colleagues and students who read chapters or parts of chapters and commented and made helpful suggestions – Mike Baynham, David Block, Emma Brooks, Mel Cooke, Marnie Holborow, Chris Jenks, Miguel Pérez-Milans, Tabitha Millett, John O'Regan, Sian Preece, Olcay Sert, Will Simpson and Scott Thornbury. We are indebted to all of them. We would also like to thank the MA students who took the 2016–17 iteration of John's module, *Language Teacher Identity and Development*, for their critical engagement with many of the chapters, as well as Bloodaxe Books for granting permission to reproduce the poem by Jackie Kay. A special 'thank you' is reserved for David Block, who generously read all the chapters and acted as a critical friend throughout.

INTRODUCTION

In my country
walking by the waters,
down where an honest river
shakes hands with the sea,
a woman passed around me
in a slow, watchful circle,
as if I were a superstition;

or the worst dregs of her imagination,
so when she finally spoke
her words spliced into bars
of an old wheel. A segment of air.
Where do you come from?
'Here,' I said, 'Here. These parts.'

Jackie Kay (1993)

THE RISE OF TEACHER IDENTITY

The Scottish poet Jackie Kay describes how she was moved to write these lines as a result of repeatedly being taken for a foreigner in her own country. As a black woman, her skin colour marked her out as someone who was frequently perceived as being alien, requiring her on occasion to give an account of herself to strangers. Such incidents are not uncommon in a globalised world (Zhu and Li 2016) where people who are phenotypically, culturally, ethnically and religiously different – the list could go on – are, if not living cheek by jowl, then at least coming into contact with one another, and frequently in settings where anxiety about foreigners and those perceived to be different is often prevalent. But such acts of identity (and for many scholars that is how Kay's assertion is to be understood) are not only triggered by questions about where we are from but also they are part and parcel of living and working in highly bureau-cratised societies where we are all repeatedly required to say who we are (Blommaert 2005; Joseph 2004). We do this in emails, on the telephone, at meetings, in job inter-views, and in the many other kinds of interactions we engage in outside our working lives, where contextually relevant aspects of ourselves are signalled in a multitude of ways. Reflecting on this ongoing identity activity, Blommaert (2005: 204) states:

Such acts are of tremendous complexity, for they involve a wide variety of situating processes: situating the individual in relation to several layers of (real, sociological) 'groupness' and (socially constructed) 'categories' (age, category, sex, professional category, but also national, cultural, and ethnolinguistic categories), situating this complex in turn in relation to other such complexes (young versus old, male versus female, highly educated versus less educated, and so on), and situating this identification in relation to the situation at hand, making selections that result in 'relevant' identity.

It is little wonder, then, that identity, as the superordinate term for all such activity in which we situate ourselves as certain kinds of people (both as individuals and as members of collectives) and the ways in which we position others (also individually and collectively) and are in turn positioned by them, has become a key term in a range of disciplines across the social sciences. This is evidenced by the proliferation of journal titles – a small selection of which include *African Identities*; *Identity: An International Journal of Theory and Research*; *Self and Identity*; *Journal of Identity and Migration Studies*; *Journal of Language, Identity & Education*; *Journal of Religion, Identity, and Politics*; *National Identities*; *Social Identities* – to say nothing of the multitude of books (including this one) with the word *identity* in the title. It has been calculated that publications in English listing *identity* as a keyword increased from just a few hundred per decade in the mid-twentieth century to tens of thousands per decade by the early twenty-first century (Côté 2006). This salience in the social sciences was mirrored in the late 1990s and early years of the current century in applied linguistics (for example, Benwell and Stokoe 2006; Block 2007; Edwards 2009; Norton 1997, 2000, 2010; Norton Pierce 1995) and in the more specific literature on second language education (for example, Barkhuizen 2010; Block 2015; Clarke 2008; Duff and Uchida 1997; Kamhi-Stein 2013; Kanno and Stuart 2011; Mayer 1999; Nagatomo 2012; Richards 2006; Varghese et al. 2005). That applied linguists should be interested in identity is hardly surprising, given that language is seen as one of several key semiotic resources drawn on in the production of identity. Nor is it surprising that researchers in the field of second language teacher education are also interested, given that, as Block (2015: 13) points out:

> [Language teachers have] an occupational identity, and specifically a language teaching identity. Such an identity may be defined in terms of how individuals, who both self-position and are positioned by others as teachers, affiliate to different aspects of teaching in their lives. Thus identity is related to factors such as one's ongoing contacts with fellow teachers and students as well as the tasks that one engages in, which can be said to constitute teaching.

This book is about English language teacher identity and in it we take the view that the process of becoming an English language teacher and the experience of working as one repeatedly raise issues of identity which are in need of exploration – particularly so at the present moment when English language teaching (ELT) is becoming ever more firmly imbricated in a complex set of marketised global educational processes

(Ball 2012). These processes combine to involve English language teachers (and indeed all teachers) in structures – institutional, national and international – which are not of their making but within which they have to negotiate their professional identities in ways which are congruent not only with structural demands, but also with their own already existing gendered, classed, raced and other identities and their own beliefs about teaching and learning.

Writing in 2009, Miller suggested that, as an area of inquiry, language teacher identity represented an emerging field. As this volume goes to press (winter 2017/18), her prediction has been shown to be prescient. In addition to the references listed above, two edited books – *Advances and Current Trends in Language Teacher Identity Research* by Cheung, Ben Said and Park (2015) and *Reflections on Language Teacher Identity Research* by Barkhuizen (2017a) – as well as a special issue of *TESOL Quarterly* edited by Varghese, Motha, Park, Reeves and Trent (2016) and another of *The Modern Language Journal* edited by De Costa and Norton (2017) are a clear indication of the vitality of research on language teacher identity. Taken together with earlier work, they provide a snapshot of how the field has developed while simultaneously signalling the kind of work that remains to be done. In line with Miller's assessment, we take the view that researching and theorising language teacher thinking, cognition, beliefs and development cannot easily be undertaken without due consideration of language teacher identity. In fact, the latter may be said to have moved centre-stage in work on second language teacher education. As Miller (2009: 175) puts it, '[w]hat teachers know and do is part of their identity work, which is continuously performed and transformed though interaction in classrooms.' To this we would add, and as we will show in the chapters which follow, identity work is not solely a feature of classroom interaction, but also of interaction in teacher education courses, group discussions and research interviews of various kinds.

In this turn to language teacher identity, the editors of the *TESOL Quarterly* special issue draw attention to a paradox we consider to be important for the field. They state:

> The research in language teacher identity builds partially upon a tradition of teacher identity research in the broader discipline of mainstream teacher education, which predicates itself on a particular understanding of teaching and teacher education. One significant proposition is that who teachers are and what they bring with them, individually and collectively, matters in what and how they teach and thus, to students, families, communities, and institutions (Varghese et al. 2016: 548).

However, and this is where the paradox arises, they go on to point out that just as second language teacher education began to engage seriously with the concept of teacher identity in the first decade of the twenty-first century, the concept had already

> lost some of its purchase in mainstream teacher education because of growing attention to standardization and accountability, leading to what may seem like an

exclusive focus on pedagogy and practice (and a lack of attention to the connection between practice and teacher identity). (550)

While it is undeniable that the topic of teacher identity is particularly vibrant currently in our own field – certainly *at the level of scholarship* – we would argue that many second language teacher education programmes are just as vulnerable to what we would describe as neoliberal recalibration as mainstream education courses. As Block and Gray (2016) have shown with regard to the situation in the UK (a setting far from unique in neoliberal times), the one-year state-school Postgraduate Certificate of Education – Modern Foreign Languages (PGCE-MFL) has been successively stripped of almost all theoretical content that does not relate to topics such as the practice of teaching, classroom management and lesson planning. Similarly, they show that a globally disseminated private sector course such as the Cambridge Certificate in English Language Teaching English to Adults (CELTA), which predated the neoliberal era and which was, from its inception, thoroughly marketised, also seeks to produce a teacher 'whose horizons do not extend beyond the micro-context of the classroom to the macro-context of the social, political and economic conditions within which the classroom is located' (Block and Gray 2016: 488). While such courses do not allow for any kind of detailed exploration of the concept of language teacher identity, they do very much presuppose an identity for course takers – namely, that of *effective practitioner*. Such an identity ascription is based on the idea of a largely experientially trained, disciplined bureaucrat with a narrowly defined knowledge base. It is precisely because of the nature of this type of initial training that we consider the concept of identity to be an important one for teachers undertaking continuing professional development (or those embarking on pre-service Masters qualifications which may have more space for such explorations). In suggesting this, we align ourselves with scholars such as Maclure (1993: 311), who takes the view that the concept of identity, when actively engaged with on a teacher education course and subsequently integrated into professional practice, can allow teachers to reconceptualise their sense of themselves as educators in such a way that it has the potential to become a useful 'organising principle' in their lives (discussed more fully in Chapter 2). In doing so, we are aware of Golombek's (2017) caveat that the mere introduction of alternative identities and the re-storying of teachers' experience on such courses is insufficient, as misrecognition and the political and institutional realities constraining teachers' lives cannot simply be rethought away. Rather, we see identity as a tool to be used in struggle, and although it carries no inbuilt guarantee of (political) success, we take the view that it serves to make the struggles teachers may engage in more feasible.

METHODOLOGICAL CONSIDERATIONS

It will be clear from the above that understandings about teacher learning, development and identity formation have undergone a significant transformation. The raft of publications just referred to is also typified by a considerable degree of theoretical diversity. Thus we see scholars drawing on poststructuralism (Nelson 2016), sociocultural theory (Golombek 2017), Bakhtinian perspectives (Hallman 2015) and sociolinguistics (Higgins 2017), to name but a few of the approaches being adopted. At the same time, the kinds of identities explored are equally diverse. A far from exhaustive sample includes teachers' professional identities (Nagatomo 2012), religious identities (Varghese and Johnston 2007), non-native speaker teacher identities (Park 2012), multilingual identities (Canagarajah 2017) and raced identities (Motha 2006), as well as teachers' *imagined* identities and the tensions between these and their *practised* identities (Xu 2012).

This wave of interest in language teacher identity is partly due to the influence of situated, practice-oriented theories which have gained ground over the more individualistic and cognitivist perspectives which dominated in the past. Theories such as situated leaning (Lave and Wenger 1991) or communities of practice (Wenger 1998) have had a strong influence, and can be seen as part of a 'practice turn' in the social sciences in which cognitive phenomena such as knowledge and beliefs are not artificially separated from actions, but seen as bound up and connected in social practices (Schatzki 1996). Within these socially situated perspectives on learning, development and identity, there has been an overwhelming (and highly productive) focus on what Barkhuizen (2011) refers to as 'narrative knowledging', largely because narratives are a rich source of information on how teachers see themselves and the work they do. At the same time, somewhat less attention has been paid to the linguistic and interactional resources through which practices and identities are established and maintained. For example, Creese (2005: 55) argues that, in communities of practice theory, 'despite its emphasis on negotiation of meaning, we are given little insight into how meanings are made and interpreted. It lacks infrastructure to explain the role language plays in social life.' Thus, there are still relatively few studies that focus on how professional practice is constructed in the moment-by-moment interactions of practitioners as they talk about what they do, or plan to do. This is true even where work on teachers' beliefs and practices does depend on discourse data, in that there is often a lack of detail on how the data were produced in social interaction (Potter and Hepburn 2005). Our own contribution to the burgeoning literature on English language teacher identity aims to build on the work that colleagues have done already by addressing interaction explicitly and consistently across the data chapters which are at the heart of this volume. We do this by focusing, in many cases as colleagues have done before, on the stories teachers tell, but in all cases we draw on a range of principled approaches to the analysis of talk-in-interaction to show, in detail, how ELT practitioners negotiate the meanings of their practices and their professional identities.

OVERVIEW OF THE VOLUME

The book is notionally divided into three sections. The first section comprises this introduction and is followed by Chapters 2 and 3. Chapter 2 explores what is meant by identity, where the concept came from, and how it has come to occupy such a central place in contemporary thinking. From there we move on to a consideration of the problems associated with it, before outlining in greater detail why we believe it remains a particularly relevant concept, not only for the exploration of teachers' sense of themselves across a wide range of settings, but also as a potentially useful concept in the working lives of ELT professionals.

Given that the book is part of a series on social interaction, Chapter 3 turns its attention to this perspective on human sociality and addresses its role in analysing talk and identity in teacher education and professional development. The centrality of conversation analysis and its shortcomings are considered, along with membership categorisation analysis and varieties of positioning theory. In addition, we consider the importance of non-verbal semiotic resources, the usefulness of Bourdieu's (1985) concepts of field and habitus, and Silverstein's (2003) notion of indexicality in allowing us to link the micro-level of speaker interaction with the macro-level of identities as more broadly socially constituted phenomena.

This is followed by the second section, which consists of five data-driven chapters in which different teacher identities are explored in a range of ways. There is a degree of overlap across these chapters with small stories, stance, positioning and alignment, and a view of the research interview as a form of interaction being recurring features. Chapter 4 begins by exploring those identities related to knowledge, competence or expertise. The focus is on the interaction between student teachers and teacher educators on a pre-service ELT course, the Cambridge English CELTA. Using detailed transcripts of lesson-planning sessions, the analyses show how the trainee teachers and tutors negotiated practical knowledge and identity, and how power asymmetries emerged in the interaction. The data also include stimulated recall interviews in which participants produce accounts of their own interactive practices. The chapter shows how knowledge construction and identity formation are mediated through social interaction at this crucial stage in teacher development, and discusses the extent to which power, in the shape of the wider social, political and institutional constraints, was oriented to in the interaction.

Chapter 5 focuses on language teachers' 'professional' identities and explores the ways in which teachers position themselves in relation to salient aspects of their everyday work, and the wider institutional and social contexts that impact on their professional practice. The teachers dealt with in this chapter all work in the English for Speakers of Other Languages (ESOL) sector in the UK – a diverse setting largely dedicated to the education of migrants and asylum seekers. The chapter concentrates on talk about 'individual learning plans', which teachers are required to complete as a means of tracking students' progress. Analytically, the chapter focuses on the small stories teachers tell in interview and the ways in which they position themselves and each other vis-à-vis these artefacts as part of their interactional identity work.

Chapter 6 addresses teachers' 'language-related identity' (Pennington and Richards 2016) and focuses specifically on the ways in which two groups of 'nonnative' teachers of English based in Spain see themselves as users, learners and teachers of English. One group of teachers works in the primary sector, while the other is from the secondary sector. The latter group work in a bilingual school and several of the teachers teach a variety of subjects through the medium of English. The analytic framework we use in this chapter is membership categorisation analysis (MCA), which is concerned with how speakers, through their talk, make certain identities relevant by ascribing themselves, and others, to certain categories. The chapter suggests that these teachers readily reproduce a 'subaltern' attitude (Kumaravadivelu 2016) with regard to so-called native-speaker teachers, although this is to some extent mitigated by counter-evidence of orientation to the membership category of 'modern non-native teacher of English', characterised by a more practical and pragmatic view of the goals of language teaching, less of an obsession with grammar and an abandonment of the view that learners need to acquire a specific accent or variety.

Chapter 7 takes its cue from Varghese et al. (2016), who argue that social class is often obscured from vision in work on language teacher identity. This chapter is written by way of a corrective and explores the centrality of social class and political identification in the identity work of three ESOL teachers in a group interview. It begins with a detailed overview of the concept of social class and the ways in which teaching, as it relates to social class, has been theorised. As with Chapter 5, the chapter features small stories told by the teachers. Here the analytic focus is on Du Bois's (2007) concept of stance taking in discourse and the ways in which speakers position themselves and align (or not) with one another as they interact. The chapter shows how social class and political identification are central to these teachers' sense of themselves as educators.

In Chapter 8 we turn our attention to non-normative sexual identity as it is made interactionally relevant in a research interview with a gay teacher as he discusses lesbian, gay, bisexual and transgender (LGBT) representation and erasure in commercially produced ELT materials. The chapter surveys the evolving cultural and political background with regard to the winning of LGBT rights and the reticence of major ELT publishers to keep abreast of social change in this regard. Analytically, the chapter uses Goffman's (1974) concept of framing, and pays particular attention to the notion of play frames (Coates 2007) and the use of smiling and laughter to establish and maintain rapport between the interactants. The chapter shows how gay educators' sexual and professional identities intersect and mutually inform one another.

The final section of the book consists of Chapter 9, which reviews some of the key issues relating to language teacher identity as dealt with in recent scholarly work, and discusses them in the light of our findings in the five data chapters. We then go on to suggest how a focus on social interaction can contribute to future research in the field, and in so doing we raise a number of methodological issues. The final part of the chapter addresses how research findings on language teacher identity may have implications and applications for language teacher education and professional development more generally.

2

IDENTITY – AN OVERVIEW

INTRODUCTION

It is significant to note that there is no entry for identity in Williams's *Keywords*, first published in 1976. Subtitled *A Vocabulary of Culture and Society*, this overview of salient terms in the social sciences, cultural studies and the humanities is a powerful reminder of identity's relatively recent arrival as a theoretical concept – although, as Block (2007) points out, related terms such as *subjectivity*, *self* and *self-consciousness* were already well established in a range of disciplines such as psychoanalysis, sociology and philosophy. Accounts of identity thus frequently seek to provide the term with a history in which its evolution is laid bare, and which at the same time can be seen as an attempt to carve out a theoretical space in which the concept can be explored and put to use. In that respect, this chapter can be seen as both a metacommentary on the histories of identity that circulate and an articulation of our own perspective. Hall's (1996) work is a good place to start, given the influence this has exerted and the poststructuralist orientation it espouses – one which, as we shall see, has been influential in contemporary thinking about identity in applied linguists and second language teacher education (for example, Norton 2000; Pavlenko 2003; Block 2005, 2007; Bucholtz and Hall 2005).

EVOLUTION OF IDENTITY

In a number of key statements on the subject, Hall (1992a, 1992b, 1992c, 1996) proposes a history in which identity evolves from an originary eighteenth-century Enlightenment understanding, through an early twentieth-century sociological one, to a late twentieth-century postmodernist or poststructuralist conceptualisation. By starting in the eighteenth century, Hall, by implication, links identity to the emergence of the individual, a figure described by Williams (2001 [1961]: 66) as 'a kind of absolute, without immediate reference [. . .] to the group of which he is a member'. As Williams argues:

> The growth of capitalism, and the great social changes associated with it, encouraged certain men to see 'the individual' as a source of economic activity, by his 'free enterprise'. It was less a matter of performing a certain function within a fixed order than of initiating certain kinds of activity, choosing particular

directions. The social and geographical mobility to which in some cases these changes gave rise led to a redefinition of the individual – 'what I am' – by extension to 'what I want to be' and 'what by my own efforts I have become'. (67–8)

Hall glosses the first of his three evolutionary stages in terms of the classically agentive Cartesian subject possessing what he calls an 'essential centre' or 'identity'. Descartes's famous philosophical proposition 'Cogito, ergo sum' (I think, therefore I am) provided this idealised figure with an enduring maxim for what would prove to be an equally enduring view of the human subject (where subject refers to the human being as the possessor of consciousness with the capacity for rational thought). As Keucheyan (2013: 183) has pointed out, '[t]he idea of a sovereign subject, transparent to itself and rational, is one of the foundations of modernity.' In turn, the sociological understanding is held to link this very individualised conceptualisation of identity to the social context in which it is formed and located. Hall (1992a: 276) writes:

> According to this view [. . .] identity is formed in the 'interaction' between self and society. The subject still has an inner core or essence that is 'the real me', but this is formed and modified in a continuous dialogue with the cultural worlds 'outside' and the identities which they offer [. . .] The fact that we project ourselves into these cultural identities, at the same time internalizing their meanings and values, making them 'part of us', helps to align our subjective feelings with the objective place we occupy in the social and cultural world.

However, Hall argued that, by the late twentieth century, both self and society were undergoing processes of transformation with serious consequences for the concept of identity. Identity was now held to be 'under erasure', which meant that it had become an unsatisfactory term – 'an idea which cannot be thought of in the old way, but without which certain key questions cannot be thought at all' (Hall 1996: 2). This was in fact something of an academic sleight of hand – a term which had not been used previously to any great extent in theoretical work was now introduced as being inherently problematic and of almost questionable serviceability. Such a questioning, and the instability it sought to index, were in fact integral to this perspective (and, as Wetherell (2010) shows, Hall was not alone in adopting this approach). The impact of what Hall referred to as the 'five great de-centrings' ushered in by Marx, Freud, Saussure, Foucault and feminism, coupled with the structural change supposedly brought about by globalisation, meant that the Cartesian/sociological subject was finished. In their various ways these 'de-centrings' represented attempts from very different theoretical perspectives to draw attention to the extent to which individual agency may be constrained by factors such as social class or patriarchal gender relations; the extent to which the rational thinking subject may be far from transparent to itself and motivated by unconscious and irrational drives and desires; or indeed that the assumed 'essence' at the heart of every human being had no ontological basis and amounted to little more than an Enlightenment fiction. 'The subject', Hall (1992a: 276–7) wrote, 'previously experienced as having a unified and stable identity, is becoming fragmented; composed, not of a single, but several, sometimes contradictory or unresolved, identities'. Such a perspective, generally referred to as anti-essentialist, adopts a pluralised, processual and socially constructed view of identity which is completely at odds with earlier understandings in which the notion of an unchanging core is assumed.

Block (2007), in his less schematised account of the rise of identity as a theoretical construct, frames it in terms of a move from a structuralist to a poststructuralist view of the subject and society. From a structuralist perspective, Block (2007: 12) suggests:

> The self is seen as the product of the social conditions in and under which it has developed. Traditionally, this has meant that individuals are determined by their membership in social categories based on social class, religion, education, family, peer groups and so on. In a broader sense, it has also meant that they are shaped and formed by their culture, understood to be the relatively fixed worldview, modes of behaviour and artefacts of a particular group of people.

Structuralism can also be seen as an attempt to shift the focus away from the individual as a separate entity with a unique essence towards one in which the structures within which individuals are located occupy the foreground. On this view the subject is seen as an element which can be understood only in terms of its relation to other elements within the structure. Such a perspective implied an assault on the agentive Cartesian/sociological subject with its unique essence, described by Lévi-Strauss as 'that intolerable spoilt brat who for too long has occupied the philosophical stage and prevented any serious work by demanding undivided attention' (Lévi-Strauss 1971, in Keucheyan 2013: 45). Elsewhere, he would argue that the individual was merely 'a crossroads where things happen. The crossroads is purely passive; something happens there' (Lévi-Strauss 1978: 4).

Poststructuralism, on the other hand, while also rejecting the idea of essences, can be seen as an attempt to recover something of a sense of agency which was held to have disappeared in the structuralist understandings of the individual and its relation to society. As Block (2007) argues, while most poststructuralists continued to recognise the role of structures in their work, it was agency which tended to be privileged. This is clearly evidenced in Hall (1996: 6), who describes identities as:

> temporary attachment to the subject positions which discursive practices construct for us [. . .]. They are the result of a successful articulation or 'chaining' of the subject into the flow of discourse [. . .]. The notion that an effective suturing of the subject to a subject-position requires not only that the subject is 'hailed', but that the subject invests in the position, means that suturing has to be thought of as an *articulation*, rather than a one-sided process, and that in turn places *identification*, if not identities, firmly on the theoretical agenda.

From this perspective, identity is about the highly agentive act of investment in, or identification with, already available subject positions. Think, for example, of the way in which a novice teacher might encounter and identify with the model of the teacher as *reflective practitioner* or *critical pedagogue* on an initial teacher education course.

Such an identification (possibly with an actual course tutor, or simply through inculcation into reflective practice or critical pedagogy as ways of doing teaching) could lead to an emerging sense of a very particular kind of professional identity with significant implications for the way in which the novice might come to construe and approach pedagogic practice. Identification is understood by psychoanalysts Laplanche and Pontalis (1988: 205) – work which is cited by Hall (1996) – as a psychological process in which 'the subject assimilates an aspect, property or attribute of the other and is transformed, wholly or partially, after the model the other provides. It is by means of identifications that the personality is constituted and specified.' Clearly, this could be held to imply something more ontologically consequential than temporary attachment to a subject position (a point we will return to later in this chapter). However, it does to serve to reinforce the centrality of agency in poststructuralist understandings of identity. In addition to providing a theoretical basis for the very heterogeneous theorisation of the fragmentation of the self described by Hall, poststructuralism also entailed an emancipatory dimension linked to the post-1968 historical moment in which it may be said to have emerged. In the words of Foucault (2003: 6–7), this moment was typified by:

> the immense and proliferating criticizability of things, institutions, practices, and discourses; a sort of general feeling that the ground was crumbling beneath our feet, especially in places where it seemed most familiar, most solid, and closest [nearest] to us, to our bodies, to our everyday gestures. But alongside this crumbling and the astonishing efficacy of discontinuous, particular, and local critiques, the facts were also revealing something [. . .] beneath this whole thematic, through it and even within it, we have seen what might be called the insurrection of subjugated knowledges.

Such a perspective implied a critical stance towards all taken-for-granted views of the social world, the socially constructed categories which were used to describe it, and the so-called 'grand narratives' which were used to explain it (and which were held to privilege certain meanings while silencing others). It also implied a key role for discourse in the construction not only of social reality but also of the individual, and crucially for the concomitant role of *de*construction as a means of challenging dominant discourses, and the opening up of marginalised and silenced counternarratives which would in turn provide discursive spaces for individuals to occupy.

But what does this mean in practice – and more specifically what might it mean for English language teachers? Pavlenko (2003) provides a good example with regard to the native/non-native speaker dichotomy which has been the source of much debate within the field and which has been held to disadvantage 'non-native' English speaker teachers in some settings. She writes:

> One powerful discourse that informs preservice and in-service teachers' views of themselves and of their students is that of standard language and native speakerness. In the case of English education, the discourse portrays standard English as the only legitimate form of the language and monolingual native speakers – who

are also implicitly White and middle-class – as its only legitimate speakers and 'owners'. (Pavlenko 2003: 257).

Pavlenko goes on to describe a study in which pre-service teachers from a wide range of international backgrounds on a Teaching English to Speakers of Other Languages (TESOL) course in the USA were exposed to academic content on bilingualism, multilingualism and the concept of multicompetence (Cook 1992, 1999), which, she claimed, had the effect of allowing some novice teachers to re-imagine their 'non-native' speaker identities and 'to construe themselves and their future students as legitimate L2 users rather than as failed native speakers of the target language' (Pavlenko 2003: 251). In this way, Pavlenko argues, the counter-narrative of multicompetence opened up a discursive space for some of her informants, thereby displacing what she calls the powerful discourse of 'native speakerness' (which constructs the monolingual speaker of English as the final authority on acceptability, grammaticality and pronunciation, and which is still frequently seen in many parts of the world as providing the basis for the best kind of teacher).

In line with Hall and Block, Benwell and Stokoe (2010) see the 1980s as the moment when identity studies take a decisive 'discursive turn' across a range of academic disciplines. By this they mean an approach to the study of identity in which language is seen as central. However, they see this as having two very distinct tendencies – one indebted to varieties of cultural theory (such as poststructuralism and neo-Marxist Frankfurt School Critical Theory) and the other to conversation analysis. These tendencies have parallels with Gee's (1999: 19) distinction between *Discourse* (capital 'D') and *discourse* (lower case 'd') – the former referring to the historically evolving, socially and institutionally shaped ways of using language, thinking, acting and construing social reality, and the latter referring more narrowly to specific stretches of talk or writing. Before going any further, it is necessary to look at little more closely at the similarities and the differences between these two tendencies and the implications they have for the study of identity.

Most researchers working in all discourse traditions would have little problem in agreeing that identities are plural and dynamic; that they emerge (or are constructed or performed) in social interaction; that they are sensitive to context; and that they are relational – or, as Blommaert (2005) puts it, that they are both inhabited and ascribed. We saw this earlier in Chapter 1 in the poem by Jackie Kay, where the poet perceives she is being ascribed a foreign identity, and then responds by choosing to inhabit a local Scottish one. Nor would researchers working in these traditions disagree with Agha (2006: 237), who states: 'Given that identity is a variable phenomenon we can only approach it from the standpoint of the semiotic activities through which its variation is exhibited.' Where they differ is in the manner in which these semiotic activities are treated when they become data for analysis and in their understanding of context. Those working within, for example, a critical discourse analysis (CDA) tradition (very much a capital 'D' perspective) begin with an a priori theorisation of the social and seek to make connections between micro-features of discourse and the larger social structures within which they occur. It should be pointed out that many working within a CDA paradigm, while accepting the role accorded to language by Foucault, are also indebted to Marx for their understanding of social structures. Wodak's (1997, 2006) work on doctor–patient interaction provides a classic example of the CDA approach, proceeding as it does from a starting point in which structural inequalities within which doctors and patients are situated are taken as given. Such an approach operates on a broad view of context as entailing both the micro-context of the specific discursive event (or written text) under investigation and the macro-sociohistorical context within which it occurs. On the other hand, those working within a conversation analysis (CA) tradition (a lower-case 'd' perspective) stick to a much narrower view of context as consisting of the interaction itself and restrict themselves to fine-grained micro-analysis of 'talk-in-interaction', which is entirely inductive and eschews all temptation to impute significance to any element which cannot be shown to be present.

Both these approaches have been critiqued. CDA, for example, has been famously criticised for its politically motivated stance and reliance on small samples of data which are (so the charge runs) selectively chosen (Widdowson 1995, 1998), its (suggested) unhappy combination of Marxism and poststructuralism (Hammersley 1997) and its (supposed) ethnographically inadequate treatment of the broader social context it claims to take into consideration (Blommaert 2005). At the same time, with regard to CA, Blommaert (2005), for all his admiration of its achievements in shedding light on the micro-aspects of social interaction and the ways in which it can show how particular identities are intersubjectively produced, suggests that its very narrowness of focus on the interaction itself – as the *only* context to be considered – is a serious limitation. He also argues persuasively that identity *can* be present and *can* be a significant element in interaction without actually being visible in recorded data:

> Identities can be there long before the interaction starts and thus condition what can happen in such interaction. A conversation between a Turkish immigrant and a Belgian police officer may not show any interactional traces of active and explicit orienting towards the categories of 'Turkish immigrant' or 'police officer'. But both parties in the interaction are in all likelihood very much aware of each other's identity, since these categories and typical relationships between them have been pre-inscribed in the interaction. Identities can also be attributed afterwards, by parties not involved in the interaction. (206)

In fact, not all researchers sympathetic to the methodology of CA confine themselves to its analytic strictures. West and Zimmerman (1983) provide a clear example of this in their study of interruptions in the talk of women and men who are unacquainted. Interruptions, which were understood as 'violations of speakers' turns at talk' (103), were shown to be a more pervasive feature of male speech than female speech. In seeking to make sense of the data, in which the participants did not in any visible way orient towards their gendered identities as women or men, West and Zimmerman argued that 'the distributional evidence prompts the inference that sex category was salient in the interaction and employed in and though the management of talk' (110). They concluded that such interruptions were 'a way of "doing" power in face-to-face interaction, and to the extent that power is implicated in what it means to be a man vis-à-vis a woman, it is a way of "doing" gender as well' (111). Other scholars, such as those working in interactional sociolinguistics and linguistic ethnography, are also happy to make use of the methodology of CA while reserving the right to interpret data in ways which CA analysts would consider unwarranted – what Rampton (2006: 396), with no negative imputation, refers to as an 'impure' approach.

Thus we can see that, for all its salience in contemporary thought, identity is indeed something of a problematic concept – not only in terms of how it is to be analysed but also in terms of the conceptual work it is required to do. How, for example, can identity be said to entail a temporary point of attachment to a subject position (and therefore to some extent be inherently ephemeral) *and* at the same time be used to discuss more enduring senses of self in terms of gender, race and class? Before outlining our own view, it is necessary to step back again and address some of the problems with identity.

PROBLEMS WITH IDENTITY

In Chapter 1 we said that identity has become the superordinate term for all activities in which we situate ourselves as certain kinds of people and the ways in which we position others. For some scholars, such as Brubaker and Cooper (2000), the range of activities encompassed by this understanding of identity presupposes a semantic load which the term is ultimately unable to bear. The fact that identity is used to refer to relatively enduring senses of self as gendered, raced and classed and so on, *and* at the same time to more transitory identities related to roles or stances adopted in interaction such as 'problematizee/problematizer' (Ochs and Taylor 1995), 'prank phone caller' (Zimmerman 1998) or 'complainant' (Stokoe 2003) mean that, for Brubaker and Cooper, any analytical potential the term might have is seriously compromised. It is clear that, for them, doing gender and being a prank phone caller are just too different to be discussed under the same analytic heading. In their survey, they look at identity across disciplines and point to what they see as an overall theoretical incommensurability in uses of the term. However, they also suggest that even where agreement might be found among theorists as to the nature of identity – as in the socially constructed, non-essentialised view most commonly found in many of the social sciences today – there is often also contradiction (a point also made by Bendle (2002) in his equally trenchant critique).

> 'Essentialism' has indeed been vigorously criticized, and constructivist gestures now accompany most discussions of 'identity'. Yet we often find an uneasy amalgam of constructivist language and essentialist argumentation. This is not a matter of intellectual sloppiness. Rather, it reflects the dual orientation of many academic identitarians as both *analysts* and *protagonists* of identity politics. It reflects the tension between the constructivist language that is required by academic correctness and the foundationalist or essentialist message that is required if appeals to 'identity' are to be effective in practice. (Brubaker and Cooper 2000: 6)

Thus queer or feminist scholars, for example, may hold the view that sexual and gender identities are socially constructed (and therefore culturally contingent) rather than always and everywhere the same across time and space. At the same time they may argue for women's rights and lesbian and gay rights in the present *as if* gendered and sexual identities were more ontologically secure than they believe them to be, and all the while believing in a post-gender, queerer future where such identities might cease to exist. Although this is not a theoretical problem, it is a political one – a point recognised by Spivak (1999), who coined the term 'strategic essentialism' to describe the practice of talking the talk of essentialism as part of a rights-claiming, recognition-demanding politics. However politically expedient this may be, clearly it also has the potential to reinforce essentialism – at least outside the academy where theoretical complexities may serve to undermine the clarity of arguments put forward in favour of recognition, law reform and social justice.

As a way out of all such conundrums, Brubaker and Cooper propose abandoning the term and focusing instead on the clusters of meaning which identity encompasses. These are identified as 'identification and categorisation', 'self-understanding and social location' and 'commonality, connectedness, groupness'. Identification is seen as preferable to identity as it connotes *process* rather than *condition*, and means that speakers can identify themselves *as* and *with* certain kinds of people, thus avoiding what they describe as the 'terrible singularity' (Brubaker and Cooper 2000: 1) of so much identity politics. As we saw earlier, Hall (1996) also recognised the usefulness of focusing on identification precisely for the same reason – although this did not lead him to abandon identity as a viable concept. With regard to the second cluster of meanings, Brubaker and Cooper (2000: 17) say that self-understanding is 'a dispositional term that designates what might be called "situated subjectivity": one's sense of who one is, of one's social location, and of how [. . .] one is prepared to act'. They add that as 'a dispositional term, it belongs to the realm of what Bourdieu has called *sens pratique*, the practical sense – at once cognitive and emotional – that persons have of themselves and their social world' (17). Thus they signal indirectly the importance of *habitus* – Bourdieu's term for the range of sedimented dispositions in mind and body which are socially acquired from the several structures within which persons are formed and which inform an individual's practical sense of how to act. Finally, they suggest that commonality, 'the sharing of some common attribute'; connectedness, 'the relational ties that link people'; and groupness, 'the sense of belonging to a distinctive, bounded, solidary group' (20), mop up the remaining meanings currently contained within the concept of identity. Such a separating out of meanings, they argue, would ultimately serve to clarify discussion and analysis by ridding the social sciences of a term which they see as 'riddled with ambiguity, riven with contradictory meanings, and encumbered by reifying connotations' (34).

Other scholars have taken the view that the constructivist/poststructuralist understanding of identity may also be inadequate at times (Bendle 2002; Block 2006; du Gay 2007). Bendle (2002: 12) argues that accounts of identity which ignore insights from psychology and psychoanalysis 'tend to assume an extreme plasticity of the self that dissolves any real conception that there exists an ongoing core or substrate to the personality at all'. While recognising that this kind of thinking is 'a strength as it avoids pessimism about the intractability of social problems and provides for maximum human adaptation and hope for the future' (that is, we are both more agentive and more adaptable than we think), he also suggests that there are serious drawbacks, as such a view:

> utilizes a very shallow and under-theorized module of the human personality that radically generalizes the notion of identity, dissipates its analytical power and is particularly weakened by the absence of an adequate depth psychology with its alertness to profound and possibly intractable psychic conflicts with important implications for the identities concerned. (12)

Bendle concludes his critique with a plea for his own discipline of sociology to become more interdisciplinary in its thinking, arguing that until it does so, its theorising on identity will remain largely superficial. Taking up Bendle's criticism of certain kinds of constructivist/poststructuralist thinking and his recommendation that identity-based research needs to engage more fully with the 'psy' disciplines, Block (2006: 46) acknowledges the possibility of an ignored inner core in the poststructuralist conception of the person and the 'need to be attentive to the subconscious deeper inner workings of the mind and how they might impact on one's sense of self and identity'. However, he also recognises that these disciplines might have little light to shed on many of the fluidic identities produced in interaction and that psychoanalysis in particular may be an inappropriate source of theory for identity research, given its ultimate therapeutic orientation.

Du Gay (2007: 11), previously closely associated with the Hall perspective outlined above, takes a somewhat different angle and argues that the time has come to redirect identity research towards a more empirically grounded, sociological–anthropological understanding of 'the specific forms of "personhood" that individuals acquire as a result of their immersion in, or subjection to, particular normative and technical regimes of conduct'. In this he is heavily influenced by Latour's (2004: 231) argument that much so-called critical theory has become irrelevant and ineffective as critique, and that if the critical mind is to renew itself, it will only be through the 'cultivation of a *stubbornly realist attitude*' (italics in original) – which, in du Gay's case, implies a reconsideration of the role of structures in identity formation. Such a position is not a great remove away from the current one adopted by Block, which sees him increasingly drawing on Marxism and critical realism. Without rejecting his previous non-essentialist orientation, he argues that social class as an identity inscription has been neglected in identity research in applied linguistics and that engaging with this necessarily presupposes an engagement with the material and economic base of society – something which is alien (if not anathema) to anti-foundational 'post' theorising (Block et al. 2012; Block 2014a).

Social class has most certainly been neglected in studies of second language teacher education and development (but see Johnston 1997). In one of the few studies to draw attention to the class location of teachers, Akbari (2008: 646) refers to the difficulties encountered by many teachers in Iran, who are often unable to transform their teaching practice in ways recommended by what he called the international academic discourse community, which is unaware of the realities of teachers' lives:

> Teachers in many contexts are not different from factory workers in terms of their working hours; in many countries, a typical language teacher works for 8 hours per day, 5 or even 6 days per week. Most of these teachers are poorly paid and 'putting bread on the table for my family,' as one such teacher put it, is their main priority. The financial and occupational constraints they work within do not leave them with the time or the willingness to act as iconoclasts and social transformers, roles that will jeopardize their often precarious means of subsistence.

And, of course, as has been suggested elsewhere, minimally qualified teachers across the commercial sector globally frequently work in very casualised conditions (Gray 2010). Engagement with social class could therefore be seen as necessary in the study of identity, but as Sayer (2002, 2005a, 2005b) has pointed out on numerous occasions, class identity is not the same as other kinds of identity:

> Class, unlike, say, ethnicity is not an identity demanding recognition as legitimate [. . .]. Low income people are not disadvantaged primarily because others fail to value their identity and misrecognize and undervalue their cultural goods, or indeed because they are stigmatized, though all these things make their situation worse; rather they are disadvantaged primarily because they lack the means to live in ways which they, as well as others, value. Certainly, some may be consigned to the working class because of racism or other identity-sensitive forms of behaviour, but these are not necessary conditions of being working class. (Sayer 2005a: 947–94)

And he adds:

> Whereas sexism and racism are primarily produced by 'identity-sensitive' behaviour and can hence be reduced by people changing their attitudes and behaviour towards others, class inequalities need a great deal more than an elimination of class contempt to erode, for they can be produced by identity-indifferent mechanisms of capitalism [. . .]: they need a redistribution of resources. (959)

It is clear, then, that if we are to include social class as a dimension of identity, an exclusively poststructuralist orientation may be inadequate. Redistribution requires more than the opening up of marginalised and silenced counter-narratives – helpful though this may be as a first step. Recall the example earlier of the 'non-native' English speaker teachers referred to by Pavlenko (2003). Although they were reported as having successfully re-imagined themselves as multicompetent speakers and bilingual teachers, there is no guarantee that in some settings this would undo prejudice against them in terms of employability – although it might allow them to begin to strategise for change. Block's solution to this particular problem is (unlike that recommended by Brubaker and Cooper) to continue to make use of identity as an analytic term, but to approach it in a more intersectional way (Crenshaw 1991) – one which recognises that identities (and, in many cases, the inequalities that can accompany them) arise out of very different social and economic processes.

So where does this leave us in terms of this introductory chapter? Having sketched out a very brief history of identity and outlined some of the problems associated with it, it now remains for us to clarify our own position on this somewhat troublesome concept.

THE CASE FOR IDENTITY

Given the book's title, it will be clear that we have decided to retain identity as a useful concept – despite the incisive critique advanced by Brubaker and Cooper. In doing so, we were guided by Joseph's (2004) assessment that the term is already well established and its problematic nature well known. To introduce a new set of terms runs the risk of complicating things even further. Like culture, the term is multidis-cursive, thus placing the onus on us to be clear about which of the many meanings we wish to invoke as we go along and to be clear about how we address specific problems that have been identified. Such multidiscursivity need not be seen as problematic though, and indeed it has been suggested that 'multiple theoretical approaches are absolutely essential if we are not to lose sight of the real-world complexity of our subject' (Varghese et al. 2005: 40). Given our focus on identity and interaction, it will be clear that we are interested in the way in which identities get done in interaction – so far, so familiar in terms of the thrust of identity-based research in applied linguistics and language teacher education. However, as we have suggested above, what gets done in interaction varies considerably. Let us begin with how we view one of the big problems identified earlier – namely, the issue of the use of the term to describe ephemeral and more enduring senses of self. One way of resolving this difficulty has been proposed by Baynham (2014), who argues that identities have to be seen as 'brought about' in interaction, but also in many cases 'brought along'. Arguing from a basic poststructuralist position, Baynham suggests that

> even from the perspective of a performative account of identity, of the speaking self, there is an enormous structuring weight of discursive formations, which are 'brought along' in the moment of discourse, part of the presupposed baggage of the locutionary agent, to be contingently rearticulated. (71)

For Baynham, this structuring weight can be understood with reference to Bourdieu's concept of *habitus*, and Butler's (1990) idea of *repetition* – a key element in the iterative construction of, for example, gender (that is, the way we come to feel about ourselves as 'women' and 'men' through the repeated performances of gendered ways of talking, walking, sitting, dressing and so on). We are sympathetic to this view of identity and to Baynham's view that narrative and 'small stories' (Bamberg and Georgakopolou 2008) in particular are privileged sites for the exploration of more enduring identities. As Baynham argues, 'those relatively stable identity positions, often thought of as essentialized, are in fact sedimented and built up over time through many repeated encounters in which identity is "brought about" performatively.' On this view, identity is always 'brought about', but it is often also 'brought along'. Baynham's reconciliation of the performative and the portable aspects of identity seems to us to provide an adequate response to the most serious charge levelled against identity by Brubaker and Cooper (2000) – namely, that of analytical bluntness.

However, although we are adopting a broadly discursive view of identity in this book, we see our own position in the long run as closer to that of Sayer's critical realism (glossed below) – largely because of his recognition of the particular nature of class identity and our own view that there is no escaping class in a class society. For Sayer (2002: npn), class is seen as:

> hugely important for *forming* subjective identities and the habitus. Both habitus and the social field are deeply classed and gendered, affecting us at subconscious as well as conscious levels so that they are evident in our comportment and tastes and pre-reflective feelings and responses. As Annette Kuhn puts it, 'Class is something beneath your clothes, under your skin, in your reflexes, in your psyche, at the very core of your being.' (Kuhn 1995: see also Charlesworth 2000)

While such a view does not imply an essence (in the sense of an unchanging and unchangeable core), it does suggest an essential sameness in the objective relationship of members of a class to the material and economic base of society, which other identities do not. And it also suggests that speakers bring along more than the weight of discursive formations to interaction – although they bring this too. Furthermore, Sayer's (2000: 2) critical realism is one in which the centrality of discourse is recognised – 'there is', he says, 'a world existing independently of our knowledge of it,' but he adds that this world 'can only be known under particular descriptions, in terms of available discourses, though it does not follow that no description or explanation is better than any other'.

Finally, we are sticking with identity for a further two key reasons related specifically to teaching: first, because – as we will suggest below – it has considerable explanatory power in enabling us to shed light on the complex process of becoming an English language teacher and the ongoing experience of working as one; and second, because it has the potential to provide teachers with a much-needed resource for becoming more agentive in strategising for change, something we see as particularly important in the face of the ever more marketised contexts in which teacher preparation takes place and the conditions under which teachers are required to work. Let us begin by looking at the first of these a little more closely. Britzman (1994), in line with much recent thinking on becoming a teacher (Mayer 1999; Danielewicz 2001; Clarke 2008; Kanno and Stuart 2011), sees the process as one which entails the construction of a new professional identity. Britzman (1994) has written with great insight on the difficulties novice teachers can experience in their initial induction into the job. She begins by making an important distinction between role and identity:

> In actuality, role and function are not synonymous with identity; whereas role can be assigned, the taking up of an identity is a constant social negotiation. One must

consent to an identity. There is a distinction between learning to teach and becoming a teacher. (Britzman 1994: 24)

And she adds:

> It is impossible to discuss identity without taking into account the antagonistic meanings of experience. This relation becomes particularly clear when we consider the identity of teacher. It is an identity that is at once familiar and strange for we have all played a role opposite teacher for a significant part of our lives and this student experience seems to tell us what a teacher is and does. The identity of teacher, however, does not seem so transparent once one steps into the teacher's role; once there, role and identity are not synonymous. That is, role speaks to function whereas identity voices investments and commitments. Function, or what one should do, and investments, or what one feels, are often at odds. (29)

From this perspective, becoming a teacher entails numerous new identifications for the novice, and consent can sometimes prove difficult and seem like compromise, something which is also borne out in Block and Gray (2016). Given that what it means to be a teacher is both ascribed by others (such as the state, teacher educators, schools, the media, society at large and so on) and at the same time inhabited by the individual teacher, it is little wonder that induction into the job can be experienced as a kind of ontological upheaval which is frequently painful. As Britzman demonstrates, identity is a useful concept in exploring changes to sense of self and the negotiation of what will be long-term investments in new subject positions. Her case study of Jamie Owl, a young, female, working-class novice teacher, shows how Jamie survived in the early stages of her teaching practice by refusing at times to inhabit an identity she believed she was being forced to assume and which she had not yet succeeded in negotiating for herself:

> I have finally decided when I enter the school building in the morning, I am not a teacher. I am a human being who's assuming a role that has been designated teacher. And I carry out some of the functions of that teacher. But when things go against my grain, [and] I don't want to do it, I don't believe in it, or just that I don't know, then I can admit that. And that way I can save my own peace of mind and I can deal with the situations that arise. And I don't know everything. I'm a human being, which, in a lot of ways, was my own expectations of what a teacher should be when I walked in there. (Britzman 1994: 37–8)

What we see here is a refusal to assume the identity of teacher at key moments in teaching practice – triggered, we are told, by (among other things) Jamie's difficulties in classroom management, which saw her acting in an autocratic manner which was supportive of school authority but which ran against the anti-authoritarianism her aspired-to teacher identity entailed. Jamie's temporary refuge in the identity of 'human being' and her intermittent refusal to self-identify as a teacher were, Britzman suggests, a coping strategy in a painful process of negotiation. Identity, therefore, as something ascribed, rejected, negotiated, claimed and inhabited, is – we would suggest – a particularly useful concept for exploring induction into teaching.

It is also useful in exploring experienced teachers' sense of self. Despite having learned to teach, they are necessarily involved in the ongoing activity of negotiating their sense of themselves as teachers – whether in the light of continuing professional development, in the face of government diktat, or under pressure from commercial imperatives (to say nothing of the interaction of their teacher identity with the many other identities they already have and the ways in which they intersect). This leads us to the final reason for sticking with the concept of identity – that of identity as an 'organising principle in teachers' jobs and lives' (Maclure 1993: 311), which we referred to in Chapter 1.

Writing in the mid-1990s, at a time when state-school teacher education in Britain was being subjected to yet further neoliberal 'reform' in the shape of a move towards a more school-based model (with a concomitant downgrading of the role of the university in teacher preparation), Cowen (1995) reflected on this situation in terms of the role of the state in determining the nature of teachers' professional identity. The move towards the school as *the* privileged site for learning about teaching was seen as a shift from the ascribed identity of the *reflective practitioner* with a firm grounding in the social sciences, 'permanently re-examining the social fabric and social assumptions about the purposes of schooling within which he or she must daily practise' (21), in favour of the more neoliberal *effective practitioner* – an altogether very different identity ascription. Such a politically motivated recalibration of teacher identity was based, he suggested, on the rejection of the idea 'that teachers should possess any significant amounts of knowledge which are not directly related to classroom teaching performance, to efficient management and administration of school routines, and to a perfected craft-like knowledge' (23). What is significant in this model of teacher education, he argued, is 'the demand that occupational competence be narrowly defined, be regularly measured, and be provided by existing practitioners. Thus the term "effective" is inserted into the discourse; and the word "reflective" exits from the debate' (23). This change in the manner of initial teacher education was accompanied by the introduction of strict government inspection regimes for schools, the grading of teachers and schools against performance criteria, the introduction of frequent pupil testing and the publication of results in league tables by way of enforcing greater accountability to what were now called stakeholders – namely, parents, employers and the state. Such change was also designed to facilitate the development of an educational market in which schools competed against each other for government funding (see Gray and Block [2012] for a fuller account).

Maclure (1993) explored the effects of these changes on teachers' identities in interviews with sixty-nine primary and secondary school teachers in the UK. What she found, not surprisingly, was evidence of a considerable degree of disillusion and evidence of what she called 'spoiled identities'. In the case of such informants, she reported that the 'most troubled of these were the teachers who were no longer able to reconcile their identities with the job in any sense' (Maclure

1993: 317) and who felt that their faces no longer fitted in the newly 'reformed' education system. In addition, she also found evidence of the disavowal of the identity of teacher:

> A surprisingly high proportion of teachers (more than half) wanted to deny at least part of the identity of 'teacher'. [. . .] Many project teachers were at pains to emphasise that they did not socialise with teachers out of school, claiming a disdain for talking 'shop', and characterising teachers as a group as boring. [. . .] Many other teachers expressed similar sentiments, suggesting that the identity of 'teacher' is associated with negative qualities such as dullness. These teachers seemed happy to embrace the *role* of teacher, but wanted to shrug off the identity. (318; italics in original)

In the light of such comments, 'spoiled identities' is a particularly apt description of what her data reveal. Curiously, Maclure does not reference Goffman's (1963) *Stigma: Notes on the Management of Spoiled Identity*, nor does she make use of the concept of stigma in her analysis to any great extent. In Goffman's (1963) remarkable book, spoiled identities are those which are stigmatised as a result of social discreditation. And indeed one feature of the discourse of much neoliberal 'reform' has been the attempt to spoil the identity of teacher through the repeated discrediting and pillorying of 'bad' and 'underperforming' teachers (see Gove [2010, 2013] for typical examples). In attempting to account for the evidence of disavowal of teacher identity, one very plausible interpretation Maclure proposes is that:

> the old iconographies of teacherhood, with their virtues of vocation, care, dedication and self-investment, are being eroded under the pressures and interventions of the late twentieth century, while the new identities of 'professionalism' which are being offered by employers and policy-makers are becoming ever more difficult to believe in. (Maclure 1993: 318)

Despite their disillusion, Maclure argued these teachers in their various ways were still laying claim to a different identity in which being a teacher was understood in very different terms. And this is in fact the overall thrust of her paper – namely, that teachers' identity claims *and* their identity disavowals can be understood 'as a form of *argument* – as devices for justifying, explaining and making sense of one's conduct, career, values and circumstances' (316; italics in original). In that sense, biographical narrative inquiry becomes a useful way of exploring teachers' identities, and as Clarke (2009) has argued, this view of identity as argument can be taken further in ways which allow teachers to become more agentive in arguing for themselves, and – we would suggest – to strategise for what kind of identities they want to lay claim to, even in the face of attempts to eradicate them.

CONCLUSION

As teachers of all subjects in both state and private sectors globally become ever more firmly imbricated in education systems which are reconfigured as 'edu-businesses'

(Ball 2012), in which the officially endorsed identities available to them are restricted, it is incumbent on those of us who think otherwise to make the case for alternatives – difficult as this may be in the current climate. To do so, as Clarke (2009) suggests, is in fact an ethical imperative. One way in which this can be seen happening today in Britain is in *The Guardian* newspaper's regular column 'The Secret Teacher'. In this feature, teachers write anonymously about their working conditions and their frustrations with government interference, disavowing the official discourse of the effective practitioner and indirectly claiming a very different kind of identity for themselves.

In the data analysis chapters which follow in this volume we will see English language teachers from a variety of settings doing something very similar – rejecting in many cases the professional identities that are on offer, arguing for themselves in ways which are indicative of their claims to alternative notions of what it means to be a teacher and in ways which are congruent with the other identities they also inhabit. Hall, in his much-cited introduction to the collection of essays in *Questions of Cultural Identity* (Hall and Du Gay 1996), having argued that identity was under erasure, famously asked 'Who needs identity?' On the basis of data we include here, this volume will suggest that English language teachers do – perhaps now more than ever.

3

SOCIAL INTERACTION AND IDENTITY

INTRODUCTION

Having described how identity and the related concept of agency have been treated in both the wider arena of the social sciences and within education, and more particularly English language teaching, we now turn in more detail to the issue of the relationships between identity, agency and social interaction. In order to explore the roles of identity and agency in English language teachers' professional lives and practices, we need to see social interaction as a primordial site where identities are produced and made relevant. However, just as there are different views on the nature of identity, there is also a range of perspectives on the role of social interaction with relation to identity. In this chapter, we examine a range of perspectives on the relationships between identity and agency and social interaction. In order to see identity and agency in terms of social interaction, we need to build conceptual bridges between the 'macro'-concerns we have described in our survey of identity in the social sciences and in education, and the investigation of the relevance of identity when we look at the details of talk in interaction. In other words, we need to shift from a focus on the identities which are inherent in dominant discourses and social structures, to the real-time, historical processes in which these identities may be taken up, adapted or resisted.

ETHNOMETHODOLOGICAL AND CONVERSATION-ANALYTIC APPROACHES TO IDENTITY

The most powerful analytic framework for investigating how identities may be oriented to, taken up or resisted in social interaction is that of conversation analysis (CA), though as we pointed out in the previous chapter, its relationship with the more 'macro-level' concerns is, at the very least, problematic. However, because our approach pays attention to the details of key social interactions in which language teachers' professional lives are played out, we draw on concepts developed in conversation analysis and its approach to identity. For this reason, we begin our overview of how identity has been seen in terms of social interaction by examining the distinct contributions of ethnomethodological and conversation-analytic approaches.

A focus on identity in/as social interaction can be seen as a shift away from more static conceptions of identity in which people are ascribed membership of various groups: for example, according to class, gender, race, nationality and so on. In this more static view, a person's identity is almost an obvious, taken-for-granted attribution. One simply *is* white, Irish, middle-class and so on. People are categorised as belonging to certain groups, such as social class (for example, C2 skilled working class), and then studies can be carried out which link their belonging to this category with aspects of their behaviour. Seeing identity as linked to social interaction is also a move away from social psychology perspectives such as social identity theory (for example, Tajfel and Turner 1986), which investigated people's self-perceptions as members of social groups, and how they treat others depending on whether they see them as belonging to the same group (the ingroup) or not. Interestingly, this work showed that ingroup favouritism or bias operated whether the groups formed were based on larger social categories such as culture or gender, or were based simply on random or arbitrary group allocation. However, as in the more macro-sociological perspectives, identity is seen as something that can be ascribed to people, or that they can claim, but there is no attention to the ways in which 'identity work' is done in and through social interaction.

In seeing identity as an interactional and discursive phenomenon, attention is turned to the work people do through talk and other modes of communication to display, claim, disavow, or make relevant in any way, their own or others' membership of any social categories. Benwell and Stokoe (2006) define a discursive perspective on identity as entailing 'who people are to each other, and how different kinds of identities are produced in spoken interaction and written texts' (p. 6). Using this interactional perspective on identity, we shift from identity being what people are or have, to what they do. And a large part of what people do consists of how they use talk-in-interaction to communicate, their discursive practices. Tracy and Robles (2013) describe this link between discursive practices and identity:

> The identities a person brings to an interaction influence how that person communicates. At the same time, the specific discursive practices a person chooses will shape who he or she is taken to be, and who the partner is taken to be. (25–6)

In this sense, identity is not just an interactional phenomenon, but a profoundly *relational* one. As Agha (2006) puts it, 'a person's self conception differs from a second figure of identity, namely a "relational self" (the way in which that person is "read" by others), a figure that is critical to social interaction' (234). This idea of identity being inherently relational, 'who we are to each other', and as having critical importance for social interaction can be traced back through a theoretical tradition in the twentieth century in which the formation or construction of selves or identities was seen as intrinsically linked to processes of social interaction (in the work of Mead, Blumer and Goffman, for example).

However, it was the groundbreaking work of Harvey Sacks that began to show in detail how people in everyday talk made sense of the social world by using what he termed 'membership categorisation devices'. Membership categorisation devices are entities such as 'family' that contain categories (mother, father, son, daughter and so on) which are linked together. In his famous example (Sacks 1974) of how it was possible to make sense of 'the baby cried, the mommy picked it up,' he showed that because 'baby' and 'mommy' are classifications which both belong to the same membership categorisation device, we are able to ascertain that it is the mommy of that particular baby who picked it up, not just any 'mommy' who happened to be passing by. Sacks also showed that certain activities are bound to categories (for example, crying to babies, caring for babies to mothers), and that these categories are often related in pairs (parent–child, husband–wife, teacher–student), with rights and responsibilities attached to belonging to the categories. In social interaction, people may design their talk in ways in which they show accountability to the rights and responsibilities inherent in the categories they may claim membership of for themselves, or ascribe to others. For example, Stokoe (2009) shows how people involved in neighbour disputes categorise themselves and others in certain ways (such as 'old man', 'kids') or describe people in ways that imply category memberships ('she's eighty-three') in order to carry out such actions as formulating complaints and making denials. As Stokoe points out, this work challenges assumptions that it is not possible to capture identity phenomena in the detail of social interaction. This kind of work shows clearly that membership categories are not things that randomly appear in conversations, but are used in systematic ways by people to carry out social actions such as complaining or denying an accusation.

Work on identity in social interaction based on membership categorisation analysis (MCA) is a distinctive strand in the tradition set in motion by the early work of Sacks. However, according to Stokoe (2012), it has the status of a 'milk float' in relation to the 'juggernaut' of the CA tradition established by Sacks and his co-researchers Schegloff and Jefferson (see Sacks, Schegloff and Jefferson 1974). Identity has been a focus of attention in this tradition: for example, in the book edited by Antaki and Widdicombe (1998). The chapters in this volume all seek to reframe identities not as something people *have* but as things they *do* in and through social interaction. As Widdicombe puts it in the epilogue to the volume, a CA approach to identity is primarily concerned with

> whether, when and how identities are used [. . .] the occasioned relevance of identities here and now, and how they are consequential for this particular interaction and the local projects of speakers. (1998b: 195)

For example, Widdicombe's study of goths and punks in an English city in the same volume (1998a) shows how the young people approached by the researchers did not unproblematically accept being categorised as members of lifestyle groups. In interactions with the researchers, they resisted being ascribed identities as unthinking or unwitting followers of fashions, highlighting their own agency as they made choices about how to affiliate with the groups they had been identified as belonging to. As Widdicombe found, it was problematic to recruit people as possible spokespersons for certain identities, as the putative members of the groups resisted going along with being categorised in this way.

Within a conversation analysis perspective on identity, perhaps the most influential work is that of Zimmerman (1998). He shows how 'proximal' identities made relevant in the more immediate local properties of interaction articulate with 'distal' identities, those which are relevant to the activity or situation in which interactants are involved. He identifies three levels of identity: discourse, situated and transportable. Discourse identities are produced in and through the sequential organisation of talk-in-interaction. Examples of discourse identities are current speaker, listener, storyteller, story recipient, questioner, answerer, repair initiator and so on. When speakers assume a discourse identity, they may project a reciprocal identity for co-participants (for example, storyteller–story recipient, questioner–answerer). Situated identities are those which are relevant to the activity that participants are involved in, often activities in which there are institutional or 'official' roles, such as teacher–student, interviewer–interviewee, doctor–patient and so on. Thus, situated identities become relevant as actors pursue particular agendas and projects, and display knowledge and skills linked to the institutionally sanctioned activities in which they are involved. Discourse and situated identities need to be articulated, as it is through the moment-by-moment organisation of interaction or production of discourse identities that participants are able to pursue the larger projects relevant to their situated identities. The third level of identity in Zimmerman's framework is that of transportable identities. These are identities that can be ascribed to people on the basis of visible or otherwise salient attributes. As Zimmerman (1998: 90) puts it, these identities 'tag along' with us and can be potentially relevant to any situation. Examples of transportable identities are teenager, woman, child and English person. It is important to note that, in a conversation analysis perspective, such identities only become of interest to the analyst if there is evidence that they are oriented to in some way by participants in the interaction. Thus, the fact that someone may notice that another person is a young person or a person with a particular ethnic background will be of no relevance unless it can be described as an interactional phenomenon.

Zimmerman's framework is extremely useful for producing micro-analyses of the identity work that goes on in moment-by-moment interaction. In the field of TESOL, Richards (2006) has used this framework to show how the introduction of transportable identities into classroom discourse in a language classroom can have a powerful transformative effect on how the discourse and situated identities emerge. He introduces the notion of 'default identities', which are those which are seen to go along with the institutional nature of the setting (that is, teacher and student). Thus, teachers, in the situated identity as 'teacher', will normally take on discourse identities such as askers of questions and evaluators, and students will take on discourse identities such as respondents to questions. However, departures from these default identities can have profound effects on interaction, particularly when participants invoke aspects of transportable identity. As Richards points out, there may be moral reasons why teachers, in classroom interaction, may choose not to engage in self-revelation in which transportable identities come into play, as, for example, when they hold beliefs that are incompatible with their roles as responsible professionals or with the cultures in which they live and work (73). Such moral concerns in relation to transportable identities will inevitably emerge across the range of social interactions in which language teachers engage, not just in the classroom, and analysis will need to pay attention to how they emerge in the detail of interaction, particularly in the interplay between discourse, situated and transportable identities.

SOCIOLINGUISTIC PERSPECTIVES ON INDEXICALITY AND IDENTITY

However, rich and revealing as micro-analytic work on identity from an ethnomethodological or conversation analytic perspective has been, in this volume we need to go beyond a 'pure' conversation analysis perspective if we are to explore the links between the 'micro'-level of ongoing interaction, and the 'macro'-levels of identities as social, cultural and historical phenomena. As Blommaert (2005) argues, and as we noted in the previous chapter, CA uses a rather restrictive notion of context, limiting it to the immediate, empirically visible evidence, as seen in the transcriptions of spoken interaction. While such discipline has been immensely productive in producing insights into the sequential organisation of talk-in-interaction (see Schegloff [2007] for a detailed account), it limits its focus to what Blommaert (2005: 67) describes as the 'strict locality' of unique, one-time, situated interactions. As such, he claims that it does not allow us to gain a purchase on higher levels of situatedness, in which what comes into view may be 'large, general, supra-individual, typical, structural, and higher than the single society' (ibid.). For this, we need to broaden the lens to find ways in which we can link the micro-analysis of interactional detail with the ways in which identity has been a focus in the wider debates within the fields of education and TESOL. For this, we turn to Bourdieu's work on 'field' and 'habitus', and sociolinguistic work on indexicality and identity as the distribution of semiotic resources.

Bourdieu's (1985) concepts of 'field' and 'habitus' allow us to begin to make connections between the 'macro'- and the 'micro'-levels. Hanks (2005) offers a definition of Bourdieu's construct of field as a type of social organisation which has two aspects:

(a) a configuration of social roles, agent positions, and the structures they fit into and

(b) the historical process in which those positions are actually taken up, occupied by actors (individual or collective). (Hanks 2005: 72)

Hanks gives the example of roles or positions which may be part of the academic field, such as 'demanding instructor' or 'motivated student'. If we shift the focus to the second aspect of field, we need to examine the 'historical process' in which such positions are (or are not) taken up in such socially situated activities as seminar discussions, grading and evaluation (Hanks 2005: 72). This gives us a way of linking the 'micro' and the 'macro', or of seeing how identity needs to be explored in and through social interaction. For example, as we have seen in the previous chapter, the field of TESOL is a form of social organisation in which there are specific configurations of social roles, agent (or identity) positions, and structures of which they can be part. However, as can be seen in point (b) above, in order to grasp how the field is constantly reproduced, we need to explore how these positions are taken up by actors as they participate in situated activities: that is, in social interaction. Social interaction, in this view, is a primordial site not only for the reproduction of the field (in this case, TESOL) but for the development of each individual's 'habitus': that is, her dispositions and ways of acting and seeing the world. As Jenkins (2008: 42) puts it, Bourdieu's notion of habitus 'resonates loudly' with a conception of identity as embodied, and both individual and collective. Although Bourdieu (1993) sees the development of an individual's habitus as occurring through interaction with the field, it is a short step to see how such development needs to occur in and through engagement with the situated activities which constitute different fields. This provides a strong justification for focusing on social interactions in situated activities as sites where not only fields such as TESOL are reproduced, but also the identities of those who participate in them.

However, Bourdieu's concepts of 'field' and 'habitus', although useful for allowing us to see both aspects of the reproduction of social practices, do not provide us with resources for examining how identity formation is carried on in and through meaning-making activity in specific socially situated activity. When actors take up, adapt or resist identities in interaction, they do so using a range of semiotic resources, including language, gesture, smiling, laughter, movement, and artefacts that they may have to hand. In this sense, identity can be reconceptualised as sets of semiotic resources, which actors deploy as they resist or take up positions in ongoing interaction. Identity in this view can be seen as what Blommaert (2005) describes as 'semiotic potential', and, he argues, this in turn requires 'fine-grained analysis of how people *practically* identify themselves and others, and how they do so through the deployment of whatever means they have at their disposal (Blommaert 2005: 210; italics in original). As Blommaert points out, this moves us away from a reductionist perspective on identity as static, pre-established categories to the practical identity work people do as they engage in interaction.

However, as Blommaert repeatedly points out, individuals do not come to social interactions with equal 'means at their disposal'. In any society, or field of activity, semiotic resources will be unequally distributed, and analysis should not start from assumptions that all are able to participate equally. Power is always at issue where identity and agency are concerned. Thus, identity may become relevant in what happens before or after any piece of talk in interaction, as unequal access to resources may condition how and whether people can participate in certain activities in the first place, and how they do participate may be taken up and interpreted in identity-relevant ways by others 'after the event' (Blommaert 2005).

Let us summarise what we have seen so far. In building our bridges between the more 'macro'-concerns relating to identity and agency and this book's focus on social interaction, we have made two key shifts. First, using Bourdieu's concepts of 'field' and 'habitus', we have moved from the social positions and roles inherent in social structures to the 'historical processes' in which they are negotiated, taken up and possibly resisted in interactions. Second, we have moved from seeing identities as fixed, pre-established entities to seeing them as forms of unequally distributed semiotic potential whose deployment needs to be examined through fine-grained analyses of actual situated interaction. The next move is now to build a conceptual structure which will allow such 'fine-grained analyses' to say something about how larger social, cultural, political and historical phenomena relevant to identity and agency are 'pointed to' or 'indexed' in and through social interaction. For that, we turn to the construct of 'indexicality'.

The notion of 'indexicality' (Silverstein 2003) allows analysts to build links between real-time moment-by-moment language and interaction practices and wider cultural and social phenomena. The semiotic resources which speakers bring to any interactional event can 'signal', in different ways, what can be seen as 'contextual' features, which in turn provide a ground for others' interpretations of who they are and what they are doing (Gumperz 1982). Thus, semiotic resources can 'point to' or 'index' wider 'macro'-level phenomena. As Silverstein (2003: 201) puts it,

> When we think of the 'context' of linguistic signals macro-sociologically, (. . .) we think of things that perdure in one or another intuitive sense beyond any particular token interactional moment, and which semiotic material in such an interactional moment may index.

Thus, in the field of language teaching, we have perduring 'macro'-level identities such as 'non-native speaking teacher', 'teacher trainer/educator' or 'trainee'. At any moment in a specific socially situated interaction, any piece of 'semiotic material', such as the use of a particular term, the design of a turn, a glance or a nod, a smile or a laugh may be working to signal some aspect of a wider context which is of relevance to the ways in which participants identify themselves and/or others. This in turn may constrain, or enable, different types of agency. In other words, identifying oneself, or others, as a specific sort of person may have important consequences for what one is able to do, both in the immediate unfolding context of interaction, and in the wider context of present and future professional practice.

Indexicality works not only at the level of the signalling of wider macro-sociological categories in interaction. As Bucholtz and Hall (2005) point out, seeing identity as an interactional phenomenon entails a shift from conceptions of identity as relating exclusively to wider social categories such as class, race, gender and so on. They put forward a 'positionality principle' in which identity can be seen at three levels:

(a) macro-level demographic categories;
(b) local, ethnographically specific cultural positions; and
(c) temporary and interactionally specific stances and participant roles.

(Bucholtz and Hall 2005: 592)

This principle expands and enriches our view of identity work in social interaction. To give an example from the field of language teaching, a teacher may, through the use of semiotic resources in interaction, index membership of the wider social category of non-native speaker of the language she teaches, a professional employed in a locally prestigious language teaching organisation, and take up an evaluative stance in relating a classroom incident or in appraising a piece of published teaching material.

Bucholtz and Hall expand the notion of indexicality in identity work to focus not only on *which* types of identity can be made relevant, but also on *how* indexicality works as a process, in what they call the 'indexicality principle'. They identify four processes through which identities can be indexed in social interaction:

(a) overt mention of identity categories and labels;
(b) implicatures and presuppositions regarding one's own or others' identity position;
(c) displayed evaluative and epistemic orientations to ongoing talk, as well as inter-actional footings and participant roles; and
(d) the use of linguistic structures and systems that are ideologically associated with specific personas and groups.

(Bucholtz and Hall 2005: 594)

As an example of the first process, in social interaction relevant to their professional activities, language teachers may invoke transportable identities (in Zimmerman's term) by overtly describing themselves or others as 'native speaker', or attribute char-acteristics to their learners which are linked to their national identities ('Japanese students are shy'). Or, using the second process, they may signal identity categories more indirectly by leaving it up to the hearer to interpret what they are saying, as, for example, by positioning themselves as relatively powerless deliverers of a pre-ordained curriculum, rather than as agents with the capacity to innovate. In terms of Bucholtz and Hall's third process of indexing identity, teachers may design their contributions to interaction in ways that display a positive or negative assessment of any feature of the talk, or their own (lack of) knowledge of that feature. As an example, teachers may construct narratives of incidents from their own practices which display positive or negative evaluations of actions and/or participants, and which may display greater or lesser levels of 'epistemic access': that is, privileged knowledge as to participants' motives and so on. In terms of interactional footings or roles, a trainer in interaction with a student teacher may shift positioning from an authoritative source of knowledge about methodology to that of a 'fellow teacher' in supporting a decision made by the trainee. As for the fourth identity indexing process, teachers may use linguistic or other semiotic resources associated with the field of language teaching, such as when teachers in training begin to 'appropriate' specific terms by using them in their descriptions of events (for example, 'warmer', 'feedback', 'controlled practice'). By doing so, they may index membership, or aspi-rations to membership, of the field of language teaching, although the interactional effect of any such actions needs to be analysed as part of the ongoing sequence of turns.

It is important to reiterate that such indexicality work as described by Bucholtz and Hall's principle is never neutral or free from issues of unequal power distribu-tion. Blommaert points out that the systems of meaning that people can index with their semiotic resources are ranked and stratified. The use of any sign may index more or less powerful identities, and if they are powerful they may relate to what Silverstein (1998, in Blommaert 2005: 75) describes as 'centring institutions'. Such powerful institutions can impose indexicalities to which others may feel impelled to orient. As we have seen in the previous chapter, in the wider field of education, and more specifically in TESOL, centring institutions, such as ministries of education, organisations which award teaching qualifications or large publishing houses, may impose indexicalities that individual language teachers may feel they have little choice but to orient to, at least publicly. A case in point may be perceived pressure to adopt versions of communicative language teaching (CLT) as they appear in different countries' curricular standards and guidelines. This may lead to tension and conflict with serious consequences for the formation and maintenance of individual language teachers' professional identities (see Tsui 2007 for an illustrative case). However, the more powerful centring institutions are not the only centres in what Silverstein (2003) calls 'orders of indexicality'. Centring institutions which distribute indexicalities exist on various different levels, from global and national systems, to more local 'centres' such as peer groups or communities of practice (Wenger 1998). Thus, what any individual may index through their use of semiotic resources in interaction will be not only ranked and stratified, but also 'polycentric', and 'not all ways of speaking have equal value' (Blommaert 2005: 75). This has important implications for the approach to language teacher identity and social interaction in this book. Teachers may orient to identities which are attributed by powerful centring institutions, but they may also orient to other centres of indexicality which are relevant to aspects of their local contexts, and through these to identity categories which may not always fit those expected of them.

The framework of indexicality as put forward by scholars such as Silverstein (2003) and Blommaert (2005) forms a backdrop to the approaches to social interaction and language teacher identity which we draw on in this volume. While we do not necessarily refer to the concept specifically in the analyses, in each chapter we explicitly draw links between the interactional phenomena we explore in detail and the wider issues which affect the professional, and indeed personal, lives of English language teachers, and which have received attention in the literature. Our intention is not to examine the detail and sequential organisation of interaction for its own sake, but to add a rich and productive dimension to the work already being carried out on language teacher identity. Thus, as we hope will become clear as the data-led chapters in the volume unfold, we have adopted a range of approaches to the analysis of English language teacher identity in social interaction, which we feel are compatible with the position we have laid out in this chapter. They are approaches that allow us to examine in detail the moment-by-moment unfolding of situated interactions involving English language teachers in a range of settings, while keeping in focus the substantive identity-related topics of interest in the TESOL literature.

INTERACTIONAL PERSPECTIVES ON NARRATIVE, POSITIONING AND KNOWLEDGE

An example of how we combine these two dimensions can be seen in the treatment of narrative in the volume. In Chapter 2 we pointed out the centrality of narrative, or 'narrative knowledging' (Barkhuizen 2011), to practitioners' and researchers' understandings of language teacher identity. A large body of research on teacher identity sees narrative as a way in which teachers construct their actual experiences (as in the influential work of Clandinin and Connelly: for example, 2000) or as a sociocultural tool which can play a role in their development (Johnson and Golombek 2011). While our approach does not deny the importance of these perspectives, and indeed aims to complement them, we focus attention on the ways in which narratives are produced and built up in and through social interactions. The main concept we use for these analyses is that of 'small stories', narratives or narrative fragments that emerge in ongoing action and which are often a means through which participants carry out socially relevant actions. We recognise, with Barkhuizen, Benson and Chik (2014: 4–5), that there is a tension in narrative inquiry between approaches which focus on the content of narratives, and those which focus on the interactional work that any piece of narrative may be doing in a given situation. The former can be said to relate to 'big stories' while the latter has a concern with 'small stories' (Bamberg 2007), (usually) small fragments of narrative which appear in conversations, and through which participants may be doing various kinds of identity work.

Another perspective which allows us to combine a focus on interactional detail with wider 'macro'-issues is that of positioning theory. Positioning theory, in its original form, was developed by Rom Harré and his colleagues (for example, Harré and van Langenhove 1999; Harré et al. 2009). Its focus is on how people, in interaction, orient to what they call 'subject positions': that is, by positioning themselves, and others, in certain types of roles or identities, which are often related to participants' beliefs about what rights and duties pertain in the situation. Subject positions can relate to broader social 'master narratives' that influence what are taken to be rights and duties applicable in any local domain. However, our approach to positioning draws on a more discursively oriented approach, such as that of Korobov (2010), which shifts the focus away from cognitive issues such as concepts about rights and duties, towards the interactional work and discursive actions through which people position themselves and each other in social interaction. In this view, positioning is closely related to identity, and the analyses focus on specific discursive actions and interactional moves, and their relevance for the positions and identities participants ascribe to themselves and each other. A discursive approach to positioning can be combined with a focus on small stories, and this has been productively used in research on English language teacher identity (for example, Barkhuizen 2010), and this is a line of work we expand on in this volume, with a sharper focus on the interactional work being done by participants.

A further example of how interactional phenomena can be linked to wider substantive issues in the literature on teachers and teaching relates to the topic of knowledge. Most work on teachers' knowledge uses categories or taxonomies grouped around constructs such as pedagogical content knowledge (Shulman 1987) or, more recently, content knowledge for teaching (Ball et al. 2008). In contrast to these approaches, we shift the focus to what participants know and take others to know (and by extension what they are entitled to do) as an interactional matter. In doing so, we draw on conversation analysis work on epistemics in interaction (such as Heritage 2012a, 2012b), and related work on deontics which examines how participants can exercise power over others by getting them to carry out certain acts (Stevanovic and Peräkylä 2012). In drawing on membership categorisation analysis (Hester and Eglin 1997; Stokoe 2012) we show how the ways in which teachers assign themselves and others to categories such as 'native speaker' and 'non-native speaker' with their respective attributes can illuminate key issues in the recent ELT literature such as native speakerism or debates around English as a Lingua Franca (ELF).

CONCLUDING REMARKS: METHODOLOGY, DATA COLLECTION AND PRESENTATION

Before we move on to the data-driven section of the book, we finish this chapter with some comments about methodology and data presentation. In this chapter we have outlined our overall theoretical approach to identity and social interaction, and have briefly glossed the specific perspectives which are used to analyse data in the book. However, rather than front-loading extensive treatments of each individual perspective to the opening section of the book, we provide relevant background on each approach in the chapter in which it is used. This allows the reader to see each approach in the context of a specific issue in the teacher identity literature and a set of data. In this sense, the data chapters can stand on their own and be read by those interested in the specific problem, and can also work as a practical toolkit to provide guidance for researchers who would be interested in applying these perspectives on social interaction to their own data.

A key theoretical and methodological issue which runs through all the data-driven chapters in the book relates to the nature and use of discourse data which are either naturally occurring or have been elicited for research purposes. As will be seen, most of the discursive data analysed in the chapters have been elicited as part of the research process, and largely consist of interview or focus-group data (but see Chapter 4, which uses interaction from a teacher-training context). While we appreciate the value of using what has been described as 'naturally occurring' (that is, non-research-elicited data), we concur with recent work on reflexivity and co-construction in the research interview (for example, De Fina and Perrino 2011; Mann 2016) that this distinction is not entirely helpful. Thus, we consider research interviews and focus groups as 'live' interactional settings where identities and positionings are at stake and are talked into being, avowed, and rejected through discursive actions and interactional moves. This approach to the research interview is most explicitly seen in the final data-led chapter (Chapter 8), which uses Goffman's (1974) frame analysis to show the shifting positionings and identity-relevant moves of a researcher and research participant in an interview set up to elicit data. While the nature of the research interview is an explicit focus of this chapter, throughout the data-driven chapters we approach interviews and focus groups as co-constructed, identity-relevant interactional events.

In terms of data presentation, there is some variety in the ways in which the extracts are presented. This is due to the fact that different interactional phenomena are of relevance to the issues explored in the individual chapters. Thus, some chapters will draw on a wider range of the transcription conventions normally associated with conversation analysis than others. For those readers who are unfamiliar with conversation analytic transcription, a list is provided at the end of the book. While the book draws on some of the tools and procedures of conversation analysis, it does not claim to be a contribution to the research agenda of this field. Rather, it should be seen as an applied endeavour in which we draw on a set of theoretical and methodological tools which we believe to be adequate to the task of exploring issues of English language teacher identity as they emerge in co-constructed social interaction.

4

KNOWLEDGE, POWER AND IDENTITY IN TRAINER–TRAINEE INTERACTION IN PRE-SERVICE ENGLISH LANGUAGE TEACHER EDUCATION

INTRODUCTION

This chapter focuses on one dimension of identity: that which relates to knowledge, competence or expertise in the field of language teaching. We present an argument that what language teachers know, and how they know it, is closely tied in with identity: that is, who they are for themselves and for others in the various contexts of language teaching. In keeping with the focus of this book, we show that it is in social interaction in the various contexts of relevance to language teaching that knowledge identities are made visible and worked on. Furthermore, wherever there is knowledge, there is often asymmetry in that some people are held to have more knowledge than others. This has implications for power relations, as those who are considered to have more knowledge are often seen to have the authority to enable or constrain the actions of others who are taken to be less knowledgeable. Thus, the examples that we analyse in this chapter all come from a language education context where, for the participants, there is an orientation to knowledge asymmetry. We show that, in a language teacher education interactional setting where teacher trainers and trainees work together on trainees' lesson plans, participants position themselves and others with an eye to roles and identities that cannot be separated from issues of knowledge and competence. In doing so, we see that for them power is very much in evidence as they accede to or resist others' attempts to act on their own fields of action.

In the following sections, we briefly survey how knowledge, and its development, have been conceptualised in the field of language teaching, focusing on work on language teacher knowledge and expertise, how these grow, and the differences between novice and experienced teachers. We then go on to show how knowledge and identity are inextricably linked, the argument being that what individuals know and can do cannot be separated from who they take themselves to be, and to how others see them. We show how knowledge, learning and identity have been conceptualised in situated learning theories, particularly Wenger's (1998) notion of Communities of Practice. This is followed by some criticisms of these theories, relating to their lack of attention to power, and to the details of how identity work is done in social interaction. We argue that a strongly discursively oriented version of positioning theory, combined with concepts drawn from recent conversation analysis work on epistemics in interaction, may be better placed to bring out the subtleties of how identity work around knowledge is done in teacher education contexts where there

36

are knowledge and power asymmetries. The data we use to illustrate these arguments come from a specific language teacher education setting: lesson planning sessions on a pre-service ELT education course, in which tutors and novice teachers work together on the latter's lesson plans. Our analyses show that, although the tutors were treated as having privileged access to certain types of knowledge, there were constant subtle shifts in positioning as trainees carved out for themselves their own spaces for exercising agency. In discussing the implications of these analyses, we link the identity work done in these interactions to the wider discourses of TESOL, and the kinds of identities made available there. We argue that teacher education courses such as the one we focus on here may be designed to produce a certain sort of teacher identity – the minimally skilled deliverer of coursebook-based lessons, and that the social interaction that takes place in these courses is a site where these identities may be acquiesced to or contested.

KNOWLEDGE, EXPERTISE AND IDENTITY IN
LANGUAGE TEACHING

The nature of teachers' knowledge, its contents and how it grows, has long been a key topic in research on teacher cognition, which Borg (2006), in the context of language teaching, defines as the investigation or study of 'what language teachers, at any stage of their careers, and in any language education context, think, know or believe in relation to any aspect of their work' (272). Beyond language teaching, early work in this tradition set itself two important tasks: distinguishing 'knowledge' from 'belief', and identifying and describing different types of the former. Pajares (1992) attempted to clear up the 'messy construct' of belief and make it a workable construct for research on teaching. He seems to have been successful in this task as work on teachers' beliefs has carried on unabated ever since, with the construct, once separated from knowledge, rarely problematised, until recent work which relocates belief within more contextual, ecological and complexity theory perspectives (Kalaja et al. 2015; Kubanyiova and Feryok 2015). However, the construct of knowledge has had a rather more chequered history, with an array of sometimes competing conceptualisations emerging, including practical knowledge, personal practical knowledge and pedagogical content knowledge. For some researchers, knowledge, or one of its types such as practical knowledge or pedagogical content knowledge, is taken to subsume the concept of belief with beliefs being now an aspect of knowledge, or at least indivisible from it. Thus, for Verloop, van Driel and Meijer,

> It is important to realize that in the label 'teacher knowledge', the concept 'knowledge' is used as an overarching, inclusive concept, summarizing a large variety of cognitions, from conscious and well-balanced opinions to unconscious and unreflected intuitions. (2001: 446)

In the field of language teacher cognition, Woods (1996) denied that knowledge and beliefs were static, separable entities, seeing them as forming a continuum, with teachers drawing on knowledge and belief structures indistinguishably in carrying out planning and teaching. He coined the acronym BAK (Beliefs, Assumptions, Knowledge) to refer to this bundle of resources teachers rely on in their decision-making and interpretative processes.

Research on language teachers' knowledge has focused on a range of key areas, including the contents of language teachers' knowledge in relation to language as subject matter, drawing largely on the construct of pedagogical content knowledge (for example, Andrews 2007; Bartels 2005); the practical knowledge necessary for language teachers to implement approaches such as communicative language teaching (Woods and Çakır 2011; Wyatt 2009); and studies of different stages in language teachers' knowledge growth, with the construct of 'expertise' used to make comparisons between novice, experienced and 'expert' teachers (Tsui 2003). More recently, with the growing popularity of more situated learning theories, the relationship between knowledge and identity has been a focus of attention, in work such as Tsui (2007) and Morton and Gray (2010).

In earlier work (Morton and Gray 2010), we showed how, in the context of learning teaching, knowledge can be seen as largely a matter of identity. Drawing on Beijaard, Meijer and Verloop (2004), we described how the concepts of knowledge and identity have been conflated, and used their definition of identity formation as 'a process of practical knowledge-building characterized by an ongoing integration of what is individually and collectively seen as relevant to teaching' (123). A view of knowledge being 'who you are or are seen to be' as much as 'what you know' has strong links with how learning is conceptualised in Communities of Practice theory. As Wenger (1998) argues, acquiring the competence which allows one to recognise oneself, and be recognised, as a fully functioning member of a community of practice, is essentially a question of identity formation. However, situated learning theories such as Communities of Practice can often paint a picture of the path to becoming competent being one in which power differences between participants are flattened out, the only problem being that sometimes learning paths are blocked by 'old timers' who refuse to allow access to full participation. We take from situated learning theory that knowledge and identity are indeed inextricably intertwined, but we add to this the dimension of power, and the acts of positioning in which power is exercised and resisted.

EPISTEMICS AND DEONTICS IN INTERACTION

Another weakness in situated learning theories is they can lack a detailed framework for the close-up description of how knowledge/identity is oriented to and worked on in unfolding interaction. In this chapter, we draw on recent work in epistemics and deontics in conversation analysis (Heritage 2012a, 2012b, 2013; Stevanovic and Peräkylä 2012). In this perspective, knowledge is seen not simply as something that people walk around with in their heads ('inside the skull', as Kasper 2009 puts it), but rather as social interaction which goes on 'out there' as people jointly engage in all types of activity, from the most mundane to the most institutionally rarefied. People position themselves, and each other, in terms of what they know, how they have access to it, and what rights and responsibilities they have for knowing (or not knowing) something. Knowing, or not knowing, is not a neutral affair, as people are held accountable by others for having or not having access to knowledge. This is what Stivers, Mondada and Steensig (2011) mean when they refer to the 'morality' of knowledge in conversation. Linked to this is the idea of epistemic authority – that is, that a person may have an identity as an 'authority' because of perceived or expected privileged access to a specialised field of knowledge – and this may be oriented to by participants as a relatively stable and enduring state of affairs (Heritage 2012a: 6). In the case of this chapter, participants on a teacher training course will thus see the trainer as having access to the specialised knowledge of language teaching (subject matter knowledge and methodology).

Another dimension of power/authority is that of 'deontic' authority: that is, the position which is associated with the rights to set rules and norms about what should be done (Stevanovic and Peräkylä 2012). As Stevanovic and Peräkylä point out, these two types of power/authority are closely linked: it is by being recognised as having access to specialised fields of knowledge that we are invested with the authority to determine others' actions. People with epistemic authority can determine 'how the world is' but they may also use deontic authority to determine 'how the world ought to be' by constraining the possible field of actions of others. Thus, this is a conception of power which is very close to Foucault's in 'The Subject and Power' (1982), where power is seen not in simple terms as the exercise of physical constraint on bodies, but as a mode of action that acts upon the actions of others.

Our specific interest in this chapter is in knowledge asymmetry: that is, how participants orient to themselves and others as having differential access to knowledge, and, relatedly, with differential power to act or act on others' ability to act. Thus, inevitably, there must be a focus on power. Briefly, the participant who is positioned as having access to valued knowledge will be enabled to structure the possibilities for action of others who are positioned as having less knowledge. For example, as will be described in more detail below, lesson-planning conferences can become a kind of 'consultancy' in which the roles, or identities, of 'expert professional' and 'inexpert novice with problem' become available. However, as we shall see in the analyses, things are rarely as simple as that, and roles or identities can be resisted and shifted, as those positioned as less expert exercise agency. For example, as Stevanovic and Peräkylä point out, participants not only may agree to or resist others' proposals for future action, but also may accept or contest other participants' attempts to distribute deontic rights between the participants in specific ways. Thus, in the lesson-planning conferences, student teachers may either acquiesce to or resist trainers' proposals for future actions (ways of carrying out activities in the lesson), but they may also (in theory) negotiate the ways in which deontic rights are distributed.

This complexity is very relevant to the interactional context of joint lesson planning on a teacher training course. The rights to decide on certain courses of action are shared between the trainee and the trainer. For example, it is probably the trainer who has decided the topic and content of the lesson slot (that is, a 'chunk' of material in the coursebook, such as a reading, speaking, listening or writing activity or some work on grammar, vocabulary or pronunciation – or a combination of these elements). However, the trainee is free, at least initially, to come up with a plan for how she will execute this lesson slot. For example, the trainee may decide to use some pictures or realia to present vocabulary, or may decide to change the order of activities in the book, or even leave out an activity altogether. Stevanovic and Peräkylä point out that such negotiations of deontic rights and responsibilities in interaction can be very complex. For example, those who are taken to have strong deontic rights in a domain may not make those rights obvious in turn design, by 'commanding', while those with fewer deontic rights may upgrade their authority by being more strongly assertive (Stevanovic and Peräkylä 2012: 299).

CONTEXT, PARTICIPANTS AND DATA

The data analysed in this chapter were collected during a pre-service CELTA training course at a UK university language centre. There were eleven trainees on the course, all of whom except one were native speakers of English. The trainees were divided into two groups (one of six and one of five) for lesson-planning and feedback sessions with the trainers. Three trainers participated on the course (the authors, Tom and John, and a colleague given the pseudonym Jenny). The interactional setting focused on in this chapter is the lesson-planning sessions, in which the trainees presented their plans and proposals for upcoming teaching slots in lessons which they shared with other members of the group. These sessions usually took place one or two days before the trainee taught his or her slot in the lesson. They had previously been assigned a 'chunk' of material to teach (usually based on a coursebook) and had had time to think about how they might approach the teaching slot.

DISPLAYING DEONTIC AUTHORITY

In the extracts analysed in this section we can see instances where the trainers, who have a priori strong deontic rights, express them in quite abrupt, unmitigated ways. In extract 4.1, the trainee, Bill, is at the beginning of describing his plan for a language-focused lesson on articles to Tom (the trainer) and the other trainees. He begins by talking about his plans for a warm-up activity ('warmer'):

Extract 4.1: The definite article

```
1    Tom:  What's the warmer then
2    Bill: Well I mean I've ideas I just
3          I have a couple of questions
4          that might sort of lead me into
5          what I'm thinking about as a warmer
6          u::h yeah
7          should I confuse students
8          with erm the everyday phrase
9          >not everyday< but the phrase the definite
10         article
11         you know not the word the
```

```
12           but like he's the definite article
13           she's the definite article
14           it's the definite article
15  Tom:     No
16  Bill:    No just drop that okay
17           ((general laughter))
18           make a note (.) right
19  Tom:     I didn't know that
20           is that an English idiom?
21           he's the definite article
22  Bill:    It's an old sort of archaic thing at the moment
23           anyway erm (.) right skipping the warmer
24           ((general laughter))
```

Bill rather tentatively proposes the idea of introducing the lesson by using the rather infrequent idiomatic expression that someone can be called 'the definite article', meaning something like 'the real thing'. His diffidence about the proposal can be seen in line 7, where he describes the proposed action as confusing the students. However, it is designed as a genuine proposal, as can be seen in the use of the present tense ('I'm thinking about as a warmer') in line 5. Tom's response is curt, to say the least, and Bill humorously positions himself as having been told in no uncertain terms that the proposed course of action is a non-starter. The humour is shared by the other participants, though it seems not by Tom, who, without pausing, goes on to ask about the idiom. At line 23, Bill is still, arguably, orienting to the still-live inferences about the distribution of deontic rights and responsibilities, by suggesting rather hastily moving on from talking about the warmer. And, again, this seems to be oriented to by the other trainees, as can be seen in the laughter in line 24.

Another example of a rather curt display of deontic authority occurs in extract 4.2, in which the trainee, Gill, proposes using a role play as part of a lesson on the topic of jobs:

Extract 4.2: Role play

```
1   Gill:  … and then and then
2          I was thinking you know
3          to get more towards the freer practice
4          at the end again
5          maybe even do a bit of like role play
6          I was thinking this is where maybe you-
7          we've crossed a bit erm
8          ((disapproving growl)) no don't go
9   John:  don't go into role play=
10  Gill:  =okay
```

Again, we can see here that the trainee, Gill, rather downplays her deontic rights by designing her proposal as something she 'was thinking' (line 2), and by various hedges in line 5 (the use of modal adverb 'maybe', partitive 'a bit of' and softener 'like'). This is followed by more tentativeness in that another trainee has proposed using role play in the same lesson (we've crossed a bit). As in extract 4.1, the trainer, John, does not downplay his deontic authority and issues a blunt, unmitigated directive, the content of which Gill acquiesces to without delay by latching her 'okay' to John's command.

In both of these extracts, then, we can see the participant in the interaction who is invested with stronger deontic authority issuing rather blunt directives which in no way attempt to downplay any sense of deontic superiority. This is noteworthy, as conversation analysis findings on 'dispreferred responses' such as disagreements (for example, Pomerantz 1984) show that blunt, unmitigated disagreements are normally not very common in social interaction, and this may be due to face issues. No reasons are offered for these unmitigated displays of deontic authority. In extract 4.1, the very curtness of the claim to deontic authority is arguably oriented to by the participants in the interaction (possibly except the trainer). By positioning himself as having been well and truly told what (not) to do, even to the point of taking a note of it, Bill in a way turns the tables on the more deontically powerful trainer. He takes up an identity position rather like that of a schoolboy who has been reprimanded for suggesting something out of order, with the laughter suggesting he has gained the sympathy and complicity of his fellow trainees. He also exercises agency by controlling the agenda: that is, by moving swiftly on to another topic. In extract 4.2, in contrast, there is no apparent second-order positioning in terms of deontic rights and responsibilities, with Gill acquiescing to both the content of John's directive (what she shouldn't do) and his right to issue it.

In both cases, the trainers, by issuing rather blunt displays of deontic authority, attempted to ward off courses of action that would be likely to prove counter-productive from the point of view of their epistemic authority: that is, they oriented to themselves as having epistemic primacy (Heritage 2012a) in the form of access to the domain of knowledge of classroom practices, in which they could see the possible negative consequences of the trainees' proposed courses of action. In the first case, the more than likely result of confusing the students, and in the second, the inadvisability, from the students' perspective, of having two very similar activities (role plays) in the same lesson. However, while, from a pedagogical perspective, these may be extremely justifiable ways of seeing the possible outcomes of certain decisions, there was no attempt to make explicit the reasons for these prohibitions. In Foucauldian terms, actions on others' capacity to act were most definitely carried out. Neither student attempted to carry out the ideas which had been rejected by the trainer in the subsequent lesson. However, as we have seen, one trainee chose to engage in second-order positioning, inserting within the overall storyline of the lesson-planning session a sub-plot of a rather heavy-handed trainer crushing a novice teacher's idea, and in so doing enlisting the sympathy of his fellow trainees.

COMMITMENT FOR FUTURE ACTION

When someone proposes a course of joint future action involving other participants, the expected response is a commitment (or withholding of a commitment) to that future action. As Stevanovic and Peräkylä (2012) point out, it is important to separate the commitment from the proposed course of action itself. That is, participants can use a 'compliance token' such as 'alright' or 'okay' to display commitment to the future action, although the proposed course of action may or may not be actually carried out. In extract 4.3, the trainer, Jenny, proposes that the trainee, Martin, adjust the aims in his lesson plan to account for the role of writing in the lesson:

Extract 4.3: Lesson aims

```
1   Jenny:  I think if you were going to then
2           get them to write a report for a newspaper
3           your main aim would be writing
4           but if you're going to get them to speak it
5           (.) your main aim is going to be speaking
6   Martin: Yeah
7   Jenny:  With a subsidiary aim of writing
8   Martin: As long as there's writing
9   Jenny:  That'll be your subsidiary aim to write - the
10          writing
11  Martin: Okay
```

In lines 1–5, Jenny's turn is designed as a kind of teaching as she makes links between what happens in the classroom and what the lesson's aims are. This is very important in the context of the CELTA certificate course, as trainees have to show that what happens in the lesson reflects a coherent and justifiable plan. At line 6, Martin's 'yeah' is an acknowledgement or display of understanding of the content of Jenny's turn, and Jenny goes on in line 7 to complete the instruction on the distinction between a main and a subsidiary aim. In line 8, Martin may be further displaying understanding of Jenny's point, and in lines 9–10, Jenny explicitly proposes a course of action – writing will be a subsidiary aim in Martin's teaching slot. Martin responds in line 11 with a compliance token, displaying commitment to the proposed course of action.

In the case of the lesson-planning sessions, it is interesting to consider the extent to which they are 'joint' future actions. Of course, in the extract just analysed, it is the trainee who will teach the lesson slot, but the plan with which he goes into the lesson is a product of his own proposed actions and the decisions emerging in the joint lesson-planning session. Martin's lesson plan, which he will be assessed on, as well as the actual teaching, is now likely to have writing as a subsidiary aim, and this will have to be reflected in the lesson: for example, in the amount of time devoted to it in relation to the main aim. But not only Martin but also Jenny are responsible for the lesson, as at least some of what the trainee attempts to execute successfully will have been based on input from the trainer. We have seen that courses of action can be strongly advised or disadvised by the trainer's exercise of their deontic authority, with which comes a measure of responsibility for the success or otherwise of the outcome. Thus, producing a 'pass' lesson on a CELTA course is a matter of joint responsibility, and such a successful result depends on a combination of the trainee's agency and the trainer's epistemically based deontic authority.

Overall, such interactions point to a 'moral world' in which roles and identity positions seem to be oriented to by participants as pretty stable states of affairs. In terms of epistemics, Heritage (2012a) points out that 'epistemic status' is usually held by participants in interaction to be a relatively settled matter. People, by dint of occupying certain roles, will be granted certain epistemic access to attributes or possessions relevant to the role. Thus, parents will be taken to have privileged access to knowledge about their children, or pet-owners about characteristics of their pets, as numerous examples in Heritage and Raymond (2005) testify. In the context of teacher education, trainers will be taken by trainees to have epistemic access to, among other things, subject knowledge, teaching methodology, a practical sense of what is possible in the classroom, and what it takes to produce a successful 'CELTA lesson'. However, this epistemic status is inextricably linked with what could be coined 'deontic status' – it is also a fairly settled matter among participants that the trainer has superior rights in proposing future courses of action, including deciding between alternative courses of action. Thus, the storyline of the lesson-planning sessions resembles a kind of consultancy, in which the trainer, with her identity as an 'expert', has the power to shape what the trainee, with the identity of 'novice', does in the classroom or writes in lesson plans.

Thus, when trainers directly propose courses of action, trainees generally respond with commitments to carry out the action, such as 'okay', or 'right'. They very rarely withhold commitment or go as far as to question the deontic authority of the trainer in proposing a course of action. However, on the relatively rare occasions that commitment is withheld, it can force interesting shifts in footing among the participants and make available different discourse and situated identity positions. This is what happens in extract 4.4, in which the trainer, John, after some discussion and negotiation, presents the trainee, Gill, with the running order of the whole lesson, a very complete proposal for future action!

Extract 4.4: Vocabulary lesson (1)

```
1    John: this could be your way in
2          it could be it could be underneath
3          you could do jumbled letters
4    Gill: Ah ah right
5    John: So each job this'll be it'll be like
6          ok coalminer so it'll be like M-I-C erm R
7          you know whatever it is
8          and then you do the first one for them
9          you say okay here are some well known jobs
10         everybody yeah what I want you to do is to put
```

```
11              the letters in the right order yeah and that's
12              their little that's your little warmer
13              your little fun intro
14 Gill: Hm
15 John: Then ok meaty stuff here ((bangs table))
16              job duty then you know these
17              erm more dictionary work
18              sort of banker banking you know
19              psychiatrist psychiatry yeah a bit of drilling
20              ((lines removed))
21              yes this is what students at this level need
22              and then moving on to okay let's have a look
23              again at Martin's little job description now
24              we're going to try and do a similar thing
25              and you know write the job descriptions
26              but they mustn't mention the name of the job
27              we're - make it really clear we're going to read
28              each other's job descriptions and try and guess
29              from the duties what the job is.
30 Gill: Hm hm
31 John: You know I think that could be really nice
```

John delivers a proposed course of future action down to the performative details of what Gill might say in the classroom (lines 9–11, 22–4 and 27–9). Gill's responses are minimal. In line 4 she produces a 'news receipt' that displays that the idea of using jumbled letters is new to her, and in lines 14 and 30 her responses are simple continuers that show that John still has the floor. John completes his run-through of the proposed course of action with an assessment – the lesson could be 'really nice' (line 31). This is a first position assessment for which the whole evaluative tone has been made 'ripe' (Heritage and Raymond 2005) by the description of the proposed lesson, and, as such, it invites a second positioned assessment (Pomerantz 1984), which, in turn, could preface a commitment on Gill's part to carrying out the course of action: that is, by delivering the lesson just the way it has been packaged by the trainer.

However, Gill produces neither the due second positioned assessment nor any commitment to carrying out the proposed action. Rather, she shifts the footing of the interaction by asking a methodological question:

Extract 4.5: Vocabulary lesson (2)

```
1 Gill: so what's like the general structure for a
2              vocabulary lesson
3              or is there not really a set one you just=
4 John: =well sometimes you see sometimes
5              you're going to be doing vocabulary on its own
```

```
6            this is like this is like a kind of segregated
7            vocabulary slot that's focusing on jobs and duties
8            that's related to the theme of the lesson erm
9            but sometimes vocabulary's going to be
10           like in in whoever's doing the reading in Bill's
11           where it's linked very much to the reading that's
12           coming up yeah
13  Gill:    mm mm
14  John:    erm but I don't think there's any one way to
15           necessarily do something yeah
16  Gill:    Okay
```

By asking a methodological question about vocabulary lessons in general (not only the one that has just been described) in lines 1–3, Gill brings about a subtle shift in footing and, by extension, identity positioning. In the previous extract, John was orienting to a discourse identity of proposer of a course of action, with the proposal dressed in vivid and evaluatively loaded terms. He was also orienting to a situated identity of more expert other, vested with the epistemic and deontic authority to propose a course of action rather forcefully and in such detail. Gill was placed in the discourse identity of listener and very likely compliant executor of the proposed actions, and in the situated identity of novice in the world of teaching, in relation to John.

By shifting the footing in lines 1–3 in extract 4.5, Gill now takes on the discourse identity of questioner, and a situated identity of actively engaged and thoughtful (if inexperienced) practitioner. She asks a question that goes 'under the surface' of a recipe for classroom behaviour, asking about the possibility of an underlying structure for vocabulary lessons. This in turn places John in the position of shifting footing from focusing on a specific plan of action for a lesson, to elucidating some underlying principles about the teaching of vocabulary. John is still in an 'expert' situated identity, but Gill's exercise of agency has resulted in him having to shift to a different domain of epistemic authority – not just how to do a particular lesson, but the possibility of there being a template to produce many such lessons. In lines 14–15, John shifts to an even higher level of generality in making the point that there is not just one way of doing things. In doing so, he indexes a possible teacher identity – the flexible practitioner who is not tied to a set of recipes, but who recognises that the same outcomes can be achieved through different means. Perhaps indexing this kind of identity is a response to Gill's own exercise of agency, in which, by withholding commitment to the expert's proposed course of action, she shifted the footing of the encounter at that moment in a way that allowed her to get something from the interaction that may well have better met her needs as a developing reflective practitioner. In any case, by line 16, she has not displayed compliance with the proposed course of action, but displays acceptance of John's response to her question.

PROPOSALS

In the lesson-planning data, what we have are proposals, not assertions or announcements. That is, neither trainers nor trainees announce what will happen in declarative indicative clauses with future reference, as in this invented example: 'you will divide them into pairs and do the speaking activity on page 43.' Rather, what we find are what Stevanovic and Peräkylä (2012) describe as proposals, in which the plans and intentions (for the speaker's own or others' actions) are expressed as non-binding and contingent, often with the use of a modal verb such as 'could'. Stevanovic and Peräkylä argue that proposals indicate deontic symmetry in that rights to constrain future actions are more evenly distributed among speakers. This orientation is maintained in second speakers' responses when they convey approval of the proposals by making positive assessments such as 'that's good' or 'I think it is quite nice.' By doing so, second speakers claim epistemic access to the assessed referent and thus rights to evaluate it.

In the lesson-planning data, there is clear evidence that the deontic playing field is not so level as in the context examined by Stevanovic and Peräkylä. First of all, there are no examples of trainees' second positioned positive (or negative) assessments of trainers' proposals. Assessments of proposals do occur, but in three sequential contexts only: trainers' assessments of trainees' proposals, trainers' assessments of their own proposals, and trainees' assessments of other trainees' proposals. We shall examine some examples of each of these before considering why trainees' assessments of trainers' proposals are absent from the data.

In extract 4.6 Julie (a trainee) and Tom (the trainer) are talking about a listening activity that Julie is going to do in her teaching slot. The focus of the conversation is the gist task she will give the students on the first listening.

Extract 4.6: Nice little listening

```
1    Tom:    That kind of gist task do you think
2            (2.5)
3    Julie: Yeah my gist task would be very simple questions
4    Tom:    Hm hm
5    Julie: Her name
6    Tom:    Hm hm
7    Julie: Where does she come from
8    Tom:    What's her job
9    Julie: And what's her job
10   Tom:    Yeah um that's fine hm hm that's fine yeah (.)
11           that's a nice little listening looks really nice
```

Following Tom's question about the gist task in the listening activity, Julie presents her proposal as contingent by using the conditional modal 'would' (line 3), and goes on to give two examples of the gist questions she would use. Tom joins in this listing of possible gist questions by suggesting 'What's her job' (line 8) and Julie approves this addition to the list by repeating it. In lines 10–11, Tom produces a strong positive assessment of the proposal, with repetition of positive adjectives and intensification with 'really' (line 11). In producing this assessment of Julie's proposal (which admittedly he has partly contributed to), Tom claims epistemic access to the plan of action as described in the preceding turns, and also rights to assess it in terms of whatever properties make it a 'good' gist listening task.

Trainers, however, do not only positively evaluate trainees' proposals. In extract 4.7, the trainee, Martin, is describing his plans for a reading and speaking activity about UFOs.

Extract 4.7: It's a little vague

```
1    Martin: read over these things discuss in pairs groups
2            (.) take away team up with the other group
3            have to solve the puzzle
4    Jenny:  What kind of information will they get?
5    Martin: I'm not entirely sure
6    Jenny:  So are you thinking about like you saw a- on the
7            19th of March
8    Martin: It will be linked to the UFO thing (.) it will
9            have to be a puzzle something for them to work
10           out
11   Jenny:  You'll have to puzzle it out ((laughs))
12   Martin: Short texts each find out what happened (.) talks
13           about what it leads on to
14   Jenny:  That's what I'm thinking (.) it's a little bit
15           vague at the minute because you haven't worked it
16           out exactly but if you could contextualise it a
17           little bit
```

In terms of epistemic access, this extract shows that it is trainees who are taken to have access to knowledge about their own plans and intentions, and it is the trainers who need to gain access to these by asking questions, as Jenny does in lines 4 and 6–7. The interaction is 'ripened' (Heritage and Raymond 2005: 16) for Jenny's assessment of Martin's proposals by Martin's display of uncertainty in line 5, and her own assertion of his need to 'puzzle it out' in line 11. In lines 14–17, Jenny produces a somewhat negative assessment of Martin's plan as it stands. However, negative assessments in the data were never blunt or unmitigated, and we can see here that Jenny downgrades the negativity of the assessment by qualifying it as 'a little bit' vague (lines 14–15). She also offers an account for the assessment ('you haven't worked it out exactly), which implies that Martin will be able to exercise agency in clarifying his plans at a later point, and offers him advice on how to do this ('if you could contextualise it a little bit'). As in extract 4.6, the trainer claims epistemic access to the content of the proposal (which she has contributed to gaining by asking questions) and also claims rights to assess it in terms of its viability as a blueprint for a piece of classroom teaching.

Turning to the second sequential environment for trainers' assessments of proposals, their assessments of their own proposals, in extract 4.8 (part of what was previously analysed as extract 4.4) we can see how the trainer, John, positively evaluates his own proposal.

Extract 4.8: That could be really nice

```
1    John: then ok meaty stuff here ((bangs table))
2          job duty then you know these
3          erm more dictionary work
4          sort of banker banking you know
5          psychiatrist psychiatry yeah a bit of drilling
6          ((lines removed))
7          yes this is what students at this level need
8          and then moving on to
9          okay let's have a look again at Martin's little
10         job description now we're going to try and do a
11         similar thing and you know write the job
12         descriptions but they mustn't mention the name of
13         the job we're - make it really clear we're going
14         to read each other's job descriptions and try and
15         guess from the duties what the job is.
16   Gill: hm hm
17   John: you know I think that could be really nice.
```

In this example, it can be argued that the proposal is, at least to some extent, a joint production, as there has been quite a lot of work on Gill's initial proposal. However, the way in which this proposed plan of action is delivered does not bear any marks of contingency or collaboration. Gill's role is to act as a recipient of the plan, and she orients to this by minimal contribution in the form of continuers, as in line 16. In line 17, John delivers an assessment of the proposal, thus claiming epistemic access to its contents (unsurprising, considering his role in its production) and the rights to assess its worthiness as a plan for classroom action.

The third context for the production of assessments of proposals is that of trainees assessing other trainees' proposals. This is the only context in which trainees produced assessments of proposals, as they never assess proposals put forward by trainers, even if, as we have seen, these proposals may be the result of at least partially collaborative efforts. It is also important to point out that the trainee who produces an assessment of another trainee's proposal is the one whose lesson plan is being worked on: that is, trainees did not produce assessments of their own proposals for their own lessons. In extract 4.9, Gill suggests the idea of turning the reporting back phase of an information gap activity into a TV report for Martin's teaching slot:

Extract 4.9: TV report

```
1    Gill:    cos if you've got different I mean I know
2             but you're gonna like have two different things
3             that they're gonna do as an exercise for the
4             information gap so then and that's where you're
5             gonna join the two bits together
6    Martin:  mm
7    Gill:    but unless you kind of like did something else
8             >I'm not sure what<
9             and then they ended up like with two different
10            report forms
11   Martin:  ( )
12   Gill:    and then they can then it can be a speaking
13            exercise
14            that's your report back
15            as though they were like a TV reporter
16            or something like that
17   Martin:  I can see erm I can generate a TV report maybe
18            that could be good
19   Jenny:   mm hm
20   Martin:  yeah that would be very good.
```

This piece of interaction represents a fairly frequent occurrence in the lesson-planning sessions. The trainer takes a back seat (Jenny only intervenes with a continuer at line 19) while the trainees provide suggestions for a trainee's teaching slot. Here, Gill presents a proposal for getting students to report back on something they have read as if they were TV reporters. In lines 17–18, Martin first claims ('I can see') and then demonstrates understanding ('I can generate a TV report maybe'), thus establishing epistemic access to the contents of the proposal. He then goes on to produce two positive assessments of the proposal, the second assessment (line 20) being an upgrade of the first. Here, Martin claims epistemic access and rights to evaluate a proposal made by a fellow trainee.

DISCUSSION AND CONCLUSION

We hope to have shown in this chapter how micro-analyses which draw on concepts from recent conversation analysis work on epistemics and deontics can highlight the subtleties of how identity work is done in teacher education contexts where there are knowledge and power asymmetries. It was claimed at the beginning of this chapter that epistemic work in social interaction displays the 'deep connections between epistemics and identity, between what we know and who we are' (Glenn and LeBaron 2011: 19), and that 'the management of rights to knowledge and, relatedly, rights to describe or evaluate states of affairs can be a resource for invoking identity in interaction' (Raymond and Heritage 2006: 680). To this we can add the ways in which epistemic authority translates into deontic authority, the right to constrain others' options for future action. As Stevanovic and Peräkylä (2012) point out, both epistemic and deontic status can be held by participants in some contexts to be pretty stable affairs. There can be shared knowledge or 'common ground' in that different participants will be treated as having primary access to certain domains of knowledge, and there may be deontic common ground among the participants as regards their institutional roles, rights and responsibilities.

There was a significant amount of shared epistemic territory in the lesson-planning sessions. All participants had access to the coursebook materials on which teaching slots were based, and most had been witnesses of previous teaching practice slots. Also, epistemic access to trainees' proposals was a feature of the unfolding interaction in the sessions, as can be seen in the fact that other participants were able to claim sufficient access to produce assessments of them. However, other epistemic domains were restricted to certain participants. Most notably, the right to produce assessments of proposals as good or deficient examples of a category of events or activities was restricted to the trainers (as in extracts 4.6, 4.7 and 4.8). In other words, trainers were granted access to knowledge not only of any specific plan of action, but of whether this plan of action met the necessary criteria to be considered a good example of its type. And, of course, linked to these epistemic rights come the deontic rights to constrain future actions if these do not conform to the criteria for adequate examples of their type. Thus we can see that trainers mitigated their deontic authority when they were putting forward their own proposals, working them up to be contingent and non-binding. Given the common ground of epistemic and deontic authority invested in the trainers, it may not be surprising that they worked to defeat any inference that they were being heavy-handed or misusing their authority. However, this authority emerged much more nakedly, as we have seen, when trainers sought to avert a course of action that in all probability would have threatened a successful outcome of the lesson.

Analyses like the ones in this chapter suggest that identities such as 'trainer' and 'trainee', or 'expert' and 'novice', need not be seen only as 'brought along' to the specific types of encounter we have examined. They are, of course, partly brought along in the sense that the epistemic and deontic 'common ground' shared by participants points to the institutional rights and responsibilities. However, for these identities to have any reality, they need to be 'brought about' by the participants in the interaction. By closely examining such practices as proposing plans for future action, displaying (lack of) commitment to them, or claiming access to certain territories of knowledge by producing assessments, we can see how identities are indexed in and through social interaction. We can also see that such rights and responsibilities which go along with certain identities are inextricably linked with agency – who you are is linked not only to what you know, but to what you can do, and get others to do. In the lesson-planning sessions in this CELTA course, the trainers displayed considerably more agency than the trainees – they could shoot down whole planned courses of action, and propose whole lesson chunks that trainees would be expected to do. They could use their wider rights to epistemic access to the practices of teaching to assess trainees' courses of action – both positively and negatively. Trainees' space for manoeuvre was much more limited. They could propose plans of action with the always real possibility that they could be shot down, and they could suggest proposals for their fellow trainees, but could only evaluate proposals made by trainees. They did not orient to having any rights to override trainers' proposals, at least in the lesson-planning sessions themselves. However, committing to a proposal in interaction does not imply that the course of action was actually carried out, and for that an examination of the actual lessons taught would be necessary.

What do these micro-analyses tell us about the wider issues of language teacher identity discussed in the first two chapters? One way to approach this is to note that the epistemic territories to which trainers claimed access as they assessed trainees' proposals were in a strong sense 'out of bounds' for the trainees. It seemed to be enough that courses of action met with approval, as being something that 'would work'. Trainees rarely trespassed on to these epistemic territories by questioning why a course of action was considered the right thing to do. That is why extract 4.5 is such an outlier. It is a deviant case in that deontic congruity is denied by the trainee and in doing so she shifts the interaction on to the epistemic territory that is the preserve of the trainer – the possibility of an underlying structure for vocabulary lessons, not just the sequence of activities in the trainer's proposal. It is an example of how a shift in footing at the micro-level of interaction can signal broader shifts in the 'brought about' identities. It may be a momentary shift, but if carried out in sufficient numbers by participants in interaction, it may be enough to change the 'rules of the game' with important implications for the identities of all concerned.

Trainees in the lesson-planning sessions generally show compliance (at least in the lesson-planning encounter) with the proposals made by the trainers. These 'micro' acts of compliance index compliance on a wider scale. It may be no exaggeration to claim that English language teachers are 'made', to a large extent, in and through the interactions that take place in the formative phases of their careers. As Asif Agha has shown (2006), identities can be seen as materially constituted through repeated semiotic acts over time. The kinds of micro-actions we have analysed in this chapter, such as presenting and evaluating proposals for courses of action, and making claims to certain epistemic territories, can be seen as 'bringing about' certain identities – often those which are consistent with being a compliant deliverer of pre-packaged ways of doing things, without access to the epistemic territories where such practices are generated, critiqued and contested.

5

POSITIONING ANALYSIS OF ESOL TEACHERS' 'SMALL STORIES' ABOUT INDIVIDUAL LEARNING PLANS IN RESEARCH INTERVIEWS

INTRODUCTION

In this chapter, we focus on what can be broadly described as English language teachers' 'professional' identities: that is, how they position themselves in relation to salient aspects of the everyday work they do, and the wider institutional and social contexts that impact on their professional practice. The language teaching context examined is that of English for Speakers of Other Languages (ESOL) in England, the teaching of students who are migrants to the UK, an 'extremely complex and diverse group' (Cooke and Simpson 2008: 1–2) which includes migrant workers, refugees and asylum seekers, and who may range in age from schoolchildren to elderly, long-established residents. The interactional context is a set of research interviews carried out as part of a large funded research project, the ESOL Effective Practice Study, which aimed to establish factors that contribute to successful learning in ESOL with the aim of improving teaching, learning and assessment (Baynham et al. 2007). Although the interviews did not have a specific focus on identity, much of what the teachers said was extremely relevant to identity issues, as shown by Callaghan (2006) in a detailed re-analysis of three of the interviews.

The data analysed in the chapter consist of a set of extracts from these interviews in which teachers talk about individual learning plans (ILPs), which are documents that many ESOL teachers are required to fill in to establish and track individual learners' goals and progress. We focus on these because, as Burgess (2008) points out, they are key texts in that they construct what is literacy and language learning according to national policy and, in so doing, 'construct the identities of teachers and learners by specifying the abilities which comprise desirable identities' (4). Thus, we analyse extracts from interviews in which teachers take up a stance towards ILPs, in narrative-like or 'small story' activities co-constructed with the researcher–interviewer. We focus on the ways in which evaluations of ILPs are co-constructed in these narratives, and the ways in which they are used and developed rhetorically to perform particular identities (complying with/resisting the requirement to use ILPS, being a teacher who attends to the individual needs of students with or without ILPs, being an agent who intervenes on behalf of students and so on). Our approach in this respect is similar to that taken by Baynham (2011) in his narrative analyses of extracts from the same corpus. According to Baynham, the interview is

an invitation for interviewees to display and comment on their professional practice, thereby indexing professional identities, through the stances they take up, and
what they align to, both towards the interview co-participant (the interviewer) and
what the talk is about (their practice and the contexts for it). (Baynham 2011: 70)

By limiting our analyses to discourse around one very significant object or text (the
ILPs) we are enabled to bring the teachers' stance, positioning and alignment more
sharply into focus, as they index identities relevant to the context of professional
practice in which they are immersed. We do so by examining relatively brief orientations to narrative activity that appear in the interviews, teachers' 'small stories' in
which they take up positions regarding ILPs. These brief excursions into narrative
are an opportunity for participants to position themselves, their learners and occa-
sionally the interviewer in relation to what the talk is about: ILPs and the practices
surrounding them.

THE CONTEXT: ESOL, SKILLS FOR LIFE AND ILPS

The ESOL Effective Practice Study was carried out at a time when the then Labour
Government 'Skills for Life' (SfL) strategy for adult education was at its height. This
was a national policy initiative for Adult Literacy, Language and Numeracy (ALLN),
in which unprecedented sums of money were released to fund this long-neglected
sector of adult education (Gregson and Nixon 2011). ESOL had been a particularly
neglected corner of adult education, with much provision being informal and many
teachers working without specific training or qualifications. However, under the
aegis of SfL, ESOL became part of the broader strategy for upgrading the workforce's
basic skills, and was thus becoming subject to much greater control and regulation
than before. Hamilton (2009) likens this process to the enclosure of common lands
in the past, where what was once a loosely defined and more informal set of practices
has stricter boundaries drawn around it, with a resulting reorganisation of student
and tutor identities.

Such 'enclosure' has not necessarily led to a greater professionalisation of ESOL
teachers. Much of the new provision for ESOL teaching certification still works with
a 'training' model of teacher preparation (Morton et al. 2006), in which teachers are
positioned as mere technicians delivering classroom instruction, often with poor pay
and working conditions. In order to avoid this de-professionalisation, Cooke and
Simpson (2008) argue that ESOL teachers need to be equipped to engage critically
with the policies and frameworks that impact on their working lives. This is arguably
more critical for ESOL teachers than for those in other areas of English language
teaching. As Cooke and Simpson put it, 'Because of the position of ESOL at the
crossroads of policy, theory and practice, ESOL teachers find themselves having to
respond to constantly changing outside pressures' (2008: 12).

One such pressure point, and one that is still 'a hotly debated and contested aspect
of SfL pedagogy' (Gregson and Nixon 2011:4), is the ILP. According to guidance
available online through the Education and Training Foundation's resources portal
'Excellence Gateway', an ILP is, among other things:

- A personalised, flexible route map to guide each learner's journey
- A dynamic working document, owned and used by the learner, supported by teachers, employers and others
- A record of learning goals and progression routes, initial and diagnostic assessment information, learning targets, progress and achievements within different contexts for learning

http://www.excellencegateway.org.uk/content/eg5377

Although the 'personal' nature of ILPs is emphasised, in reality tutors are expected to do the work of translating learners' individual goals into the language of the ESOL national curriculum in order to produce targets that are measurable. These are what are known as SMART (Specific, Measurable, Achievable, Relevant and Time-related) targets. As Hamilton (2009) points out, tutors are positioned as brokers or mediators between their students' aspirations and demands, and the system's requirements for accountability. Tutors may respond in different ways to this positioning. Some may opt for a kind of 'strategic compliance' (Seddon 1997; Shain and Gleeson 1999), in which they pragmatically use the parts of the system that they find most useable or workable, while others may engage in less willing compliance (Shain and Gleeson 1999) by simply going through the motions of filling in ILPs retrospectively, with little or no negotiation with students.

Previous work on ILPs using ethnographic, literacy practices and actor network theory frameworks (Burgess 2008; Hamilton 2009) has shown how tutors are co-opted as active agents in the implementation of the wider SfL policy framework and specific aspects of it, such as ILPs. Official documentation provides what Hamilton (2009) describes as 'permissive guidance', leaving practitioners some leeway or 'surface autonomy' in exactly how they adapt ILPs for use in their own institutions. Thus, while ILPs do constrain which desirable identities are available in terms of what is counted as learning, the regime of 'permissive guidance' leaves room for a range of identities to emerge in response to policy and institutional demands. Burgess and Hamilton's literacy practices approach aims to show how 'texts themselves are central to such projects of social ordering and to the constituent processes of aligning and materialising identities' (Hamilton 2009: 239). Our approach complements this work in that we share an interest in these same texts (ILPs) and in the processes of aligning and materialising identities. However, in line with the perspective of this volume, we shift the focus to examining how tutor identities are aligned and materialised in ongoing social interaction in a research interview, in sequences where these objects (ILPs) are topicalised. There is no further 'interpretation' of what the tutors' identities might actually be (cf. Callaghan 2006), but the analytic focus is on how they 'do' identity by positioning and aligning themselves and others with regard both to the immediate interactional context of the research interview and the interlocutor, and to the people and events they portray in their accounts and descriptions of practice concerning ILPs.

DATA: THE RESEARCH INTERVIEW AS SOCIAL INTERACTION

The extracts selected for analysis are drawn from a larger corpus of forty interviews conducted with ESOL teachers in London and the north of England, collected as part of the ESOL Effective Practice Study. The interviews were carried out after observation of a lesson given by the teacher, and were designed to 'shed light on effective classrooms "from the chalkface", as well as giving insights into the effects on practice of broader, institutional factors such as the ESOL curriculum and college structures' (Baynham et al. 2007: 35). According to Callaghan (2006), the approach to the interviews was 'ethnographic' as their purpose was to gain an emic view of the teachers' worlds of professional practice by 'encouraging them to talk freely, using personal narrative and linguistic choice to give insight into their views, priorities, and concerns, without being overly directed or led by the interviewer' (Callaghan 2006: 7).

As Callaghan points out, even though the interviews were not designed to focus on identity, many issues relevant to the teachers' professional identity emerged in the talk. He argues that the interviews produced more – and better – identity-relevant data than would have been the case if identity had been an explicit topic in the interviews. This leads interestingly to what can be seen as a neglected topic in work on identity in social interaction – the research interview. It is the case that some researchers interested in social interaction, particularly from a discursive psycho-logical or conversation-analytic perspective, eschew the interview as a source of data, preferring 'naturally occurring' interaction (see Potter and Hepburn 2005 for an extensive treatment). However, as De Fina (2011) points out, the research interview is a particular context in which professional identities play a role, and it is a domain that has been 'conspicuously absent from identity studies' (225). In this sense, the research interview is no less a 'naturally occurring' context than any other interac-tional setting, with the difference being in how the ensuing data are treated by the analyst. Broadly speaking, this refers to the distinction between research interview transcripts as 'resource' and as 'topic' (Byrne 2012). When interview data are seen as a 'resource', they are used to provide access to the interviewee's inner thoughts and world outside the interview. When interview data are seen as 'topic', the focus is on the joint construction of versions of reality between the interviewer and interviewee. As Mann (2011) argues, much interview-based research in applied linguistics has underplayed the co-constructed nature of the data elicited, preferring to use inter-views as a resource to be mined for 'themes' relating to the topic and contexts of interest. In this use of interview data, 'context' is an already given background to what is going on, and the features of interest have usually been decided upon already. The problem for the analyst is to find evidence of these features in the transcribed talk, usually concentrating only on the interviewee's answers.

A more interactionally sensitive approach (and one in line with the focus of this book) is to concentrate on how features of context are made relevant by partici-pants in the interaction. Such features may coincide with topics of interest already identified from researchers' knowledge of the literature or immersion in the setting, but this should not be taken for granted. Richards (2011) points out that a more interactionally aware stance to context is advantageous as it allows analysts to pay attention to 'participants' orientation to context rather than beginning with assumptions about relevant features of the professional context and seeking to interpret speaker meaning in terms of these' (202). As he argues, using the latter approach is more likely to obscure our understanding of participants' positioning than shed light on it. In re-analysing these interviews taken from a study which had a more 'ethnographic' approach, we shift the focus to the ESOL teachers' orientations to relevant features of context. The emergence of ILPs as identity-relevant artefacts is as much a feature that was made relevant by the teachers themselves in the interviews as it was a feature of the macro-context (the performance measurement or 'audit culture' within the SfL agenda). This is seen in the fact that ILPs were as likely to be brought up initially as a topic in the interviews by the teachers as by the interviewers, thus providing evidence that ILPs were indeed a salient feature of the teachers' professional landscapes. However, how they actually positioned themselves in relation to these artefacts as they co-constructed the interview with the researcher revealed more levels of complexity in identity-relevant positioning than would be the case if the analysis was limited to identifying 'themes'. Crucially, a major resource used by the teachers in their positioning and stance taking was that of narrative, particularly those brief excursions into narrative activity that have been described as 'small stories'.

SMALL STORIES, POSITIONING AND IDENTITY

Narrative has long been of interest to researchers working in the broad field of second language teacher cognition, the study of what language teachers think, believe and know, and how this relates to what they do (Borg 2006). Narrative has been seen as an essential means by which language teachers come to know and gain an understanding of their own practices. Much of this research has set out to claim legitimacy for narrative as a form of knowing, deserving of equal importance with other more 'paradigmatic' forms of knowledge (Bruner 1986). Teachers tell stories about their practices, about their own life histories and professional trajectories, and in so doing, develop understandings which they can use as a resource for further development, and which researchers can use to gain insights into what teachers know, and how this knowledge is gained and undergoes change. Barkhuizen (2011) describes the ways in which narrative is implicated in how teachers come to understand their practices as 'narrative knowledging', and leading advocates of narrative inquiry such as Johnson and Golombek (2011) trace how it has evolved from being seen as a tool for bringing about change in teachers' practices, to one which allows for teacher professional development, and is potentially transformational for the entire field of second language teacher education.

In general, the work that goes under the label of 'narrative inquiry' has tended to focus on larger narratives that have been written down or elicited in research interviews, and which can cover relatively long periods in teachers' lives and careers, such as Tsui's (2007) study of a language teacher's identity over a large portion of his career. These are examples of what Bamberg (2007) refers to as 'big stories', the production of which entails participants' stepping back from their everyday activities to reflect on them. 'Big stories' are specially produced as part of a research project, carried out either by teachers themselves or by researchers from outside the teachers' contexts. They are in a sense a 'time out' from the hurlyburly of the types of activity research participants are normally engaged in and, as such, as Freeman (2007) puts it, they represent life 'on holiday'. In terms of analysis, the main interest is in their content, what it is the stories are about – the characters, events and plots, and how they develop.

In contrast, 'small stories' are types of narrative which emerge in the course of other activities. They are the types of stories we tell each other when we are doing other things, such as having a conversation, teaching a class, or even participating in a research interview that is not necessarily focused on eliciting narrative. These can include a wide range of discursive activities that go beyond canonical personal narratives about events in the distant, or recent, past. Georgakopoulou (2007: 2) gives a useful, brief definition of small stories as 'an umbrella term to cover a gamut of under-represented narrative activities'. Thus, Baynham (2011) shows how, in talk about their professional practices, ESOL teachers produced a wide range of narrative activities, indeed 'small stories', which included not only personal narratives, but also generic/iterative narratives, hypothetical or future narratives, narratives as examples, and even negated narratives (of things which did not happen).

Whatever the type of narrative activity, small story research is interested not just in the internal content and structure of the story itself, although these are important, but also in how the story came to be told at all, what its function is in the surrounding interaction, and what the teller was accomplishing by telling it. An important aspect of what anyone may be accomplishing by engaging in these types of narrative activity is in conveying and indexing a sense of identity. As Freeman (2007: 156) puts it, small stories 'are extremely valuable for showing how identity gets renegotiated and reconstructed in and through social interaction'. And, in the context of language teaching, Barkhuizen (2010: 291) shows how a pre-service teacher's small story can be seen as a way of constructing an answer to the question 'who am I?'.

As Vásquez (2011) points out, small story research shifts the focus from narrative inquiry to narrative *analysis*. In narrative inquiry, researchers are interested in the 'what' – that is, the content of the elicited stories – whereas in narrative analysis, the focus shifts to the 'how' of narrative activity. As Vásquez puts it, 'Narrative analysts are interested in how individuals construct, project, claim, negotiate, or resist various identities, and they closely examine speakers' discursive choices in order to do so' (2011: 543). In narrative inquiry, researchers, and teachers, may be concerned with how the narrator reveals 'who they really are' through self-reflection, while, as Bamberg observes, narrative analysis is 'interested in narrators who are engaging in the activity of narrating, that is, the activity of giving an account; for instance, when we engage in making past actions accountable from a particular (moral) perspective for particular situated purposes' (2007: 170). It is the emphasis on the situatedness of narrative activity and its moral accountability that make a small story narrative analysis approach a powerful tool for the study of language teacher identity. As Vásquez reminds us, identity is always socially situated, with identities performed in local, situated contexts (2011: 539). She argues that, as language teaching and learning are situated and relational processes, it is time that we paid more attention to how language teacher identities are performed and invoked in and through the small stories language teachers tell.

As for accountability, small story analysis allows us to focus on what the story is doing at the moment it is being told. To extend an idea from conversation analysis, we can ask, 'why this story, told this way, now?' Where a story is produced at a point in an interactional sequence, and how it is constructed, will accomplish some social action, such as warding off competing (possibly negative) interpretations of what was going on, or inferences about a participant's character or competence. People do not generally tell stories out of the blue for no apparent purpose, but, in Potter's (1996) terms, they have a stake and interest both in the depiction of characters and events in the story and in what this may mean for the ongoing interaction in which they are currently engaged (in which the telling of the story is a component). Thus, teachers' accounts of their practice in any context (including research studies) will not be a neutral or 'innocent' description of what went on, or what they were thinking or intending, but will be designed to carry out a social action of relevance to how they are positioned both in terms of the events depicted in the story and in relation to the interlocutor(s) to whom they are telling the story.

However, these shifts from big to small story research and from narrative inquiry to narrative analysis leave open the questions about what specific procedures can be used for the analysis of narrative data. Pavlenko (2007) criticises how narratives have generally been analysed in applied linguistics, and offers some guidelines for researchers to help them broaden their analytic foci. She argues that much of the narrative-based research in applied linguistics limits itself to focusing on what she calls 'subject reality': that is, how events in stories are experienced by the teller. Narratives are subjected to some kind of content or thematic analysis in which themes or categories emerge from the data, often without any reference to any exist- ing theoretical concepts which might throw light on the origin of the categories and how they relate to each other. However, and importantly for our concern with identity, Pavlenko suggests that the most problematic aspect of this approach to narrative in applied linguistics is its 'lack of attention to ways in which storytellers use language to interpret experiences and position themselves as particular kinds of people' (2007: 166–7). Pavlenko argues that work on narratives in applied linguistics needs to attend to not only subject reality, but also life reality (findings on how things are or were in the storyworld) and text reality (the ways things or events are narrated by storytellers). To reflect this widening of the lens, analysis needs to go beyond the coding of themes or content, to take in analysis of context (both at the sociocultural and historical level, and at the micro-level of the setting of the production of the narrative) and of form (the ways in which narratives are structured and the devices used by storytellers to accomplish interactional purposes).

Turning to the more specific procedures for the analysis of small stories, Bamberg (2007) offers a useful framework, which draws heavily on the construct of position- ing. With its emphases on how participants negotiate and resist certain identities and orient to their own and others' moral accountability both in the storyworlds and in the telling of stories, small story research has a clear affinity with positioning theory. And, indeed, small story researchers such as Bamberg and Korobov (Bamberg 1997, 2004; Korobov and Bamberg 2007) draw heavily on the construct of positioning in their analyses, as indeed does Barkhuizen (2010) in his small story work in applied linguistics. Bamberg and Korobov's work is a version of positioning theory which is somewhat removed from the original work of Harré and his colleagues, in that it takes a much stronger discursive and anti-cognitivist stance (Korobov 2010). It is also a view of positioning which links it explicitly to identity, with Korobov describing a discursive approach to positioning as 'the identity-relevant force of certain discursive actions' (2010: 272). In this sense, positioning theory is a means by which identity work carried on through discursive actions can be explored, rather than positions being some kind of normative moral order or 'rules' that participants invoke in interaction.

Bamberg's (2007) framework for the analysis of small stories consists of three levels of positioning:

- the content of the story itself and the ways in which characters and events are represented
- the coordination of the interaction between the storyteller and audience
- the ideological positions or master narratives with reference to which narrators position themselves and others.

Analysis begins with a focus on the content of the story itself: its characters, spatial and temporal coordinates, and plotlines. The aim is to describe how the storyworld is built up, how people and events are represented in relation to possibly relevant social categories and their attributes. The analysis then shifts from the 'there and then' of the storyworld to the 'here and now' telling of the story in real time. At what point in the interaction does the narrative emerge? How are the different elements of the story put together in the unfolding interaction between the storyteller and his/her audience? What interpretations does the telling of the story encourage or attempt to ward off? By bringing together the two worlds (the 'there and then' of the story and the 'here and now' of the telling) speakers can make a 'position' visible, not only for themselves but also for their interlocutors. In carefully analysing the first two levels of positioning we can come full circle by moving to the third level, in which we focus on how, in their positioning work in the first two levels, speakers may comply with or counter wider ideological master narratives or discourses by which they themselves are positioned. This analytic process is depicted in Figure 5.1.

In this chapter, we draw on both Pavlenko's wider recommendations and Bamberg's more specific positioning analysis procedure to examine the small stories produced by ESOL teachers in research interviews as part of a large research project (Baynham et al. 2007). Following Pavlenko, our interest is not only in how these teachers interpret their experiences of events, but also in how the world of their practices is constructed, and how their accounts are structured and sequenced in the interactive context of their production. As Bamberg suggests, we proceed by first examining the content of the story in the 'there and then', before moving on to how

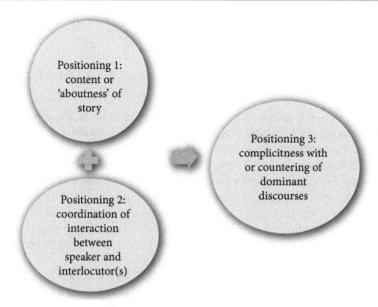

*Figure 5.1   Positioning analysis procedure for small stories
(based on Bamberg 2007: 170–2)*

it is co-constructed in the coordinated interaction between storyteller and audience in the 'here and now'. We then relate the positions emerging in the way these two positioning levels are brought together to the wider 'macro'-context of the dominant discourses of adult education and ESOL. In doing so, we can see whether and how these teachers resist or comply with the identities that are available to them, and what other identities may emerge in and through the positions they take up.

In taking up identity-relevant positions, participants take up an evaluative stance with regard to objects (such as the ILPs), and in doing so, align themselves and other interlocutors with regard to these objects and other salient features of context (Du Bois 2007). Moreover, a positioning and 'small stories' approach sees the use of evaluative expressions as an aspect of social practice (Wiggins and Potter 2003), rather than as a means of recovering participants' underlying attitudes to key objects and aspects of the wider 'master narratives'. Wiggins and Potter highlight a distinction between 'subjective' and 'objective' evaluative practices that is useful for the analyses of these teachers' small stories. Subjective evaluations refer to those in which participants express an individual preference or dislike for something, using words such as 'love', 'enjoy' or 'hate' to display subjective experience. Objective evaluations are those in which participants indicate directly some quality of the object itself, whether it is 'good', 'bad', 'beautiful', 'disgusting' and so on. In their analysis of evaluative practices at meal times, Wiggins and Potter suggest that one function of subjective evaluations is to account for the speaker engaging in specific activities. This is an interesting line of analysis to follow with the present data, as teachers' evaluations (whether subjective or objective) may be linked to their accounts of practice: that is, whether and how they engage in the literacy practices related to ILPs.

POSITIONING AND EVALUATIVE STANCE TOWARDS ILPS IN TEACHERS' 'SMALL STORIES'

In order to select the sample of interview extracts for analysis, the following procedure was used. First, the corpus of interviews was examined to identify any identity-relevant themes which were topicalised by the participants, and which involved the kinds of narrative practices described in the previous section. It quickly became apparent that ILPs were a prominent focus of concern, and that these were often brought up by the teachers themselves, without prompting. All extracts in the corpus of interviews where ILPs became a topic, and in which teachers produced 'small stories' in positioning themselves in relation to them, were isolated and subjected to further analysis, using Bamberg's procedure as described in the previous section.

The four data extracts analysed here are chosen to be illustrative of two broad evaluative stances in the ways teachers positioned themselves in relation to ILPs. They are from interviews with two different teachers. The first (extracts 5.1–5.2) adopted a generally accommodating and at least partially positive stance towards ILPs, while the second (extracts 5.3–5.4) shows a more critical stance. However, whether or not a teacher adopted an explicitly positive or negative stance towards ILPs, the positions taken up were complex in that there were descriptions of various types of compliance or non-compliance. In keeping with the focus on 'small stories', all the extracts have narrative elements, so that IPLs as objects, tutors, learners, and other actors such as managers are positioned within these narrative activities, mostly generic/iterative, but with some personal narrative and exemplars. The participants in the interviews were the interviewer (a member of the Effective Practice project research team), always marked by the letter 'I', and the teacher (identified by the letter 'T').

In extract 5.1, the teacher positions herself as someone who is familiar with ILPs and uses them routinely, and as knowledgeable both about her students' needs and how to 'translate' them into measurable 'SMART' targets reflecting elements in the ESOL curriculum.

Extract 5.1: 'I try to get them to narrow it down a bit'

```
1   I: I hadn't thought about that because you do map the
2      worksheets to the curriculum. And you do have the
3      codes. So what do you tell the students?
4   T: Well when they're doing the ILPs when we're going
5      over them every few weeks I say have a look and see
6      if you can find any of these codes on the work.
7      Have you done these? So they can tick their own
8      ILPs of what they've covered.
```

```
 9  I: So when you devise an ILP you map the outcomes to
10     the items in the curriculum?
11  T: Yeah
12  I: So what do you do if the student says- What do you
13     want to do? I want to learn English.
14  T: You say well why do you want to learn English? Is
15     it for a job? Is it for (.) er to speak to your
16     neighbour? Okay. Is it to watch television and
17     understand it? Is it to go to your child's school?
18     And put those as individual goals and make them
19     slightly more measurable.
20  I: And how do you get from say I want to talk to my
21     neighbour to an item in the-
22  T: Well there are things that are like swapping
23     personal information. So swapping personal
24     information with another student they can then do
25     with their neighbour. There's a student in my E2
26     class who talks with her neighbour and her
27     neighbour practises with her. That was one of her
28     goals. She comes in and said my neighbour told me
29     this vocabulary. Er people say I want more words
30     with spelling. I say well how do you think you can
31     do that? I sort of try to get them to narrow it
32     down a bit.
33  I: mm
```

In 'small story' terms, the whole extract is a generic/iterative narrative in which the teacher describes her regular or usual practices when using ILPs. The ILPs appear in the story as something unexceptional and 'going over them' as a regular occurrence ('every few weeks' – line 5). At various points, the teacher adds a performance element by inserting direct speech, as in lines 5–7 where she reproduces her words to the students as she gets them to work on their ILPs. As Baynham (2011) points out in his analysis of a set of interviews from the larger corpus from which these extracts are drawn, performance appears throughout the range of narrative types in teachers' 'small stories' of practice, not just in personal narratives.

In terms of the co-construction of the interview, the researcher–interviewer does not, as in other examples, ask the teacher explicitly to evaluate ILPs, but rather asks questions to confirm understanding (lines 9–10) and to elicit more detail on the teacher's practices. Interestingly, the interviewer uses performance in his questions (lines 12–13), setting the scene for the teacher to respond with a turn which is almost completely composed of performance elements, apart from the last turn constructional unit. In this turn, the teacher positions herself and the students as involved in a dialogue, with the students' self-expressed goals being translated into something 'slightly more measurable'. The teacher is positioned as a skilful practitioner who is concerned with the students' agency, but who is able to form a bridge between the students' goals and the demands of a performance measurement culture. Thus, talking to a neighbour can be matched to the curricular item 'swapping personal information' (lines 22–3). The positioning of students as agentive can be seen in lines 29–32, where the teacher uses a mixture of performance and diegetic summary to show how she involves the students in working on narrowing down their goals or finding ways to achieve them. In sum, what Hamilton (2009) describes as 'permissive guidance' here allows the teacher to create a space in which she can construct an identity by positioning herself as compliant with the 'master narrative' of a performance measurement culture by showing skill and regularity in the types of practices expected of those using ILPs, but also allowing for her students' and her own agency as they negotiate what goes into the ILPs.

However, in extract 5.2, which is the continuation of 5.1, we can see a subtle shift in the teacher's positioning, especially in response to an evaluative comment by the interviewer which positions the teacher in a very explicit identity-relevant way as someone who has 'bought into' the performance measurement culture.

Extract 5.2: 'You've bought into it yourself I suppose'

```
1    T: So you're trying to train them really into what
2       you- What set-up you've got.
3    I: mm mm
4    T: Trying to get them through the system.
5    I: And do you- Do you run against insurmountable
6       problems there or do you find that things seem to
7       work quite well or-
8    T: I'm quite a good sales person ((laughs))
9    I: ((laughs)) yeah (.) you've bought into it yourself
10      I suppose.
11   T: Well some of it I have and some of it I haven't.
12      It's kind of top heavy. But if you can say to them
13      it's for you to keep and if you come back to
14      college in three years you can show me what you've
15      learnt before and then we can look at what you need
16      to learn next to see if you can remember these
17      things. It's personal to you so- That's how I try
18      and- I say we need to have evidence you know. And
19      um if that's- You know for education things have
20      changed and we do need to have evidence that you're
21      learning rather than me just saying that you're
22      learning.
23   I: And they're okay about that?
24   T: Yeah
25   I: They tend to take on board everything that you've
26      said.
27   T: Well they're accommodating I think that group.
```

At lines 1–2, we can already see a subtle shift in the teacher's self-positioning, and that of her students. The practices she has described in her previous turns are meant to train them into 'the set-up' and 'get them through the system', leaving open an inference that such actions may not necessarily be exclusively in the interests of the students achieving their own learning goals. This inference is supported in line 8, in which the teacher positions herself in this ongoing generic small story as 'quite a good sales person'. This positioning by the teacher, as someone who is trying to train students into the 'set-up', 'get them through the system' or is acting as a 'sales person' could be seen as taking up an identity that is somewhat distanced from that of someone with a solid commitment to the intrinsic worth of such practices.

However, in lines 9–10, the interviewer seems to take up another inference, one in which the teacher is showing willing compliance with the system, having 'bought into' it. Here, the interviewer is positioning the teacher in relation to the perfor-mance management culture, which the ILPs represent, by depicting her as having a positive evaluative stance towards that 'system'. Interestingly, he does not explicitly align himself with the teacher in this way, especially as the term 'buy into' can have a slightly negative connotation. However, this positioning is resisted by the teacher, who steps back from a full to only a partial commitment to the system which ILPs represent. Here, the teacher positions herself as having autonomy and agency, she 'buys into' what she values in the system, but rejects other aspects of it: for example, the fact that it is 'top-heavy' (presumably referring to bureaucratic imposition from above).

Having shown agency in negotiating the space allowed by permissive guidance, the teacher in the rest of the turn creates a space to elaborate on the aspect of the system she does position herself as 'buying into': that is, there is a need for there to be evidence of learning, both for students themselves (it's personal to you' – line 17) and to meet the needs of the system. This she does by again introducing performance into her generic/iterative narrative, using direct speech to show how she addresses the students. The students are positioned in the story as participants who need to be convinced of the benefits of 'evidence'. Indexing the wider master narrative of the shift towards evidence-based practice, the students are also positioned (along with the teacher herself) as being part of a wider culture of education in which 'things have changed' (lines 19–20). The role of performance is worth commenting on here. It not only seems to appear across the range of narrative types as argued by Baynham (2011), but also may have the function of contributing to a positioning of higher commitment to a stance, by putting one's own voice directly into the narrative, the voice itself taking up a positioning or stance in relation to the topic under considera-tion, by being seen to persuade others of its benefits.

The following two extracts (5.3 and 5.4), which again come from one interview, represent the examples in the data where teachers took up an explicit negative stance towards ILPs, with the use of objective evaluations. In 5.3, in her long turn, the teacher combines generic and personal narrative to describe her past and present practices in relation to ILPs, positioning herself as someone who practises a rather less willing compliance with a system she does not believe in.

Extract 5.3: 'It's absolute codswallop'

```
1    I: So what do you think about the demands that are
2       being made of teachers now to do individual
3       learning plans?
4    T: Oh we do those anyway
5    I: For each student?
6    T: We do them anyway
7    I: Do you think it's useful?
8    T: No it's rubbish it's absolute codswallop just sit
9       making it up at home (.) tough well you do don't
10      you (.) well you can't say can you ((laughs)) well
11      it's absolute well no you'll- when you're writing
12      them (.) OK at ((name of college)) I was really
13      good I did all the assessments and I sat and did
14      all these grids and graphs and bloomin tables and
15      worked out exactly what what the students needed
16      you know from these assessments things you know
17      like oh six of them were absolutely dreadful at
18      form filling three of them didn't know their
19      alphabet you know things like this (.) and then
20      tried to incorporate these (.) tried to make a
21      syllabus from these things which you can't do it
22      because there's there's no backbone to it and
23      you've you've just got to fill it in so when then
24      when you're filling in your ILPs you like just get
25      your syllabus and your work scheme and your lesson
26      plans and just see what you've done and then I
27      preferably fill them in half termly and then just
28      get the students to sign them (.) and put smiley
29      faces on or depressed faces as the case may be
```

In this extract, in contrast with 5.1 and 5.2, the interviewer does invite an evaluative response ('So what do you think about …' and 'Do you think it's useful?'), and this is forthcoming in the teacher's long turn beginning at line 8. Interestingly, before responding with her evaluation of ILPs, the teacher positions them as part of the normal routines in her institution ('We do them anyway'). This can be seen as a claim of agency, as if ILPs would be part of her and her colleagues' practices, whether or not they were being externally demanded. However, as can be seen in the long turn from line 8 to 29, doing ILPs 'anyway' is in no way to be construed as endorsement of their worth.

Beginning at line 8, the teacher takes up a very negative stance towards ILPs and the practices surrounding them by using objective evaluation. Describing them as 'rubbish' and 'codswallop', she positions herself as someone with the epistemic authority to condemn ILPs as worthless, based on her experience of using them. This strong negative objective evaluation needs to be backed up with some evidence of epistemic access, and thus occasions the narrative activity that follows, the generic and personal small stories. In lines 8–9, there is a generic narrative in which she describes her current practices relating to ILPs, which basically consist of 'making it up at home'. This can be seen as a clear case of unwilling compliance, or even straight disobedience as 'making it up' flies in the face of what is expected of ILPs. The teacher here adopts an identity of someone who is willing to resist the external demands made upon her by subverting or even sabotaging the expected practice. Interestingly, this account of not engaging in ILP-related activity in the expected ways is juxtaposed with objective, not subjective, evaluation as in Wiggins and Potter (2003). It seems, then, that both types of evaluation can be linked to accounts for (not) engaging in certain activities.

In line 12, the teacher shifts into personal narrative to contrast her current practices with a 'there and then' in which she was compliant with what was expected ('I was really good' – lines 12–13). The use of the term 'good' (an objective self-evaluation) here is interesting, as it indexes a kind of childish identity, as in being well-behaved (she actually uses the term 'naughty' later in the interview – data not shown). It produces an effect in which ESOL practitioners are treated like children who have to comply with demands that make no sense to them or have no worth. The personal narrative in lines 12–21 paints a picture of someone attempting to comply with the external demands made of them in a positive spirit, but who is eventually defeated by the absurdity of what they are being asked to do. Thus, her lack of compliance in her current practice is not construable as something capricious (she just cannot be bothered filling in ILPs properly) but as born out of the painful experience of having once been 'good' and of having tried to comply. In this way, a professional identity is maintained, and any inference that might point towards a lack of professional seriousness is warded off. As in extracts 5.1 and 5.2, the personal narrative is also enhanced by the use of performance-like elements. These are seen in lines 17–19, where the teacher's own voice 'at the time' is invoked as she tried to incorporate learners' needs into the ILP format. This use of performance enhances the effect of epistemic access, positioning her as 'really there' at the time, struggling with the unreasonable demands made of her, but with the students' interests at heart.

From lines 23–9, the teacher shifts back into generic/iterative narrative as she provides further description of what she does now. Her description of the practice of retrospectively filling in the ILPs based on the syllabus, lesson plans or schemes of work is worked up as something she is forced to do by the circumstances (by being juxtaposed with the previous narrative in which she tried to comply in a previous job), and indeed reflects a practice which was reported by a large number of the teachers in the other interviews. As for the students, in this small story they are positioned as having very limited agency, just retrospectively signing what has already been decided on their behalf. The addition of the detail of putting smiley or depressed faces on the ILPs reprises the childish theme indexed in being 'good' (or 'naughty') and indeed may add a mocking element to the already clearly negative stance that has been established.

A little later in the interview, the interviewer shifts the topic to an explicit focus on the differentiation of learners' individual needs, to which the teacher responds with a long turn which combines generic, exemplar and hypothetical narrative to construct a professional identity of someone who is very aware of students' needs and tries to cater for them in her practices.

Extract 5.4: 'Why can't you spend your time doing something you know more constructive?'

```
1   I: Do you think that students do have different needs?
2   T: Oh definitely yeah and you try and address those
3      but why you've got to write it down on a stupid
4      piece of paper I've no idea it's just stupid I mean
5      we know in this class that there are two ladies who
6      can't read and write they're very very illiterate
7      well I try me best but without sitting one to one
8      one to one one to one they're never going to get to
9      be as good as the grade fours at writing writing
10     are they (.) unless you can give them but you've
11     got to just try and incorporate that and make
12     either make allowances for them or pair them with
13     someone better or give them extra time or and then
14     give them extra little bits you know now and again
15     but you just can't do it all the time otherwise the
16     rest of the students would disappear wouldn't they
17     if you were just sat with two students all the time
18     I find that difficult but I'm aware of it you're
19     aware of it and you try and address it but (.)
20     instead of filling out these stupid pieces of paper
21     for every flipping student why can't you spend your
22     time doing something you know more constructive to
23     help them?
```

The use of the emphatic auxiliary 'do' in the interviewer's question (line 1) raises a possible inference that the teacher, in evaluating IPLs so negatively in her previous turns, rejects the underlying assumption that students' individual needs have to be recognised and acted on. Rejecting this assumption would indeed position the teacher outside what is generally accepted to be good practice in teaching, so her long turn can be seen as a way of fending off any such interpretation. In this turn, she constructs a narrative in which she shows herself to be knowledgeable not just about students' individual needs, but also about professional practices which are more effective at meeting them than filling in ILPs. At the beginning of the turn, she sharply distinguishes between addressing students' needs and writing things down 'on a stupid piece of paper' (lines 3–4). This constructs an identity of a professional who knows what students' needs really are, and can find ways of meeting them, but this professional agency is restricted by absurd external requirements.

Beginning at line 5, there is an example or exemplum narrative (Baynham 2011), in which she describes two women with literacy problems in her class, and what she does to try to support them, mentioning such practices as 'making allowances', pairing them with more able partners or giving them more time. Again, providing detail of professional practices builds an identity of someone who not only is knowledgeable about pedagogical options, but has values that lead them to look for ways to help students with particular difficulties. However, having this practical knowledge also has the effect of showing that the teacher is aware of the limitations of what can be done (perhaps in contrast to those behind the introduction of ILPs?). This is shown in the shift to hypothetical narrative in lines 15–17, where she paints a picture of what might happen if she were to go beyond certain limits in meeting students' individual needs in class. At lines 20–3 she summarises her argument and deftly brings the focus back to the interviewer's question: professionals *are* aware of students' individual needs (she has demonstrated this in this turn) and know how to help them, but are impeded in doing so by the requirement to fill out 'stupid pieces of paper' instead of doing 'something constructive to help them'.

DISCUSSION AND CONCLUSION

These illustrative analyses suggest that taking up identities in relation to ILPs in the ongoing interaction of these interviews is far from a simple matter. Instead of there being stable identities and underlying attitudes, the identities which are made available through discursive actions keep shifting in response to actions in previous turns. Evaluative practices, in the form of subjective or objective evaluations, are used in the pursuit of rhetorical goals, such as providing accounts for (not) engaging in certain activities. Participants may seem to take up one position but then withdraw from it, only to shift towards it again, as in the analysis of the first two extracts above. This is not surprising, as a policy of 'permissive guidance' as described by Hamilton deliberately leaves space for some agency, but in doing so may also allow for a certain ambivalence in terms of the extent to which ESOL practitioners position themselves as having 'bought into' the system. And this agency and ambivalence is very much alive in the co-constructed interaction of a research interview with an interviewer who, as in the case of this study, was very likely to have been an ESOL practitioner themselves, someone who will have their own positioning towards the policy environment in which the profession has to work.

The analyses suggest how a 'small stories' approach linked to more interactionally aware versions of positioning theory and discursive work on stance and evaluation can balance the demands of focusing on identity both in terms of wider 'master narratives' and in terms of the co-constructed interaction in interviews. These 'master narratives' can be seen in terms of an 'official narrative', in which state-funded bodies advocate for the need for accountability in tracking adult ESOL students' learning. This is contested by an alternative, critical narrative, which sees ILPs as an example of a top-down imposed bureaucratic practice, which seeks only to control teachers and students and is not actually beneficial for establishing and meeting learning goals. In their ethnographic and literacy practices-based work, Burgess (2008) and Hamilton (2009) show how ILPs operate as 'key texts' in the ways in which both tutors and learners are aligned or positioned with regard to the pervasive performance management culture in adult education.

The type of 'small story' analysis we offer here can complement such ethnographic and literacy-based work by adding another layer – showing how salient features of the context are oriented to and made relevant by participants themselves. We would suggest, then, that an ethnographic approach such as that used by Burgess and Hamilton could be combined with a more rigorous approach to the co-constructed nature of the interactions in which identity-relevant talk is produced. As Latour (2005) convincingly shows, investigating the social needs to begin with topics and phenomena which are already controversial to actors in a social setting. ILPs are an example of this type of phenomenon, and thus a productive place to begin in exploring language teacher identity in this context. However, such an exploration requires a more stringent empirical focus on the discursive actions through which identities are constructed in naturally occurring interactions, including research interviews.

6

THE CONSTRUCTION OF LANGUAGE-RELATED IDENTITY BY NON-NATIVE TEACHERS IN GROUP DISCUSSION

INTRODUCTION

The aspect of English language teacher identity which is the focus of this chapter is what Pennington and Richards (2016) describe as 'language-related identity'. They include as components of this identity the teacher's own proficiency in the language they teach, their 'native' or 'non-native' speaker status, and their autobiographies as learners of the language. Thus, in this chapter, we focus on how a group of non-native teachers of English see themselves in relation to their own competence in the language, their status as non-native speakers, and their own experiences as learners of English. We also examine how, through their talk, they position themselves in relation to others who are relevant to their language-related identities: that is, the teachers who taught them, their students, native-speaking language assistants who accompany them in their classrooms, and native speakers of different varieties of English. The data analysed in the chapter are drawn from two group discussions which were held with two different groups of state-school teachers in Spain: one group of primary teachers and one group of secondary teachers. The framework for analysing these data is membership categorisation analysis (MCA), which originates in the work of Sacks (1974, 1992a, 1992b) and is discussed extensively by Hester and Eglin (1997) and by Stokoe (2012).

The chapter is organised as follows. In the next section we provide an overview of teachers' language-related identities, organised conceptually into three dimensions: identities as 'users', as 'learners' and as 'teachers'. We then go on to outline the key features of MCA, showing how it can be of benefit in investigating the issues of teachers' language-related identity. After a brief description of the context of the data collection and the participants, we present analyses of data extracts which show how teachers in their talk positioned themselves in various ways in relation to categories which are relevant to these three dimensions of teachers' language identity. We conclude with some implications for further research and practice in this area.

ENGLISH TEACHERS' LANGUAGE-RELATED IDENTITIES

Pennington and Richards (2016) posit 'language-related identity' as one of what they call the 'Foundational Competences of Language Teacher Identity', which also include disciplinary identity, context-related identity, self-knowledge and awareness, and student-related identity. From their discussion can be drawn out three key dimensions of (especially non-native) teachers' language-related identity: how they see themselves as *users* of the language; their autobiographies as *learners* of the language taught; and their involvement as *teachers* with classroom experiences and practices. This chimes neatly with Sayer's (2012) observation, based on his ethnographic study of three teachers in Mexico, that the teachers engaged with the English language in three main ways, as 'L2 teacher, user, and learner, simultaneously' (Sayer 2012: 79). He describes these three 'engagements' as 'synonymous with 'multiple identities' (87). However, Sayer goes on to point out that these are not simply roles or identities that they switch between, but are convenient labels for describing the different ways in which the three teachers engage with English. This is the approach taken in this section, in which these three ways of engaging with English are used as a means of conceptually organising the key topics and findings on non-native English teachers' language-related identities. There is no assumption that teachers categorise themselves in these ways, and it is an objective of the analysis to explore how teachers construct the various identity-relevant categories that they refer to in their talk, and what social actions such identity-relevant talk performs.

TEACHERS AS L2 USERS OF ENGLISH

The 'user' dimension of language-related identity for those teachers of English who do not speak it as a first language revolves to a great extent around the categories 'native speaker' and 'non-native speaker'. The concept 'native speaker' has been under attack from a sociolinguistic perspective for some decades now (Davies 2004; Leung et al. 1997; Rampton 1990), but, as Moussu and Llurda (2008: 316) point out, 'even though a dichotomy vision of the native speaker–non-native speaker discussion does not appear to be linguistically acceptable, it happens to be nonetheless socially present, and therefore, potentially meaningful as an area of research in applied linguistics.' The dichotomy can be seen as meaningful in two spheres: in the world of ELT practice and in applied linguistics research. In the former, it can be seen in methods and materials used, teachers' and students' attitudes, and institutional hiring practices which discriminate against non-native-speaking professionals. In the latter, attention has increasingly been devoted to two tasks. The first is that of exposing the ideologies underpinning what Phillipson (1992) called the 'native speaker fallacy' (the idea that the ideal teacher of English is a native speaker). The second task is that of advocating for and empowering non-native teachers, as seen in what Braine (2010) describes as the 'nonnative speaker movement'. In recent years, critical applied linguistics work which interrogates ideologies underpinning what is seen as the continuing dominance of native-speaking teachers in ELT has been carried out by researchers such as Jenkins (2007), Holliday (2015) and Kumaravadivelu (2016).

Jenkins (2007) argues that, even in Lingua Franca English communication, which is predominantly between those who would be labelled as non-native speaker, there is still a deference to native speaker norms. This is not in the old, colonial manner, when people could actually be punished for deviating from the standard language, but is a power which is 'less overt, more subtle, and can perhaps better be described as an ideological undercurrent that quietly pervades most aspects of ELT' (194). This idea of the power of the native speaker as an ideology within ELT is labelled by Holliday (2015, for example) as 'Native Speakerism'. Native Speakerism is, for him, a pernicious ideology which serves to privilege those within the ELT profession who are labelled as 'native speakers' and discriminates against the majority of English teachers around the world, those who are labelled, and label themselves, as 'non-native speakers'. To overcome this discrimination, Holliday claims that what is needed is 'cultural belief': that is, the idea that all teachers of English, regardless of their mother tongue, have equal professional worth. Braine (2010) argues for the importance of non-native teachers linking up with colleagues in professional organisations. Becoming members of such organisations and taking on active roles within them is one important way to prevent isolation of these teachers and ultimately empower them.

Sayer (2012), in an ethnographic study of English teachers in Mexico, draws on Bourdieu's (1991) ideas about being a 'legitimate speaker', to show how these non-native teachers are engaged in a struggle to be seen as competent, legitimate professionals who can work effectively to help learners achieve their goals. In order to do so, they need to acquire a 'postcolonial accent' which allows them to create a 'third space' in which they can recontextualise, for their local settings, some of the dominant ideas and discourses in ELT, such as the native speaker, authenticity, and 'real' contexts of language use. In similar vein, Kumaravadivelu (2016) argues that teachers labelled as 'non-native' are in a 'subaltern' position within world ELT, and he calls for a 'grammar of decoloniality' in which it is these teachers themselves who must act to upset the existing order in which ELT is still dominated by those who are seen, and see themselves, as 'native speakers'.

What these studies can be seen to have in common is a desire to expose a pernicious ideology, and take action to overturn an unjust existing order in which there is still a flagrant power imbalance between ELT professionals identified and/or self-identifying as 'native' or 'non-native'. Along with this can be seen the hope that these terms may eventually be abolished. Holliday points out the difficulty in writing about this topic 'because there is the necessity to use terms, 'non-native speaker' and 'native speaker', which should not be in use at all' (Holliday 2015: 12). In fact, Holliday advocates the removal of other labels which abound in the world of ELT, such as ESL (English as a Second Language), EFL (English as a Foreign Language), EAL (English as an Additional Language), ELF and EIL (English as an International Language), and Kachru's inner, outer and expanding circles, but is aware that doing so may cause difficulties for teachers for whom these labels provide a sense of stability (2015: 22–3). The question as to whether these labels provide a sense of stability, and whether teachers themselves show any orientation to the 'native speakerism' ideology with its assumed power imbalances, is something that can explored, as in this study, by examining to what extent teachers make these ideas relevant and adopt positions towards them in their talk about their professional lives and practices.

Indeed, in the studies on teachers of English around the world who do not speak it as their L1, it is very clear that 'nativeness' and 'non-nativeness' are very real concepts to them, and impact on their self-perception and perception of others in very significant ways. These can be grouped into issues such as awareness of lack of proficiency (fluency and accuracy), 'non-native' accent, stigma attached to speaking a local variety of English, feelings of inadequacy, self-doubt and lack of authenticity, and lack of professional legitimacy. Often, these self-perceptions are juxtapositioned with perceptions of native speakers in their contexts, such as 'imported' teachers and teaching assistants.

In terms of non-native teachers' feelings about language proficiency, Pennington and Richards (2016) note that they often 'feel concerned' about their language skills, and see improving their proficiency as a priority for their professional development and in establishing an identity as competent professionals. There is evidence that lack of language proficiency or gaps in linguistic knowledge seem to affect non-native teachers more negatively than native-speaking teachers. Moussu and Llurda (2008) cite studies which show that, for native-speaking teachers, it is not such a big problem to have the occasional slip or lack metalinguistic knowledge about English. However, for non-native teachers, it appears that when they make mistakes or show gaps in their knowledge, their ability to teach effectively is questioned. This chimes with the findings of Sayer (2012) in the Mexican context, where students would often put the teachers to the test to see if they could expose gaps in their knowledge, thus challenging their professional legitimacy. Braine (2010) notes that non-native teachers in his context (Hong Kong) often seem to have a good knowledge of methodology and classroom management, but where they have problems is in their mastery of English. He warns that the students who are taught by teachers who have insufficient knowledge of the language 'may receiving confusing if not erroneous versions of English' (82). Valmori and De Costa (2016) show that non-native language teachers' proficiency is not a once-and-for-all static construct, but that it changes over time in response to contextual factors and is strongly associated with teachers' imagined future selves, and their opportunities for, and willingness to participate in, professional development activities.

An aspect of language use that is salient for non-native teachers is that of their accent, with the belief that, in order to be recognised as a competent English teacher, it is necessary to have a 'native' accent, or as near to one as possible. In Jenkins's (2007) interview study with seventeen non-native teachers, many of the participants claimed to prefer native speaker English because of its perceived authenticity, with native speaker varieties such as British English described as 'original' or 'real', and non-native speaker varieties as 'not real' or 'fake' (210–11). This links to what Holliday (2015: 13) describes as 'a widespread belief that "authenticity" in English lessons derives from "native speaker" language and cultural content'. All of the participants in Jenkins's study expressed in varying ways the belief that a native speaker accent is 'good' and a non-native speaker one 'bad'. Some of the teachers related negative 'accent experiences' (that is, negative comments about their accents, or perceived problems with intelligibility) which had a profound impact on their identities and attitudes. From these studies it can be clearly seen that teachers readily use categories and assign evaluative attributes to them, and this shows the potential for the approach taken in the present study, MCA, which examines how they do this in talk-in-interaction.

Another contextual factor that may impact on teachers' language-related identities concerns the varieties of English which are dominant in their geographical setting. Citing an earlier study by Andreasson (1994), Jenkins points out the difference between speakers in Kachru's (1985) 'outer circle', who may be happy to express an identity through the variety of English they speak (such as Indian or Nigerian English) and speakers in the 'expanding circle', who orient to a 'native' model (such as American or British English) and who will most definitely *not* take it as a compliment to be identified as a speaker of, for example, 'Spanish' English. Thus, as Jenkins points out, there is a persistent 'deficit' model of non-native accents among teachers, teacher trainers, and ELT testing institutions in the 'expanding circle' countries. The teachers in the study may not have approved of this situation, but they were aware of a link between the extent to which their accent was 'native-like' and their career prospects as teachers.

While it seems that most non-native teachers who participate in research studies orient to the superiority of 'native' varieties of English, few of them seem to be aware of the varieties that they actually use, or of the possibility that this might be some form of EIL or ELF. Pedrazzini and Nava (2011), in a small-scale study of a group of five L1 Italian teachers of English in Italy, found that the teachers did not show awareness that the English they were using represented any emerging Lingua Franca model or variety, and these teachers 'cling to their identity as English language teachers who in their professional role aspire to English nativeness' (280). In Young and Walsh's (2010) study, none of the twenty-six participants showed awareness of what variety they had learned. Looking back on their schooling, they felt that the model had been a 'local' variety of English but based on native speaker norms, while at university they had been exposed to more 'authentic' native speaker varieties, such as British or American English (Young and Walsh 2010: 135).

This lack of awareness of concepts such as ELF seems prevalent not only among non-native teachers of English, with Dewey (2015) finding that teachers on a pre-service training course (Cambridge ESOL CELTA) had low awareness of ELF as a concept. However, when introduced to the concepts of EIL or ELF, there is evidence that teachers may find the ideas attractive. This was the case in Young and Walsh's (2010) study, where most of the participating teachers in the study (19 out of 26) were attracted to the concepts of EIL/ELF at least in theory, but stated that they would find it difficult to operationalise these concepts in their own classroom practices.

In spite of a generally low awareness of concepts such as EIL or ELF, there is evidence that non-native teachers of English, as bi-/multilinguals, are aware of how they use the different languages in their repertoires. It is not so much an awareness of varieties of English per se, but their control over different registers across the languages they use. For example, Swan (2015) reports the case of one Vietnamese teacher in her study who claims that his use of English was at a more 'academic' level than his use of Vietnamese and that this enabled him to help his students access this more academic language. As Swan points out, this teacher was able to distinguish between his normal everyday use of Vietnamese and his professional needs in English, thus showing 'a sophisticated understanding of the place of each language, and of the necessary skills related to that place' (69).

Overall, then, these studies suggest that non-native English teachers around the world still see native varieties as being more 'authentic' and as being the ones to aspire to, even at the risk of causing some identity conflicts for themselves. They do not seem, on the whole, to have much awareness of being users of, or have much desire to teach, any versions of English such as EIL or ELF that deviate from standard forms associated with, say, British or American English. However, an interesting issue is the extent to which such attitudes may shift if teachers are involved in awareness raising which takes the emphasis away from stable forms such as 'standards' or 'varieties' and focuses on how English is used in communication, especially when the speakers do not share it as a first language. This is what Seidlhofer argues when she points out the 'need to question fixed ideas of the over-riding primacy of native speaker English and, above all, to give critical consideration to how the language is actually put to communicative use' (2015: 23). Thus, the focus should be on how non-native speakers 'make do' with the communicative resources they have, rather than worrying about what they are told they 'can do' in relation to native-speaker models (25). As will be seen later in this chapter, MCA can show how teachers orient to different groups of English language users, attributing to them a range of attributes and attitudes related to their acceptance of and tolerance for those non-native speakers who are 'making do'.

This focus on communicative processes, rather than fixed 'products', is also echoed by other researchers. For example, Sayer (2012) shows that legitimacy is not a static, pre-ordained quality; nor does it have to depend on reproducing 'the right accent' or demonstrating a high degree of fluency and control over linguistic forms, but is something that is constantly up for grabs, (re)negotiated in ongoing social interactions. Golombek and Jordan, in their 2005 study of two Taiwanese pre-service teachers, argue that by seeing legitimacy not as a static construct, but as something that can be developed over time through interactions with others, language teachers can gain 'a greater sense of agency in constructing their teacher identities' (529) – much more than is the case in more 'traditional' approaches which focus on intelligibility. This focus on the dynamic nature of legitimacy, and the construction of identities over time through interaction can also be applied to the concept of 'nativeness' itself, as in Luk and Lin's view that it is 'sociohistorically constructed, constantly evolving and transforming, and needs to be achieved and reachieved in moments of talk' (2008: 188). These writers' focus on communicative processes, interaction, negotiation, dynamism, co-construction and moments of talk fit very well with MCA and its concern with the construction of, and orientation to, identities in talk.

TEACHERS' AUTOBIOGRAPHIES AS LEARNERS OF L2 ENGLISH

If the 'user' dimension is concerned with how teachers see themselves as belonging to different categories of English speaker and the varieties they use, the 'learner' dimension focuses on their experiences and struggles to acquire the language they now teach or are training to teach. One vivid and powerful account of an English language teacher's experiences of learning English is Tsui's (2007) narrative study of a Chinese teacher (Minfang) who struggled with the communicative language teaching (CLT) lessons that were part of his university course. As Tsui mentions, CLT was 'much celebrated' at this university, but Minfang was not at all impressed and was very clear about his own learning preferences, which were 'being able to understand what he was reading and doing and to clarify what he did not understand' (665). As a learner, he was very perceptive and reflective about the limitations of the CLT approach, seeing it as 'soft' because it did not make language points explicit, 'unrealistic' because it demanded of teachers pragmatic competence that they were very unlikely to have, and culturally inappropriate as it required learners to act in ways which went against local Chinese culture – for example, by expressing opinions spontaneously in class. Minfang's experience is perhaps somewhat unusual in that he 'complained' about the use of CLT, whereas in other contexts teachers relate unhappy experiences of rote learning and a heavy emphasis on grammar, translation and memorising vocabulary. For example, the three Mexican teachers in Sayer's (2012) study all claimed to have learned 'basically nothing' at school from teachers who themselves had little English and depended on activities such as translating pages of a textbook using a bilingual dictionary. In contrast, these three teachers all spoke English and had been exposed to communicative methodologies on their TESOL programmes.

In terms of the varieties that non-native teachers are exposed to in their learning experiences, most of the teachers in Young and Walsh's (2010) study reported that, at lower levels, they had been taught the 'local variety' of English spoken by their teachers, which was nevertheless modelled on 'native' norms. However, as they advanced in their learning of English, the participants in this study claimed that they had gained more awareness of different varieties, even though the 'default' variety was likely to be a 'native' model such as British or American English, with this depending on what materials were used in the local context, and to what varieties the teachers had been exposed.

Apart from their past experiences of learning English, non-native teachers can see maintaining and improving proficiency as a life-long project. As Valmori and De Costa (2016) point out, there are two important decisions teachers have to take in this respect: whether to engage in professional development activities for this purpose; and maintaining their engagement in these activities whether or not they have a supportive network or community on which to rely. Valmori and De Costa's work draws on Markus and Nurius's (1986) 'possible selves' theory, and Kubanyiova's (2009) concept of 'possible language teacher selves' to show the importance of a future orientation in non-native teachers' engagement with a learner identity. This also comes across very strongly with the Mexican teachers in Sayer's (2012) study, who all displayed a desire to 'perfect' their English, as this would open up professional opportunities for them, such as presenting at ELT conferences, pursuing further study in the US, or becoming teacher trainers or coordinators.

THE 'TEACHER' DIMENSION OF L2 ENGLISH TEACHERS' LANGUAGE-RELATED IDENTITY

In Moussu and Llurda's (2008) review of the literature on non-native teachers, they paint a relatively positive picture of the 'teacher' aspect of their language-related identities, pointing out that studies have shown that teaching skills more than compensate for any perceived language proficiency deficiencies. As they put it, 'professional skills (such as knowledge of their subject, preparation, being able to make lessons interesting and fun and to motivate students, etc.) were more essential than language skills' (327). Encouragingly, they also claim that the research supports the view that students do not have a negative perception of their non-native teachers, recognising the value of experience and professionalism over being a native speaker. However, the question of students' perceptions of native and non-native teachers is a complex one, with one study (Watson-Todd and Pojanapunya 2009) finding discrepancies between students' explicit and implicit preferences, with students explicitly favouring native-speaker teachers, but implicitly showing no preference and actually explicitly expressing more warmth towards non-native teachers.

A common theme on research on non-native teachers is that their engagement with an identity as learners can be drawn on as an asset in their teaching, based on their 'personal history as second-language speakers and their knowledge and experience of education and communication in second-language contexts' (Pennington and Richards 2016: 8). They point out that teaching experience and concentration on lesson preparation and meeting students' needs can counteract any 'deficiency' orientation and can help non-native teachers to build strong professional 'insider' identities. In this sense, higher levels of engagement with the 'teacher' dimension can allay fears about inadequacies in the 'user' dimension. Along these lines, Swan (2015) shows how 'practitioners' own reminiscences about their learning experiences are presented as evidence of the strengths they acquired through learning English as a second or subsequent language' (59). In this respect, non-native English teachers can draw on resources which are generally unavailable to their native-speaking counterparts.

In Luk and Lin's (2008) study of Hong Kong English language classrooms, nonnative teachers from the local context were able to draw on the resources of the students' L1 (which they could use to establish rapport and relationships, deal with discipline issues and generally facilitate learning), and their shared experience of upbringing and the local education system. These resources allow teachers 'to interpret students' learning styles, attitudes, and problems in the classrooms' (Luk and Lin 2008: 187). In this sense, 'local' non-native teachers can be very well aware of the respective strengths of themselves and their native-speaking colleagues, and in no way see themselves as inferior. For the non-native (or multilingual) teachers in Swan's (2015) study, she shows that their worlds are 'well populated with "native speakers" but they are not necessarily seen as the dominant side of a dichotomy' (73), and they were in fact able to 'exploit' native speakers as a resource. In doing so, they attributed less merit to the native-speaking teachers' teaching skills, with their value being seen more as providers of models of the target language, teaching oral skills and having cultural knowledge related to English.

In Young and Walsh's 2010 study, they found that none of the participants showed resentment about their non-native status nor saw it as a threat to their professional identities. It seems instead that these teachers were more concerned about practical issues in their local contexts, one example being the influence of publishers on what varieties are presented for teaching purposes in materials. In this respect, Seidlhofer's (2015: 26) suggestion that textbooks can be used more as 'prompts' than as 'scripts' to follow would be useful. In terms of what varieties they were teaching, most of the teachers in the study were initially not clear about this, but further probing revealed that they were all teaching to a 'standard' native speaker model, which in most cases was American English. As stated above, the teachers in this study found EIL/ELF conceptually attractive, but not practical for their own teaching. They saw their teaching approach as having a focus on meaning and mutual understanding, rather than on aspects such as pronunciation or a specific variety of English. These teachers also highlighted the importance of clarity and comprehensibility for their lower-level learners, and, when asked which varieties might best meet these requirements, most opted for native speaker models (Young and Walsh 2010: 133). This is in line with Dewey's (2015) finding that although there is growing awareness of terms such as 'World Englishes', 'there is generally limited meaningful integration of these terms and the concepts they represent in existing practices' (180).

Although the studies reviewed here do not generally paint a picture of non-native teachers in an inferior or 'subaltern' position, there is a darker side to the ways in which non-native-speaking teachers can be positioned by others, notably by native-speaking colleagues and fellow professionals. There may be overtones of racism in some native-speaking teachers' attitudes to their non-native colleagues from different parts of the world, as shown in Holliday and Aboshiha's (2009) report on Aboshiha's (2008) doctoral study of seven British teachers of English. She found that in their discourse they positioned non-native colleagues and students from Japan, the Gulf and Portugal as 'culturally deficient' in all manner of ways, such as being hostile to change and reliant on memorisation, lacking academic skills and, as teachers, not wanting to encourage creativity in their students, lacking autonomy, being afraid to lose face by having their authority undermined, and lacking knowledge of 'the real world' (Holliday and Aboshiha 2009: 679). Similarly, in a study of native-speaking English teachers (NETs) in Hong Kong, Trent (2012) found that the NETs produced an antagonistic discourse in which they positioned themselves as 'real' teachers who used interactive methods such as games, activities, songs and drama and their local non-native colleagues as 'traditional' teachers who used textbooks, worksheets and dictations, and whose prime focus was on enabling the students to pass examinations.

There is also evidence that pressure to conform to certain mandated teaching approaches such as CLT can have a debilitating and disempowering effect on non-native teachers' professional legitimacy. Dewey (2015) points out, drawing on findings from Choi's (2013) doctoral thesis, that the use of a communicative teaching approach exerts pressures on a teacher's level of language proficiency. While Choi's study focuses on the Korean context, it confirms studies in other contexts, such as Tsui's (2007) study of a Chinese teacher referred to above, which suggest that pressure to conform to a CLT approach has implications not only for language teaching methodological expertise (the ability to put such methods into practice) but also for the pragmatic and communicative manipulation of language forms and skills that are part of a teacher's repertoire as a user. Along similar lines, Jenkins (2007) observes that teaching materials based on native models of pronunciation can have a delegiti-mising effect on non-native teachers. However, on the whole, studies suggest that the deeper non-native teachers' engagement with the 'teacher' dimension of their language-related identities, by developing a repertoire of methodological options suited to their local conditions, the more they will be empowered and legitimised as professionals.

MEMBERSHIP CATEGORISATION ANALYSIS

The approach used in this chapter to analyse how non-native English language teach-ers' language-related identities are constructed in and through the social interaction of a group discussion is MCA. MCA is concerned with how people, through their talk, make certain identities relevant by ascribing themselves, and others, to certain categories. There are three main dimensions, or components, of MCA: membership categories, membership categorisation devices and category predicates (Hester and Eglin 1997).

Membership categories are ways of classifying persons into social types. For the purposes of the topic of this chapter, some relevant classifications would be 'teacher', 'teaching assistant', 'native speaker', 'non-native speaker' and 'student'. Hester and Eglin (1997) point out that classifications can be extended beyond the description of persons to 'collectivities', such as specific institutions (such as a school or university), or wider collective bodies (such as the 'education system'). Membership categorisa-tion devices (MCDs) refer to how membership categories can be linked together in interaction to make up larger classes. This is because, when they are used in social interaction, some of these categories are heard by participants as fitting together to make a collection. Thus, the MCD 'family' is heard as including such membership categories as 'mother', 'father', 'son', 'daughter', 'uncle', 'aunt' and so on (Hester and Eglin 1997: 4). MCDs may take the form of 'standardised relational pairs', such as 'husband–wife' or 'parent–child', and these can be based on occupational roles, such as 'teacher–student' or 'doctor–patient'. Category predicates refer to the idea that, in social interaction, participants may link certain activities with specific membership categories, examples of these 'category-bound activities' being crying for babies (as in Sacks's classic example (see Chapter 3) or evaluating or correcting students' utter-ances for teachers. Apart from activities, it is important to recognise that category predicates can also include rights, entitlements, obligations, knowledge, attributes and competencies (Hester and Eglin 1997: 5).

MCA, then, is concerned with the ways in which participants in interaction either openly refer to certain membership categories (for themselves or others), make infer-ences about such membership based on how certain categories go together (MCDs), or link actions, rights, entitlements, knowledge or competences to certain categories. To give an example relevant to the topic of this chapter, participants may refer to themselves, or others, as 'native speakers' or 'non-native speakers', and may, through their talk and its organisation, link certain activities, knowledge or competence to these categories, as in constructing 'native speakers' as having special knowledge of English, making their English 'real' or 'authentic'.

The use of MCA has some advantages over other qualitative approaches such as content analysis of research interviews. The main benefit is that MCA takes an empirical approach to showing how attributes are linked to categories by participants themselves in interaction, rather than by carrying out an a priori logical or conceptual analysis (Schegloff 2007). Logical or conceptual analysis and study of the literature (as we have seen in previous sections of this chapter) will provide us with plenty to say about such categories as 'native speaker' or 'non-native speaker'. However, if we want to know more about how people in their own local settings construct their worlds of practice, it is necessary to examine how these categories become relevant, if at all, during social interactions. Another benefit of an MCA approach is to demonstrate that what Stokoe (2009) describes as 'topic-based' research (that is, on identity as a topic) can be done without directly asking participants about identity as such (see also Chapter 5 on ESOL teachers' attitudes to ILPs). Stokoe argues that it is possible to make claims about 'the specific, designed, and occasioned use of categories and category-resonant descriptions' (2009: 93), and that doing so contrasts with the view that it is impossible to carry on such 'topic-based' research in settings other than research interviews.

MCA and MCA-related studies have been carried out in the field of ELT. In a study of classroom discourse in different contexts, Richards (2006) uses an MCA-related approach, drawing on Zimmerman's notion of discourse, situated and transportable identities (see Chapter 3). He shows how shifts in orientation to different identities in talk (particularly transportable identity) are associated with changes in patterns of classroom discourse. MCA has also been used by Jenks (2013a, 2013b) to explore how participants in what are described as 'ELF' interactions (that is, where English is being used as a lingua franca among speakers of other languages) construct themselves and their interlocutors as 'non-native speakers' or even 'foreigners' and display orientations to identities such as 'learner' through mentions of category-bound activities such as 'practising' English.

Even where MCA has not been used, it can be clearly seen to be relevant to work on identity in ELF interactions, as in Baker's (2015) assertion that 'we are interested in the social groups which participants in ELF interactions orientate towards or are allocated to, and in particular we are interested in participants' identification with various cultural groupings' (108). The question of whether interactions between speakers of English who do not use it as a first or main language can be labelled 'ELF' is a delicate one, which, as Jenks (2013a) argues, has ethical dimensions: that is, researchers should take care not to use labels, or at least be reflexive when they do, that are not used by the participants in the interaction which is the object of study. In the case of the data which will be subjected to illustrative analyses in this chapter, the participants were informed that they would be responding to prompts about the English they use, had learned, and teach and want to teach, but at no time did the construct 'ELF' come up in the discussions. Before moving to looking at some of these data extracts, in which participants oriented to various identity categories and their attributes, we briefly describe the participants and the data.

PARTICIPANTS AND DATA

The data extracts which are the object of the illustrative analyses in this chapter were collected as part of an ongoing research effort which aims to explore non-native English teachers' beliefs about the varieties of English they use, learned and teach (see Young and Walsh 2010 for a report on an earlier phase of this research). The data comprise two discussions, one with a group of primary teachers, and one with a group of secondary teachers, which were held in Madrid, Spain[1]. In the primary group there were four teachers (three female, one male), and in the secondary group there were eight (four female, four male). In the secondary group, five of the teachers taught English as a subject, while three taught other subjects (history, geography, art) through the medium of English, as the school is a bilingual one in which part of the non-language curriculum is taught in English. While the purpose was to have a group discussion (rather than interviews), both discussions were built around key questions or topics that the researchers wanted to explore: which varieties of English the participants thought they had learned themselves; the variety (or varieties) they taught; the variety (or varieties) they would like to teach; the varieties they thought their students preferred; and the varieties they thought would be dominant in the future. The discussions lasted approximately 15 minutes (Group 1) and 25 minutes (Group 2) and were video-recorded and transcribed.

ILLUSTRATIVE ANALYSES

The analyses presented in this section are organised according to the three types of engagement that were described above. This is not to claim that the participants in the discussions themselves oriented to any such categorisation of three 'types of engagement'. However, each of the three ways of engaging did emerge in the membership categories that were made relevant by the participants, in the attributes predicated to these categories and in their stances towards them, often within the same short sequence of interaction.

ENGAGEMENT AS USERS OF ENGLISH: NATIVE AND NON-NATIVE VARIETIES

In the two group discussions, 'Varieties of English' emerged as an MCD, or a 'collection' of membership categories (MCs), which includes 'British English', 'American English', 'Australian English', 'Irish English' and so on, and these MCs have predicates attached to them. Interestingly, 'Spanglish' and simply 'Spanish' are MCs that are included by the participants (perhaps ironically) in the MCD 'Varieties of English', as can be seen in this extract:

---

[1] These discussions were set up, moderated and video-recorded by Ana Llinares and Steve Walsh. We are very grateful for their permission to use extracts for the analyses in this chapter.

Extract 6.1: (DG1) (M = moderator; T1, T2 and so on identify individual teachers; TT = unidentified teachers talking in overlap)

```
33. M:   so (.) can you remember what-
34.      or what do you think you learned
35.      what variety do you think you learned?
36. T1:  British? American? (.)
37.      and eh Spanish variety as well ((laughs))
38. T2:  Spang-
39. T1:  Spanglish also
40. M:   Spanglish ((laughs)) yeah
41. T2:  Spanglish yeah British
42. T3:  British we (do) learn
43. T2:  [we have learned British English]
44. T5:  [you have native teachers?]
45. T2:  no (.) no not me
46. T5:  Spanish teachers (.) okay
         ((some lines omitted))
59. M:   yeah? Same (S4's name) yeah?
60. T4:  u:h more or less the [same]
61. M:                        [yeah]
62. T4:  um: (xxx) Spanish a mix of (.)
63.      maybe sometimes British and American (.)
64.      it was a mix yeah
65.      but de- def- definitely would be Spain as well
66. M:   yeah same as well?
67. T3:  Spanish teacher
68. M:   Spanish  [teacher]
69. T3:           [Spanish]
70. M:   so it was eh- it was like a (.) local variety
71. T4:  yeah
72. T3:  yeah
73. M:   Spanish variety of English let's say [yeah]
74. TT:                                        [yeah]
```

At line 37, T1 includes 'Spanish variety' as an MC in the collection 'varieties of English'. This can be seen in the use of 'as well' as it is added to the list which includes 'British' and 'American' (line 36). At line 38, T2 begins to say 'Spanglish', which is cut off and completed by T1 – showing alignment with the idea that 'Spanglish' could be a variety of English. The laughter in T1's turn (line 37) and in M's at line 40 suggests that this term is oriented to as being humorous or striking in a way that, for example, 'British' or 'American' English would not be. At lines 62–5, another teacher, T4, also includes 'Spanish' and 'Spain' as varieties learned along with 'sometimes' British and American. The idea of a 'local' or 'Spanish' variety' of English is taken up by the moderator (lines 70 and 73) and this receives agreement from the participants.

However, later in the discussion it emerges that 'Spanglish' may not refer to a variety per se, but to the practice of alternating between languages:

Extract 6.2: (DG1)

```
183. M:  now you've- you've all said the word 'Spanglish' (.)
184. TT: yeah ((nodding)) ((laughing))
185. M:  right? (.) what do you mean by that?
186. T3: because sometimes you have to explain the words in
187.     Spanish (.) the meaning of the word (.)
188.     so (.) it's like a mixture of Spanish and English
189. M:  so it's (.) it's when you move from one language to
190.     another?
191. T3: yeah
192. M:  Spa- but it's not the (.) the type of English you're
193.     using (.) i- it's this- it's this (.)
194.     what we call 'code-switching'
195.     so you move from English to Spanish and- okay (.)
196.     alright
197. TT: ((nodding))
```

Again we can see the word 'Spanglish' used in M's turn (line 183) being followed by laughter among the group, again showing an orientation to it as something perhaps shared as an in-group source of humour or at least recognition of some striking properties. T3's response (lines 186–8) to M's request for clarification provides a description of what 'Spanglish' refers to: that is, the practice of explaining words in Spanish, with the result being 'a mixture of Spanish and English' (line 188). At line 192, M appears to repair T3's (and by inference the others') displayed understanding of what is meant by 'Spanglish', stating that it is not a 'type' (variety) of English, but the practice of moving from one language to another. In what could be seen as an example of what Potter and Hepburn (2005: 291) describe as 'flooding' – the introduction of the researcher's social science terms and categories into the discourse – the moderator uses the technical term 'code-switching'. This change in what 'Spanglish' is taken to mean seems to be accepted by the teachers, as seen in their nodding in assent. Thus, what we can see here is how a shift in the attributes of one MC, 'Spanglish', is effected interactionally, with the result that it may now belong to another MCD – not 'varieties of English' but 'multilingual discursive practices'. Such a move can also have implications for the teachers' identities, as they would now belong to the category of multilinguals who use languages for different purposes (for example, Spanish for explaining), rather than speakers of 'Spanglish', which may be seen as a low-prestige variety.

Moving to the categorisation and attribution of predicates to 'native' varieties and their speakers, we can see orientation towards the idea seen in the studies reviewed above that authenticity is linked to nativeness, as when the participants in Group 1 are talking about having Australian and Canadian teachers:

Extract 6.3: (DG1)

```
345. M:   well that's something (.) you know (.)
346.      if and when you do the teaching
347.      you could actually use that (.) tha- those
348.      experiences (.) cause they'll- you'll be able to say
349.      you know you remember that teacher from Australia
350.      (.) did you like her accent what did you of that
351.      and (.) you'll be able to use that (.)
352.      that's quite useful
353.      (11:00)
354. T1:  Canada
355. M:   Canada ( ) that's fabulous
356. T5:  that's great ( ) because it's educative for: (.)
357.      for the school and the kids
358. T2:  and each one has a proper (.) pronunciation so
```

At line 356, T5 highlights the educational benefits for the children in the school of being exposed to the accents of Australian and Canadian speakers of English, to which T2 adds (line 358) that these speakers have a 'proper' pronunciation. So we can see here that the MC 'native speaker' of English (as in Australians or Canadians) has attributed to it the predicate being able to pronounce properly. This idea of the benefits of having a 'native' teacher is taken up by T7 in Group 2, when she talks of her own experience as a learner:

Extract 6.4: (DG2)

```
128. T7:  eh: secondary school I was really lucky
129.      because my teacher was British (.)
130.      and I really liked her
131.      and she's the reason actually that I learned English
132.      (.) and studied English and I became a teacher
133. M:   now you said lucky there (.)
134.      that's an interesting word (.)
135.      you said you were lucky you had a British teacher
136.      can you say why y- you think you were lucky
137. T7:  I was lucky because I w- I was exposed to REAL
138.      English you know
139. M:   okay (.) now again (.) real English (.)
140.      th- these are (.) just interesting (.) descriptions
141.      (.) what do you mean by (.) real English
142. T7:  well I mean she was a native
143. M:   okay (.) yeah
144. T7:  she was a native (.) so
```

At lines 128–32, T7 links her own identity trajectory from being a student to becoming a teacher of English to her good fortune in having had a British teacher of English. T7's stance towards this teacher is very clear ('I really liked her'), and she is given as the actual reason why T7 went on to learn English and become a teacher. At this stage, however, it is not clear exactly which attributes of this teacher (apart from simply belonging to the MC 'British') led to all these positive associations and outcomes. In the next turn, the moderator skilfully uses the interactional move of asking for clarification of the use of the word 'lucky', and this leads to a further unfolding of the categories underlying T7's positive attitude to the experience of having had a British teacher. At lines 137–8, T7 links the idea of being exposed to 'real English' to having had a British teacher. Although not explicitly stated, the inference is that MC 'British' has as a predicate 'speaker of real English'. Further prompting by the moderator in lines 139–41 is followed by T7's explicit formulation that her teacher's English was 'real' because she was a native. In this short sequence of interaction, then, we can see a rich interplay of identity categories, their attributes and stances towards them. 'British' is linked to 'native speaker', which has in turn the attribute 'speaker and model of real English'. When this identity comes into contact with the identity 'non-native learner of English', we can see the category of 'fortunate person', which is then, on this occasion, linked to the possible (and in this case, real) future identity of 'English teacher'.

However, native speakers, especially British ones, were not unanimously invested with positive attributes in the ways they were represented in the teachers' talk, as can be seen in this comparison of American and British attitudes towards non-native speakers' speech:

Extract 6.5: (DG1)

```
128. M:   Ame- now why do say th- that's interesting
129.      why do you say American is easier?
130. T1:  I don't know I feel that I don't know
131.      I think it's easier the pronunciation
132. M:   [to pronounce]
133. T3:  [yeah the pronu-] to pronounce yeah
134. M:   right
135. T2:  and the grammar (.) as well
136. M:   yeah? Do you think so?
137. T1:  I don't know I guess it (always depends)
138. T4:  Supposed to be the same grammar
139.      but maybe it's the way we see the British people
140.      (like) British strict and
141.      I don't know maybe it's a topic
142. S2:  and American is like you are saying a mistake
143.      maybe it's okay
```

In this sequence we can see the MC 'American English' interactionally constructed as having the attribute 'easier'. After having been asked by the moderator to expand on his assertion that American English is 'easier', T1 responds with some uncertainty but identifies pronunciation as a possible factor, to which T2 adds 'the grammar' at line 135. However, at line 139, T4 shifts the focus away from the language varieties as MCs, to a focus on a collectivity, 'British people', to which the attribute 'strict' is predicated. This is contrasted with the collectivity 'American', to which is attributed the predicate of seeing it as okay for a non-native to make a mistake. Thus, we have, constructed in the interaction, a contrast between two collectivities in the extent to which they are relaxed about, or tolerant towards, non-native speakers' attempts to communicate. Further evidence of a somewhat negative stance to the collectivity 'British people' in connection with language use can be seen in this anecdote:

Extract 6.6: (DG2)

```
338. T4: yes when I was in-
339.     I was doing a summer course in:
340.     I think it was in Cambridge (.)
341.     and I had to repeat everyday I wanted-
342.     I drank Coke (.) so (.)
343.     uh: can I have a Coke? uh: can you repeat please?
344.     (.) a Coke a cook a 'keowk' (.)
345.     I didn't know how to pronounce it (.)
346.     I spent one month (.) asking for a Coke
347.     and nobody gave it to me I mean- (xxx)
348.     (.) if they had like thirty
349.     varieties of beverages fine
350.     but they were Coke Fanta and water so
351.     (please can I get my Coke)
```

This repeated incident is constructed in such a way that the protagonists represent identity categories which have clear attributes attached to them in terms of intentionality, and, by inference, more permanent negative dispositions such as a wilful refusal to accommodate a non-native speaker's attempt to communicate. The MC 'British person' (or at least 'local' living in Cambridge) is constructed as having the attribute 'unwilling to make allowances for a foreigner's pronunciation'. The way the story is told suggests that the local person really understood which beverage she wanted, and was just pretending not to understand out of spitefulness or perhaps hostility. This version is built up through the supply of contextual background (there were only three types of drink on sale), thus producing the strong inference that any reasonable person would have been able to work out which beverage was required. This anecdote can be seen as an example of the negative 'accent experiences' related by some participants in Jenkins's (2007) interview study.

In common with previous studies, which generally find that non-native teachers do not explicitly refer to terms such as 'ELF' unless prompted to do so, there was no mention of this or similar terms in the two discussions. However, one participant, T5 in Group 2, did construct himself as using English for lingua franca purposes when travelling abroad:

Extract 6.7: (DG2)

```
607. T5: and for example I travel a lot
608.     and in fact when you are (.) travelling
609.     you are not speaking with British people ( )
610.     from German from other countries
611.     in the hotels in the (counter) the reception ( )
```

The statement in line 609 ('you are not speaking with British people') clearly shifts this speaker's use of English away from 'native' varieties, and points to its use as a lingua franca for use with people from a variety of other countries. This is evidence, albeit limited, that there may be a shift in attitudes away from aspiring towards native varieties and towards a recognition that the MC 'English user' can have rather different attributes from that of 'failed native speaker'. In relation to the anecdote in extract 6.6, it is worth speculating that 'negative accent experiences' would be less frequent in such lingua franca communicative contexts.

ENGAGEMENT AS LEARNERS OF ENGLISH: OVERCOMING UNFAVOURABLE CIRCUMSTANCES

The teachers' accounts of their learning experiences tell of (mostly) negative experiences of studying English at primary and secondary school and their subsequent efforts and struggles to gain a degree of communicative competence in the language. The MC 'Spanish teachers of English' is often given negative attributes, such as using outdated methods which result in students learning nothing. In extract 6.8, T5 builds his account in such a way that it was easy to infer that he only 'really' learned English by travelling abroad:

Extract 6.8: (DG2)

```
101. T5: for me- for me the school it was a nightmare (.)
102.     yeah (.) the English I hated it (.) completely
103.     because it was Spanish teachers
104.     and um: I was supposed to try to memorise
105.     the list of the verbs (.) (every year)
106.     and (afterwards) I didn't speak a single sentence
107.     in English (.) and when I finished the Bachillerato
108.     (.) okay I didn't know anything really
109.     the verbs (4.0) only this (.)
110.     and later I had to try and improve my English
111.     travelling and looking (.) for a way because it-
112. T9: travelling where
```

```
113. T5: uh: to: United States
114. T9: okay (.) you chose the United States
115. T5: yeah the United States (.)
```

The account begins with very negative objective and subjective evaluations (Wiggins and Potter 2003) of the learning experience – 'it was a nightmare', 'I hated it completely' (lines 101–2). He singles out the MC 'Spanish teachers' as the cause of such a horrible experience, and links to them the attribute of using such presumably useless methods as asking students to memorise lists of verbs (lines 104–5). The result of this negative experience was that by the time he finished the Bachillerato (the Spanish equivalent of the Baccalaureate), he 'didn't know anything really'. This chimes with the accounts of the Mexican teachers in Sayer's (2012) study, who claimed that they had learned 'basically nothing' at school. From line 110, he paints a picture of himself as an agentive person who makes an effort to improve his English by travelling to the United States. However, this is also depicted as an obligation ('I had to try and improve my English' – line 110), which reinforces the sense that he was let down by his schooling and had to use his own initiative to compensate for these failings.

Another teacher, T8, describes his experiences of learning English as being so bad that he 'ran away' and learned another language – Arabic:

Extract 6.9: (DG2)

```
202. T8: I ran through- ran away and-
203.     and went through uh: other languages like Arabic
204.     for example and I was very attracted by Arabic
205.     and I was (.) eh learning Arabic (.)
206.     by studying Arabic by more than seven years (.)
207.     I'm not a (.) very proficient speaker Arabic speaker
208.     but I can get by okay um especially I can read (.)
209.     very easily a text in Arabic
210.     so uh: I- I- I- I had to- to be grateful to my eh:
211.     primary school and secondary school English teachers
212.     (.) because they (.) pushed me to: learn Arabic.
```

Here, the representatives of the MC 'Spanish teachers of English' are ironically granted and thanked for having the attribute of having pushed this teacher to learn another language – Arabic (lines 210–12). The upshot of the story is, though, that the English lessons he experienced were so awful that he was forced to escape to another language. Of course, he did not have to learn any language at all, as it is conceivable that this experience might have put him off learning languages for life. The inference to be taken from the way the two accounts of negative experience are constructed is that the speakers are in fact motivated to learn languages, and have the ability to do so, but this is somehow crushed by the incompetence of the (usually) non-native teachers of English they had at primary and secondary school. The teachers in this way position themselves in the identity category of 'motivated and competent language learner', with predicates which relate to their tenacity in overcoming adversity on the road to attaining a respectable degree of competence in English, at least enough eventually to claim the identity of 'competent English teacher'.

However, not all the stories of language learning experiences were negative. As we saw in the case of T7 in extract 6.4, being 'lucky' enough to have a native teacher changes the experience to a positive one. This experience goes beyond the native-speaking teacher's attribute as being a model of 'real' English, as it also includes the attribute of using a more communicative teaching approach:

Extract 6.10: (DG2)

```
146. T1: that happened to me with the Australian one
147.     (.) and I mean we were playing games
148.     for the first time
149.     and we were (.) using English
150.     as a language to communicate (.)
151.     not just memorising the verbs or- (.) you know so-
```

Here we have the MC 'Australian teacher', which is part of the MCD 'native teachers of English', with the attributes of being able to use games in language lessons which encouraged the use of English for communication – as opposed to the presumed usual practice (used by Spanish teachers) of asking students to memorise verbs. This stark contrast between the attributes assigned to the MCs 'native-speaking (for example, Australian, British) teacher of English' and 'non-native (Spanish) teacher of English' relates not only to these teachers' experiences as *learners* of English, but also to their identities as *teachers* of English.

ENGAGEMENT AS TEACHERS OF ENGLISH

In talking about their teaching practices, the teachers in both groups expressed the idea that they were flexible about which varieties they taught. They described students as being exposed to both American and British varieties (through textbooks, for example):

Extract 6.11: (DG1)

```
296. T4: so (.) they can choose eh: (.)
297.     I'm not trying to: to show my preference
298.     (for) the American one (.)
299.     so th- they're gonna choose (.)
300.     the books are b- based on the British English
301.     so it's up to them
```

T4 had previously indicated his preference for American English, but here he states that he does not want to impose his preference on the students, leaving them the freedom to choose which variety they want to learn. Thus, this teacher constructs the MC 'English learner' in his context as having the attribute of agency, of freedom to choose which variety to learn. This theme of flexibility in terms of which varieties to teach is also expressed in T8's description of his teaching practices in Group 2:

Extract 6.12: (DG2)

```
279. T8: for instance I write (.)
280.     the eh: American spelling of colour
281. M:  yes
282. T8: why because it's shorter (.)
283.     but my students are used to the British (.) eh:
284.     spelling ( ) okay? (.)
285.     that- that's where I think mine is
286.     the kind of mixed
287. M:  okay
288. T8: of many different because ah: some words (.)
289.     because I- I (.) draw my vocabulary
290.     from almost everywhere eh:
291.     an- and I try to- to make a kind of mix
292.     and I don't pay attention to
293.     what the- the word is English or British English
294.     or American English or Australian English
295.     I just use a word because I (.) eh see that it works
```

T8 constructs his own identity here as a teacher with a pragmatic outlook, with a focus on what works (line 295). Versions of words such as 'colour'/'color' (line 280) are not chosen because of their belonging to hard-and-fast MCs such as 'American English', but because of their practical value ('because it's shorter' – line 282). This is part of an overall eclectic strategy where words are drawn on from 'almost everywhere' (line 290), with no strict adherence to any one variety such as 'British English', 'American English' or 'Australian English'.

This pragmatic orientation can also be seen in T6's explicit formulation of the purpose of language learning in this context:

Extract 6.13: (DG2)

```
582. T6: but anyway our- our purpose of learning
583.     is (.) to communicate (.)
584.     to make (.) students communicate
585.     so it doesn't matter their- the accent
586.     it's just (.) make them (.) well understand
587.     what they are being said (.)
588.     and the other way round (.) ((laughs))
589.     they speak (.) and they understood
```

```
590. T3: exactly I agree
591. T6: so it doesn't matter the variety I think
```

Here, T6 states explicitly that the purpose of teaching English is to 'make students communicate' (line 584) so that they can understand and be understood (lines 586–8). Neither the 'accent' (line 585) nor the 'variety' (line 591) matters, as long as communication is achieved. Thus, both teachers (T3 and T6), in their engagement with the 'teaching' dimension of their language-related identities, downplay any strict adherence to the teaching of identified varieties. The MC 'Spanish teacher of English' can be seen, in their case, not as having the attribute 'obsession with grammar' or 'forcing students to have a British or American accent', but as eclectic pragmatists with a pedagogical focus on 'what works' in achieving the ultimate outcome of language teaching, communication.

In constructing such an identity, we can see a turning away from the idea that more communicative teaching practices have to be inevitably linked to the MC of 'native-speaking English teacher'. We saw earlier, in one teacher's descriptions of her own learning experiences, an orientation towards imbuing the MC 'native teacher' with the attribute of being a competent user of more communicative, interactive teaching styles. However, this view does not go uncontested, as we can see in extract 6.14, where T4 relates the use of more or less communicative teaching practices more to changes in methodological preferences over time than to the teacher's membership of either of the two MCs of 'native' or 'non-native' teacher:

Extract 6.14: (DG2)

```
216. T4: but I think that is (.) um: (.)
217.     it doesn't depend at all on: the:-
218.     if the teachers were native or non-native or
219.     whatever it's because (.)
220.     it's- it depends on how much (.) teaching languages
221. T2: and how ( )
222. T4: have changed- yeah
223. T2: because practising grammar and-
224. T5: in Spain we have an obsession with grammar
```

There is an implication here that age-related MCs may be involved: that is, that members of the MC 'younger teachers of English', whether or not they are native, will have been exposed to a more communicative methodology, and may be moving away from the 'obsession with grammar' (line 224). Thus while 'native-speaking English teacher' can include a range of attributes which are constructed as inherent to the category, such as using 'real' English and having 'proper pronunciation', it can be argued that these are attached just to the 'nativeness' aspect of this MC, and not necessarily to the 'teacher' aspect. Thus, the attributes which relate to teaching practices are open to change over time, such that a non-native-speaking teacher can just as well use communicative methods as a native-speaking teacher. This may be accentuated if the teacher is younger, and has thus experienced more recent changes in language teaching methodology in which communicative practices are encouraged.

DISCUSSION AND CONCLUSION

The ways in which the participants in the two discussions built up identity categories, assigned attributes to them and adopted stances towards them play off the themes which have emerged in the literature on 'non-native' teachers, where more typical qualitative methods such as interviewing were used. The MCDs 'native' and 'non-native' speaker, with their respective MCs such as 'speaker of American/British English' and 'Spanish speaker of English', were very much alive in the teachers' talk. The attribution of predicates to native speakers as being users of 'real English' or having 'proper pronunciation' partially echoes Holliday's (2015: 13) description of the commonly held belief that authenticity resides in native speaker language and cultural content – partially, because there was no evidence in these discussions of linking the attribute 'carrier of cultural knowledge' to native speakers. This is not to say that the individual teachers did not have any such beliefs, but, interestingly, at no time did it become relevant in their talk.

Although there was clear evidence of this attribution of authenticity to the MC 'native speaker', there was also evidence of an emerging perspective that loosened the link between the goals of English language learning and teaching in their contexts and 'native' varieties of English. This can be seen in the teacher in extract 6.7's description of his use of English when travelling, which did not involve communication with native speakers. It could also be seen in the ways in which the teachers emphasised the practical goals of communication, rather than focusing on specific varieties, when they talked about their teaching practices. This suggests that, while ELF as a term did not come up (they were not prompted to use it), it appears that the context in which these teachers work might be a fertile ground for reflecting on the extent to which English teaching should or should not be linked to 'native' varieties, and for encouraging teachers to explore the implications for teaching and learning of an ELF perspective.

In portraying the non-native Spanish teachers of English as being unable to provide a positive learning experience, especially when contrasted with glowing accounts of the fun and games in classes run by native teachers, the teachers echoed the negative discourses around non-native teachers voiced by native teachers in Holliday and Aboshiha's (2009) and Trent's (2012) studies. This would seem to be an example of a 'subaltern' attitude (Kumaravadivelu 2016), in which the dominated party takes as their own the discourses produced by the dominant party, and which serve to keep them in an inferior position. What seems to be missing is a resolute defence of the benefits of local teachers, as in Luk and Lin's (2008) and Swan's (2015) studies. However, this may be nuanced by the fact that these are narratives of past experience, and that the teachers who participated in the discussion may see themselves as more 'up to date' in their methodology and their sense of the importance of encouraging communicative language use. Here, we might see an emerging MC of 'modern non-native teacher of English', which shares such attributes as having a more practical, pragmatic view of the goals of language teaching, and has moved beyond an 'obsession with grammar' or the need to force learners to adopt any specific accent or variety.

In this chapter, we hope to have shown the benefits of MCA for shedding new light on topics that have been explored in the ELT/TESOL literature using other, mostly qualitative, methods such as interviewing. MCA shows that the different concepts and categories identified in the literature are often oriented to by teachers in their talk, but in the subtle, shifting ways in which identity work is carried on in talk-in-interaction, rather than through more static themes and categories that may be predetermined by those interested in exploring these topics.

7

ENGLISH LANGUAGE TEACHERS' SOCIAL CLASS AND POLITICAL IDENTITY CONSTRUCTION IN GROUP INTERACTION

INTRODUCTION

One feature of the arrival of neoliberal governments across much of the world from the late 1970s onward has been the progressive marketisation of education at all levels from pre-school through to university and the accompanying politically motivated recalibration of initial teacher education designed to produce efficient and disciplined professionals with a narrowly prescribed knowledge base (Block and Gray 2016; Gray and Block 2012). From the perspective of neoliberal governance, education is about the production of workers with the skills and dispositions needed to compete in the global economy, and teachers' specific remit is to facilitate this. As these 'reforms' were being rolled out in North America and the UK in the early days of what might be called the neoliberal era, many dissenting education theorists saw such changes in terms of the deprofessionalisation and the proletarianisation of teachers (Filson 1988; Giroux 1985; Harp and Betcherman 1980; Ozga and Lawn 1981), a phenomenon which was linked to the then much discussed proletarianisation of educated labour more generally (Larsen 1980). At the same time, another feature of neoliberalism was the attempted ideological erasure of social class as a way of thinking about human society and one's place in it and the concomitant promotion of individualism – 'a theory not only of abstract individuals but of the primacy of individual states and interests' (Williams 1976: 165). This move was only partially successful. While mainstream politicians and media commentators, including some on the political left (such as Gorz 1982), largely eschewed the term, for some academics – in particular sociologists and educationalists – social class remained an important theoretical concept (for example, Ball 2003; Bourdieu 1984; Maguire 2005; Sayer 2005b; Skeggs 2004; Wright 2005). However, the financial crisis of 2008 and its aftermath brought social class firmly back into political and media discourse, as well as into our own field of applied linguistics (for example, Block 2014a), within which we locate English language teaching. It is against this background of a broadly based return to social class that this chapter is written.

This chapter addresses two currently neglected aspects of English language teachers' sense of who they are and what they do: namely, those identities which are related to their understanding of social class as a factor in their lives and their political identifications. In doing this, we draw on data from group interaction in which a group of ESOL specialists discuss their practice, and in our analysis we pay particular attention to the ways in which their social class and political identities are indexed and made interactionally relevant. Methodologically, the chapter is indebted to Baynham's (2011) work on stance, positioning and alignment in small stories of professional experience. It begins with a necessarily detailed overview of the concept of social class (which draws on a considerable amount of historical literature) and the way in which it relates to teachers and the ESOL sector. This is followed by a more detailed account of our methodological approach, an analysis of the data and a short conclusion on the issues arising.

SOCIAL CLASS

In any consideration of social class a number of questions initially present themselves – what do we mean by social class?; what social classes are there?; and what are the criteria for ascribing or claiming membership of a particular social class? As Williams (1976) shows, terms such as the 'middle classes' and the 'working classes' appear in English only in the late eighteenth and early nineteenth centuries against the background of the Industrial Revolution and the social and political upheavals triggered by the French and American revolutions. Thus the emergence and naming of these recognisably modern social classes (more familiar to us today as singular rather than plural terms) are linked on the one hand to a change in the basic mode of production: that is, the rise of industrial capitalism, the shift to the factory as a key site of production, the conversion of rural peasants into urban wage-labourers, the ensuing growth of the city and the rise of mass education. On the other hand, they are linked to the dilution of the political power of land-owning aristocracies in favour of those who owned the new means of production and the rise of what has been described as 'bourgeois democracy' (Lenin 1982 [1919]), or (more recently) as 'democratic capitalism' (Streeck 2011). This can be understood as a system in which – despite the progressive and hard-won extension of the right to vote – political power remains firmly tied to those who are economically dominant. Marx and Engels were to prove hugely influential in the description and theorisation of these changes, and we are indebted in this chapter to their foundational work. However, despite producing a detailed analysis of the workings of early industrial capitalism (Marx 1976 [1867]), as well as ethnographic descriptions of the lives of working people (Engels 2009 [1845]), no definition of social class is found in their work – although it is clearly implied.

As Harris (1982) and Block (2014a) point out, we have to turn to their political heirs for the kind of definition they might have written. Both cite the following example as encapsulating the core of the classical Marxist view:

> Classes are large groups of people which differ from each other by the place they occupy in a historically determined system of social production, by their relation (in most cases fixed and formulated in law) to the means of production, by their role in the social organization of labour and, consequently, by the dimensions and method of acquiring the share of the social wealth of which they dispose. Classes are groups of people one of which can appropriate the labour of another owing to

the different places they occupy in a definitive system of social economy. (Lenin 1982 [1919]: 57)

From this early twentieth-century perspective we can say that the classical Marxist view of social class is relational and presupposes the existence of more than one class; it also assumes the exploitation of one class (the working class or proletariat) by another (the capitalist class or bourgeoisie), and considers the relation of all classes to the means of production as fundamental. Although Marx and Engels refer to several classes (such as the peasantry, the lumpenproletariat, land owners, the aristocracy), their model is essentially a dichotomous one (Giddens 1973) in which only the working class and the capitalist class are seen as crucial to the capitalist mode of production. Although their analysis of class society was revolutionary, a dichotomous view of social class (admittedly from a very different angle) was not entirely without precedent. As the early socialist Charles Hall, writing in 1805 in *The Effects of Civilization on the People in European States*, put it:

> [T]he people in a civilized state may be divided into different orders; but for the purpose of investigating the manner in which they enjoy or are deprived of the requisites to support the health of their bodies or minds, they need only be divided into two classes, viz. the rich and the poor. (Williams 1976: 67)

A recent example of this view is to be found in the Occupy movement's concept of 'the 1 per cent' and 'the 99 per cent'. Dorling (2014: 4) has written that the bottom 99 per cent in the UK – basically those with an annual household income of less than £160,000 before tax, all the way down to those living on welfare – now 'have more in common than has been the case for a generation', while the top 1 per cent exist in a stratospherically remote region where their wealth insulates them from the austerity demanded of the 99 per cent, and which is required to keep them in their position of privilege. However, as we shall see, such binary perspectives, while having the value of lending themselves readily to political mobilisation, have also been critiqued for being sociologically simplistic.

From the Marxist perspective, capitalist exploitation consists in the appropriation of *surplus value*: namely, that part of the value which is created by workers but which is withheld from them when the goods they have produced are sold for profit. Of course, not all labour contributes to the production of surplus value – soldiers (the example given by Marx) do not directly produce surplus value, and as such are deemed part of what is collectively referred to as *unproductive labour* – although their paid activities may be seen as necessary for the overall functioning of a system that depends fundamentally on the appropriation of surplus value. On the other hand, Marx categorises all factory workers, including the 'manager, engineer, technologist [. . .] overseer [. . .] manual labourer or even drudge' (Marx 1976 [1867]: 1040), as collectively part of *productive labour* because, despite the very different nature of their individual roles, their aggregate product creates surplus value and therefore profit for the factory owner. Clearly it does not follow from this that all types of pro-ductive (and unproductive) labour are equally invested in the system, as the manager might be held to do better out of capitalist arrangements than the drudge (or indeed the soldier). This is a point we will return to below in our consideration of teachers.

Integral to this view is the concept of class struggle, which Marx saw as coming about when workers having a shared relationship to the means of production, living 'under economic conditions of existence that divide their mode of life, their interests and their culture from those of the other classes' (Marx 1978a [1852]: 608), united politically to pursue their class interests. In doing so, they moved from being what he describes as a 'class in itself' – that is, a social formation whose members have a shared relation to the means of production – to becoming a 'class for itself' (Marx 1978b [1847]: 218) – that is, a group that is politically conscious of itself as a class and of its class interests. However, as capitalist societies developed, not all scholars were convinced by the Marxist argument of class struggle either as inevitable or as necessarily leading to the kind of revolutionary social change Marx anticipated. Many also saw Marxism as economically reductive – despite the fact that the centrality of alienation in his theorising of life under capitalism provided ample evidence to the contrary. These scholars argued the need to pay greater attention to the cultural dimensions of social differentiation, putting the 'mode of life', 'interests' and 'culture' Marx alluded to more firmly centre-stage (for example, Durkheim 1984 [1893]; Veblen 2007 [1899]; Weber 1968 [1922]; Thompson 1963) – in some cases to the near-total exclusion of the economic. Collectively, this theorisation served to complexify the concept of class, particularly as it is understood in disciplines such as sociology. As Block (2014a) shows, many contemporary understandings of social class are indebted to the work of Bourdieu, who tried to combine the material and the economic focus derived from Marx with the cultural focus derived from those who came after him. Thus, for Bourdieu:

> [C]lass or class faction is defined not only by its position in the relations of production, as identified through indices such as occupation, income, or even educational level, but also by a certain sex-ratio, a certain distribution in geographical space (which is never socially neutral) and by a whole set of subsidiary characteristics which may function, in the form of tacit requirements, as real principles of selection or exclusion without ever being formally stated (this is the case with ethnic origin and sex). A number of official criteria: for example, the requiring of a given diploma can be a way of demanding a particular social origin. (Bourdieu 1984: 102)

Bourdieu construed this highly nuanced view of social class in terms of the possession of and access to a variety of capitals. In addition to the possession of economic capital (for example, money, stocks and shares, property), then, people were seen as having varieties of cultural capital (such as educational qualifications, the ability to speak the prestige variety of a language, particular artistic and culinary tastes) and social capital (such as access through family, schooling, professional organisations and other institutions to advantageous social networks).

Some scholars (for example, Bolin 2012; Harvey 2014) have taken issue with this notion of a plurality of capitals, and in our own field Holborow (2015) has argued that Bourdieu's capitals are not equivalents and that varieties of cultural and social capital are qualitatively different from economic capital and not directly convertible into one another in the way that way that money, stocks and shares, and property are. She also argues that what she sees as the over-extension of the metaphor of capital in Bourdieu's work paradoxically contributes to neoliberalism's attempted extension of the market to all aspects of human interaction, totalising in effect that which he seeks to critique. That said, Bourdieu's reworking of the concept of social class has been pervasive and to date it has proved enduring – and for that reason we refer to it here. While agreeing with Holborow's basic point about such capitals not being equivalents and recognising that their convertibility (in some cases, as will be suggested below) can be unsuccessful, we recognise that they can *on occasion* be deployed by their possessors to their advantage.

One consequence of such complexification has been the proliferation of class categories in sociological research, often taking income from occupation as its starting point (for example, Erikson and Goldthorpe 1992). However, Marx (1966 [1865]: 886) repudiates the view that 'the infinite fragmentation of interest and rank into which the division of social labour splits labourers as well as capitalists', along with their varying financial rewards, can be used as the basis for labelling classes. At the same time, he freely admits that classes can appear difficult to pin down and that '[m]iddle and intermediate strata [. . .] obliterate lines of demarcation everywhere' (885). One relatively recent attempt to address the problem posed by the evident 'fragmentation of interest and rank' within groups who have the same (or similar) relation to the means of production, as well as the previously mentioned factors of 'mode of life' and 'culture', is found in the Great British Class Survey (hereafter GBCS) (Savage et al. 2013). The authors take Bourdieu's perspective explicitly into account and have as their starting point the view that

> a focus on occupations as the sole measure of class occludes the more complex ways that class operates symbolically and culturally, through forms of stigmatisation and marking of personhood and value. Such an appreciation requires a more culturally sensitive mode of analysis. (Savage et al. 2013: 222)

Hence the questions on the GBCS fall into three categories related to Bourdieu's concept of economic capital (for example, Do you own or rent a property?), cultural capital (Which of these cultural activities do you take part in?) and social capital (Which of these people do you know socially?). The analysts – all social scientists – adopted what they describe as a bottom-up inductive approach to the data and concluded that those taking the survey (*n* 161, 400) fell into seven new social classes, which they describe as shown in Table 7.1.

The challenge, for those who see social class in political terms, is how to reconcile such a stratified perspective with the more easily mobilised and dichotomised view found in Marx and those influenced by him. Standing's (2011) work on the precariat is representative of one attempt to mobilise (theoretically and politically) new perspectives on social class. Standing sees the precariat – a term which links the idea of the precariousness of work in the era of globalisation typified by low wages and

Table 7.1. Great British Class Survey social classes (adapted from Savage et al. 2013: 230)

Social class	Description
Elite	Very high economic capital (especially savings), high social capital, very high highbrow cultural capital
Established middle class	High economic capital, high status of mean contacts, high highbrow and emerging cultural capital
Technical middle class	High economic capital, very high mean social contacts, but relatively few contacts reported, moderate cultural capital
New affluent workers	Moderately good economic capital, moderately poor mean score of social contacts, though high range, moderate highbrow but good emerging cultural capital
Traditional working class	Moderately poor economic capital, though with reasonable house price, few social contacts, low highbrow and emerging cultural capital
Emergent service workers	Moderately poor economic capital, though with reasonable household income, moderate social contacts, high emerging (but low highbrow), cultural capital
Precariat	Poor economic capital, and the lowest scores on every other criterion

short-term or zero hours contracts with the established category of proletariat – as 'a *class-in-the making*, if not yet a *class-for-itself*' (11; italics in original). His argument is that the precariat (a growing and very diverse group with no clearly defined set of occupational identities) needs to become conscious of itself as a class if neoliberalism and the neoliberal state are to be effectively challenged. Although precariousness is clearly a feature of contemporary capitalist societies, it should be pointed out that Standing's view of the precariat as a *class-in-the-making* has been severely critiqued by scholars such as Seymour (2012), who argues that 'precarity exerts effects right up the chain of class strata, throughout the working class and into sections of the middle class' (see also Breman 2013).

Harris (1982), writing from an explicitly Marxist perspective, argues in line with Poulantzas (1973, 1975) that it is not enough to focus on identifying the gradations of class *location* (where groups appear to slot in, as in Table 7.1); it is also necessary to focus on class *position* (how groups align themselves in the confrontation with capital).[1] He writes:

> [I]n any social formation there may exist a larger number of classes than focus on the dominant mode of production might suggest. [. . .] Not everybody in a capitalist society can be neatly labelled either 'worker' or 'capitalist', and it is a misconceived exercise to attempt to squeeze all people into one or other of these respective classes. All people can, however, be identified not necessarily in terms of which of the two major classes they belong to but in terms of which particular class's interests they predominately serve. (Harris 1982: 39)

[1] Poulantzas distinguishes between class determination and class position. Harris uses the term class location as broadly equivalent to class determination.

This perspective introduces a political, ideological and subjective aspect to the issue of social class, and it is to this that we now turn our attention, and in particular to the problematic case of teachers.

CLASS LOCATION AND CLASS POSITION OF TEACHERS

In the light of the above, what – we might ask initially – can be said about the class location of teachers, the majority of whom are employed by the state and tasked, as stated earlier, with the job of producing citizens with the dispositions deemed appropriate for servicing the economy? Although there are few references to teachers in the work of Marx, in his discussion of productive labour he presents the following case:

> If we may take an example from outside the sphere of materials production, a school-master is a productive worker when, in addition to belabouring the heads of his pupils, he works himself into the ground to enrich the owner of the school. That the latter has laid out his capital in a teaching factory, instead of a sausage factory, makes no difference to the relation. (Marx 1976 [1867]: 644)

It is clear that Marx is referring here to the school as a privately owned institution. Certainly, many teachers in the non-unionised commercial ELT sector globally today may be said to work in conditions resembling those of the factory, where their main function is to produce profit for their employers (for example, Japanese *eikaiwa* or Taiwanese *bushibans*). The requirement for minimal qualifications across the commercial sector, the lack of career structure, the (generally) low wages and non-unionised working conditions, the lack of sick pay and holiday pay in many settings, and the high turnover of young, migrant teachers from English-speaking countries are indicative of the sector's basically exploitative nature. Such teachers clearly fulfil a fundamentally proletarian role in the 'edu-business' economy (Ball 2012), although in some cases their access to other forms of Bourdieusian capital may be said to mitigate the consequences of this. For example, their ability to present and be perceived as speakers of standard British or North American English and the type of qualifications they possess, as well as the extent to which they signal distinction through their dress and other semiotic means, may enable them not only to find employment in better schools, but also to make local social contacts and participate in the social life of the host country in ways not open to the local working class.

What, though, of teachers in the state-school sector who are employed by the state? Here things are less clear. In one of the most thorough explorations of teachers and social class, Harris (1982) argues persuasively that although the state in capitalist democracy functions as the representative of capital, teachers in this sector occupy a particularly liminal location.

> Teachers are basically workers: they are salaried labourers contracted to perform specific activities; and in common with the working class they have little occupational independence, little control over the labour process, and no access to the means of production. They are, however, unproductive labourers, outside of the

valorisation process, and they do not directly produce surplus value. They belong to that stratum of unproductive labour which is employed by the State to maintain the overall conditions of capitalist production; and thus, even though they share many characteristics with the working class, they do not belong to the working class. (Harris 1982: 128)

Clearly, this does not protect them from being subjected to processes of intensified proletarianisation in the neoliberal era – if that is seen as the downgrading of 'craft mastery' (Braverman 1974) in favour of 'scientifically' measurable skills (where the former is understood as the recursive interplay between personal knowledge of materials and processes and access to theory and research [Block and Gray 2016]); the institution of rigorous inspection regimes in which the demonstration of particular classroom behaviours is obligatory; the requirement to meet government targets in terms of examination results; the compilation and use of league tables to ensure school competitiveness; and the narrowing of the academic knowledge base in favour of subject knowledge and basic classroom management.

Harris argues that the class position of liminal groups such as teachers cannot be predicted on the basis of their class location, although he suggests they have much to gain from serving capital. That said, he does not consider the way in which teachers from working-class backgrounds may take – as Maguire (2005) shows – their class habitus and their class-based political identifications with them into teaching and the ways in which these may be retained in the face of middle-class teacher hostility. In addition to asserting (somewhat too mechanistically, in our view) that teachers, as state functionaries, 'are in the business of constituting individual ideological subjects as willing bearers of labour power for capital' (Harris 1982: 129), he also takes the controversial view that the quest for professionalism which has typified teaching in many parts of the world throughout the twentieth century has had the effect of distancing teachers from other workers who are not accorded professional status. This view is stoutly resisted by Lawn and Ozga (1988: 84), who argue that '[a]ll education does not serve the purposes of the state all the time,' and they make the case for professionalism as a means of claiming greater workplace autonomy for teachers.

However, Harris does argue presciently (he was writing in the early days of the neoliberal era) that, as capitalism evolved, teachers would find the processes of proletarianisation were soon to be intensified. In such circumstances, Harris hypothesised that teachers might come to identify more closely with other workers and the working class more generally. With this thought in mind, we now turn to the case of teachers in the ESOL sector.

THE ESOL SECTOR

One feature of the uneven development of capitalism globally and the concomitant social upheavals this has entailed has been the mass migration of people in ever-increasing numbers from the second half of the twentieth century onward. Simpson (2016) points out that it is estimated that 1 in 35 of the world's population today is a migrant – propelled to move in pursuit of work, to join family abroad, or in flight from war, persecution, environmental degradation or poverty. Simpson (2015: 210) describes the UK as a 'reluctant host state', where 'immigrants are needed,' but paradoxically one in which they are 'not welcomed', and where 'political leaders present any fall in the numbers of inward migrants as a victory for "tough" practices.'

In such an environment the teaching of English to migrants in the UK has become a highly charged political issue, subject to ever-changing policy directives related to citizenship and 'integration'. ESOL classes generally take place in Further Education (FE) colleges, which also provide training in literacy and numeracy, as well as vocational courses in areas such as catering and construction. However, the FE sector – and ESOL provision in particular – has been particularly vulnerable to government funding cuts in the wake of the 2008 financial crisis and the subsequent implementation of austerity. Against this background, it is hardly surprising that ESOL and political activism on the part of teachers have gone hand in hand. Simpson (2015) provides a good account of a wide range of teacher activist organisations dating back to the 1970s, all of which sought improved funding for the sector and greater recognition for ESOL teachers, while arguing for more awareness of multilingualism and multiculturalism in migrant education and a less top-down approach to curriculum content. One of the most recent groups to appear is Action for ESOL, which was formed in 2010 in response to government austerity measures. Their manifesto (Action for ESOL 2012), which comprises thirty-five points, is divided into seven sections: Defending our sector; Funding; The right to learn the common language of the UK; Language, community and diversity; Defending the ESOL identity; Professionalism; and Pedagogy. The manifesto is a highly political statement, which argues inter alia that classrooms cannot be isolated from the social contexts in which they are located; that teaching is an inherently political activity; and that the knowledge base of ESOL teachers needs to include awareness of the social, cultural and economic conditions shaping migrant language learners' lives and the mechanisms whereby they are frequently marginalised and socially excluded.

INFORMANTS, METHODOLOGY AND ANALYSIS

Three ESOL colleagues known to us agreed to take part in a group discussion (moderated by John). All three are associated with Action for ESOL – two are ESOL teachers and teacher educators (referred to pseudonymously as Peter and Susan), and one is an academic who has written extensively on ESOL and who was previously a teacher (referred to hereafter as Liz). They all have undergraduate and postgraduate degrees from prestigious institutions. We decided to use a group discussion rather than a traditional interview format, given that such an approach is better suited to shedding light on the issue we were interested in exploring – namely, the ways in which social class and political identities are indexed and made interactionally relevant as the participants collectively addressed a discussion topic set by the moderator. Although the moderator did ask questions, the aim was to allow the participants to talk and respond to one another in a relatively uninhibited and spontaneous way. In terms of relationships, the three informants were friends of long standing, and John and Liz were good friends. Peter and Susan did not know John socially, although all parties

Table 7.2. Materials used in the group discussion

Materials	Author(s)	Year/publisher
Citizenship Materials for ESOL Learners	National Institute of Adult Continuing Education (NIACE)	2010/NIACE
Problem posing at Work: English for Action	E. Auerbach and N. Wallerstein	2004/Edmonton: Grass Roots Press
New Headway Elementary	L. Soars and J. Soars	2011/Oxford University Press

were aware that they shared a lot in common politically. In the hope of triggering talk about social class and political identification, the informants were shown three pieces of pedagogic material on the topic of work and asked to say what they thought of them (Table 7.2). Two were written specifically for migrants and one was a piece of EFL material (on the basis that such materials are often used in ESOL settings).

The NIACE material comprises a set of online resources for ESOL teachers and deals with various aspects of life in the UK. The informants were given a downloaded copy of a section entitled 'Working in the United Kingdom', which consists of exercises on such topics as how to understand a wage slip, information about minimum wage law, and a short reading about discrimination at work (which contained no reference to trade unions). Although clearly focused on the perceived needs of migrants in the UK, the NIACE material could not be further removed from *Problem-posing at Work*, a copy of which was also given to the informants. This is a textbook aimed at migrants in North America, which draws on Freirean critical pedagogy and which has acquired a talismanic status among some teachers in the years since it was first published. The Grass Roots Press promotional material states that the textbook aims to give migrant students 'greater power over their circumstances' and to enable them to 'strategize together for changes' in the workplace. Thus students are presented with documented case histories of migrant workers' battles and successes with exploitative employers, information about their legal rights, and about the role of unions and how to get involved. The third piece of material was a photocopy of a unit entitled 'Work hard, play hard!' from the *Headway Elementary* textbook. The approach to work in this unit is typical of much commercial EFL material in that work is presented as a matter of freely exercised individual choice in the pursuit of self-fulfilment. Thus the unit introduces Lisa, a fictional character who lives in New York and has two jobs. By day she works in a bookstore and by night she sings in a band, activities which, readers are told, she loves and make her happy.

In terms of analysis, we looked at the data after they were recorded. It was immediately clear that small stories were relevant, as were the informants' stance, positioning and alignment with regard to each other, the sectors of ESOL and EFL, and the small stories (discussed earlier in this volume) themselves. Stance has been defined by Du Bois (2007: 163) as

a public act by a social actor, achieved dialogically through overt communicative means, of simultaneously evaluating objects, positioning subjects (self and others), and aligning with other subjects, with respect to any salient dimension of the sociocultural field.

Stance is thus seen as a three-part act involving evaluation of a stance object (or objects); positioning – understood as 'the act of situating a social actor with respect to responsibility for stance and for invoking sociocultural value' (143); and alignment – understood as 'the act of calibrating the relationship between two stances, and by implication between two stancetakers' (144). Alignment (and the means by which it is achieved, as well as the extent of convergence or divergence) is seen as a key element in the overall management of intersubjectivity between speakers. An illustrative example of this comes from the beginning of the focus group discussion. John had taken orders for tea and coffee and briefly left the group alone to look at the three sets of materials.

Extract 7.1: 'I can't believe I'm like living without that book'

```
P: So let's have a little look at these things
S: I really / I wish I had this (picking up Problem-
posing at Work)
P: I know it's awesome isn't it=
L: You have a look at that (handing Peter Headway
Elementary)
S: =Yeah
L: I'll have a look at the citizenship stuff
P: I've only seen it (referring to Problem-posing at
Work) as a title / not in the flesh before=
S: =No me too
L: I bet / you can probably get it on Amazon
S: [Inaudible] I just can't / I can't believe I'm like
living without that book
```

Although all three pieces of material were on the table, Susan immediately oriented to *Problem-posing at Work* – what Du Bois calls the object of stance – with an affective evaluation ('I wish I had this'), which is followed immediately by Peter's alignment with her position. Peter's alignment is both epistemic ('I know') and affective ('it's awesome'). His reference to never having seen the book 'in the flesh' before is followed by Susan's use of what is referred to by Du Bois as an intersubjective alignment marker ('No <u>me too</u>') (as indeed is Peter's earlier 'isn't it' tag) and a second hyperbolic evaluation ('I can't believe I'm like living without that book'). Meanwhile Liz, who has taken responsibility for allocating the remaining two pieces of material, contributes with a suggestion on how to obtain a personal copy, thereby aligning herself with Susan's initial declared position and her colleagues' joint evaluation. All three might thus be said to align with one another vis-à-vis this particular shared stance object – an alignment which already indexes indirectly their implicit shared professional and political identities through their collective endorsement of the textbook's approach to teaching English to migrants. This can be seen as the first move in what will be a series of dialogically unfolding stance utterances related to a shifting set of stance objects which the speakers introduce.

TALKING ABOUT WORK

One notable feature of the interview is the way that the EFL sector is repeatedly invoked as a negatively evaluated stance object (both indirectly and directly) by the three informants in their overall stance taking, particularly with regard to their sense of themselves as ESOL teachers. They are, of course, positioned to take up a stance on EFL by virtue of the inclusion of *Headway Elementary* as part of the discussion activity. However, it is the way in which EFL is repeatedly invoked that we wish to focus on here.

The negative evaluation of EFL first raises its head in two utterances by Peter just after the exchange in which *Problem-posing at Work* was positively evaluated by the group. Neither utterance triggers immediate alignment from the others beyond non-verbal phatic sounds of recognition of his contributions – but as Du Bois points out, stance taking is frequently a cumulative process in which utterances are echoically built on by speakers over time. Having cast his eye over the *Headway Elementary* unit, Peter says:

```
In terms of / I haven't looked at this yet / but erm I
would imagine it's not from a (.) union perspective
```

In view of the positive evaluation of *Problem-posing at Work*, in which trade union membership is viewed as an important way for workers to defend themselves and fight for their rights, this could be interpreted as a probable negative evaluation of the EFL material – although this is not something that is clarified until later in the interaction. The same is true of his follow-up comment on the three pieces of material overall:

```
But maybe there's three categories then / there's the
kind of EFL / and then there's the more political ESOL /
and then there's the less political ESOL
```

The implication of this utterance is that the EFL material is not 'political', or at least not political in the way that the two sets of ESOL materials are. Commenting on the dialogic nature of stance taking, Du Bois writes that '[d]ialogicality makes its presence felt to the extent that a stancetaker's words derive from, and further engage with, the words of those who have spoken before' (140). Although he is concerned with the echoic nature of what he calls dialogic syntax, we take the view that dialogicality is also achieved through the repeated choice of (in this case) the same negatively evaluated stance object as part of the overall (implicit or explicit) positive evaluation of another stance object (here the Action for ESOL approach to teaching). This can be seen in a subsequent comment by Susan, who was responding to a suggestion from John (not present when Peter's comments were made) that ESOL teachers' are generally on the political left. While agreeing that political commitment and ESOL do generally go together, she nuances this by adding:

```
there's a very large sector of completely / people who
would consider themselves not political [L: hmm] / who::
are there as kind of just [L: hmm]/ for language teachers
who have come from EFL o::r / their focus is language /
there's been a huge drive over the past ten / twenty
years to depoliticise ESOL / and [L: yeah] for it to be
like a profession / and technical / technical language
teachers
```

Thus we see here an echo of Peter's association of EFL as not 'political' in the suggestion that EFL teachers who move into the ESOL sector come with a focus on language – rather than with a focus on language *and* politics. This limited perspective (signalled by the use of 'just') is associated with a depoliticising professionalism (cf. Harris's point above) and a technical approach to language teaching, presumably unlike the Freirean approach espoused by Action for ESOL. The professionalism point is not taken up by the others, although as we shall see, EFL continues to be used as a negatively evaluated stance object, particularly as the informants begin to index their own class position more explicitly.

The others agree with Susan's assessment and Liz adds to this by saying that some ESOL teachers have what she describes as a 'charity take on [ESOL] as opposed to a political take on it', which she describes as meaning that they do not have a political analysis of society which goes beyond merely wanting to help migrant language learners as members of potentially marginalised groups. In responding to this, John asks the group why they feel the way they do. Susan replies with a small story about how she became an ESOL teacher. In terms of the point made in Chapter 5 regarding the question 'why this story, told this way, now?' we can conclude that Susan's small story seeks to position her *and* the group as specific kinds of teachers for whom political analysis is primary.

Extract 7.2: Susan's small story

```
J: why do you feel the way you do about all of this↑
S: well for me: / certainly my interest in (2) / in
becoming an ESOL teacher in the first place=
P: =yeah=
S: =you know / one that / erm it (.) / my political
interest preceded the / the interest to become an ESOL
teacher / that kind of combined with an interest in / a
geeky interest in language / which I still have / and (.)
/ kind of interest in politics and activism / it s- / it
was the perfect job / you know when I was (.)
```

```
L: hmm=
P: =hmm=
S: =21/ 22 just graduated / there was no bet- / you know
it combined all of the interests of my life / and so:: /
you know / and I think a lot of people felt like that as
well
L: so you sought it out as a job=
S: =yeah=
L: =in a way=
S: =absolutely yeah / [inaudible] I think rare / I think
we're quite rare though because / a lot of ESOL teachers
have done loads of other things / and then come into ESOL
later / I think quite few people (.) / actually it's / it's
the only thing I've ever done↓
```

From this perspective, ESOL is projected as an ideal site which allowed Susan to combine her already existing political views and activism with an actual job. Although she tells this as her story, she includes the others in this 'small story-as-answer' when she says 'I think we're quite rare,' thereby positioning Peter and Liz through her use of the first person plural pronoun as somehow similarly located. In fact, although the others may be said to share her political views, their routes into ESOL were different – something Susan would have known. Although appearing to suggest a similar trajectory, Susan may be said to be positioning all three of them in the situated speech event of the group discussion as sharing the same orientation to ESOL. Liz picks up on this immediately with two small stories of her own, both of which parallel Susan's in their assessment of teaching ESOL and in terms of alignment at the affective level. Significantly, these are told explicitly in terms of a move away from teaching EFL, while providing the first clear indexing of class position.

Extract 7.3: Liz's first story

```
L: because that's / I I I fell into it / because I was in
Spain so I was doing EFL [J: hmm] / (whispering to Peter
and Susan) so you know 'cause that's where we met /
J: what↑
L: that's / you know / 'cause that's where we met=
J: =yes=
L: =in Barcelona / but (.) [J laughing] / and so I was
very political / and / and always have been since I was
younger / but I didn't really connect this stuff while in
Spain AT ALL to my politics=
S: =hmm=
J: =hmm=
L: =it was much more like my own (.) marginalisation (.)
within Barcelona that I was more interested in / and/ and
```

```
I was mainly teaching posh people (.) / not too [J:
laughing] / not totally posh but [J: yeah] by the very
dint of the fact that people were going to private
language schools meant that they were prioritising that
for their kids / or that they themselves thought it was
going to help their careers / so they were going to kind
of further themselves / this is a / you know / string to
their bow [J: hmm] / to have English / so I always felt a
bit like a service provider in a way / in the EFL sector
in Barcelona / so it was much more about /you know / me
as a (.) / as my position in that / and then when I came
into ESOL in London / then I felt a bit like Susan / like
OK erm / I understand this world better (.) / it feels
more / more constructive and helpful and useful to be in
this world (J: hmm) / than to feel like I'm serving the
[P: hmm] future careers of rich people /
```

Liz's experience of teaching in the fee-paying EFL private sector is here presented negatively. In line with Susan's small story, her political identification is shown to precede her entry into teaching. Teaching is presented as an activity disconnected from her politics, in the sense that it is not seen as a way of doing politics. Much of what she says is couched in affective terms – her sense of marginalisation as an EFL teacher in Barcelona caused her to *feel* like a service provider and to *feel* that she was serving the future careers of rich people. On the other hand, her move into ESOL on return to London caused to her to *feel* 'like Susan' and to *feel* that teaching ESOL was more 'constructive', 'helpful' and 'useful'. With no pause for comment from the others, Liz then launched directly into a second small story.

Extract 7.4: Liz's second story

```
L: erm I also worked in EFL in London and that was the
worst thing I've ever done / 'cause they really were
elites
J: hmm
S: (softly) I can imagine
L: erm I couldn't stand it / did it for about 3 months=
J: =and where did you do that↑
L: XXX in XXX
J hmm I didn't know that (slight laugh)
L: yeah [P: inaudible] I got the job / it was the first
job I had when I came back from Spain [J: yeah] / and erm
I was teaching mainly business people from Switzerland
and Japan / and erm / it was just mad and I was just crap
/ and they made / but this is just coming back to me now
/ they actually said to me / you know / you've got / you
```

can't dress like that / you have to dress like [S: hmm] /
they wanted me to dress like an office girl=
P: =wow=
L: =of course you WERE really regarded as the person who
was gonna / g- (.) / you / you were like an extension of
their kind of (.) business world [P: hmm] / to a certain
extent / that's what they wanted you to be / and so I was
a complete fish out of water and they didn't renew my
contract [J: hmm] / and I was quite devastated by this /
it never happened to me before [P: hmm] / 'cause I had
like my distinction in my DELTA and everything / and I
was like you know really good (.) / and I just didn't fit
in / and this is much more the worlds that you know the
global executive world (.) /and the business world / and
the ESP and things / and I just didn't fit into that at
all [J: hmm] / one moment / and I wouldn't say it's
because of CLASS so much as / as my take on the world (.)
[J: hmm P: hmm] / actually [J: hmm] / because I just
never have aligned with that kind of thing / so ESOL was
a huge (.) [S: hmm] relief [Peter: hmm] / in many ways↓

In this second story Liz recounts what happened in what was clearly for her a worse EFL situation, where the students 'really were elites' and where she was positioned as 'an extension' of the business itself and required to dress like 'an office girl'. The use of 'girl' here is significant in that it connotes a perceived loss of adult and professional status (and a possible sexualisation), while the metaphor of being an extension reinforces the absence of professional autonomy, which resulted in her being 'crap' as a teacher. In both these stories, the EFL teacher is presented in terms of social marginalisation, low status and loss of agency in which the possession of appropriate accreditation (such as a distinction in the Cambridge English Diploma in English Language Teaching to Adults, DELTA) was insufficient to guarantee contract renewal. A DELTA distinction (at the time referred to by Liz) was indicative of a very high level of knowledge in areas such as language analysis for pedagogical purposes, language testing and language teaching methodology, as well as the ability to plan and execute effectively appropriately staged and timed lessons for specific groups of learners. This lends credence to Holborow's suggestion above that Bourdieusian capitals are not equivalents and in certain circumstances are not directly convertible into what Bourdieu (1991: 55) has referred to as 'a profit of distinction'. The picture which emerges in these two small stories is one that is entirely congruent with proletarianisation. That said, Liz explicitly states that not fitting in was not related to her own class location, but rather was a consequence of her 'take on the world' (that is, her political world view) and her lack of alignment with 'that kind of thing' (that is, the business world and the teaching of elite students). On this assessment it can be interpreted as a statement of her class position (as understood by Poulantzas and Harris above), indexicalised through her repudiation of the world of EFL, which is repeatedly associated with business, elite groups and service provision. This is contrasted with her embrace of the world of ESOL, which – in a clear echo of Susan's small story – represents a coming together of her political beliefs with work. It should be added that Liz's direct reference to 'class' in this way may also have been for John's particular benefit, as she knew of our interest in exploring teachers' class-based and political identities in this book, and she may have wished to clarify the point for the record.

It will be recalled that John's original question about why they felt as they do about teaching occasioned these small stories of becoming a teacher. At this stage John asked Peter how he got into teaching, which triggered a further two small stories. In the first of these he describes going to Argentina, aged eighteen, to teach EFL. He explains that he always had an interest in 'political economy', thereby signalling affinity with Susan and Liz in terms of having a political outlook that predated entry into teaching. He describes being in Argentina during its financial crisis in 2001 as a 'political education'. On his return to the UK he embarked on a Master's in Development Studies and began teaching migrants and doing various other kinds of part-time teaching. This provides the background to his second small story, in which EFL is again featured as a negatively evaluated stance object. It is also clear that Susan (at least) knows the story already – so her first comment ('this is the best bit of the story') functions as an endorsement of the story's 'tellability' (Baroni 2014): that is, its worthiness of being told, and its relevance to the context in which it is being produced.

Extract 7.5: Peter's story

```
P: I got a call saying would I do three months' tutoring
a Belgian baroness on a yacht (laughing) / this was
February
J: yes (laughing)
S: this is the best bit of the story
P: all right then=
S: =all right then (imitating Peter)=
P: =all right then=
L: =on a yacht /this is like bobbing around (in the sea
or whatever) ↑
P: it didn't turn out to be quite / quite on a yacht /
but erm there was some yacht involved (.) / and so / so
then I had this totally weird experience of teaching a /
an aristocrat
J: what / one to one↑
P: one to one [J: hmm] for six months / following her
around the world
L: fucking hell (laughing)
P: erm so / so bizarre (laughing) kind of EFL experience
J: but what / she'd say=
```

P: so I was using this kind of stuff (indicating *Headway Elementary*) / and just teaching her for between one and four hours a day / erm

J: and what you / when you say following her around the world / (inaudible) she would say I'm going to=

P: =to China / to Paris

J: you'd go too

P: I'd go with her / yeah

J: God

P: flying around with her

J: how did you feel↑ / I mean how=

P: =massively conflicted /angry the whole time

J: what did you feel your role was↑ (inaudible comments from the others)

P: yeah (in response to the inaudible comments by Susan and Liz) I hated a lot of it erm / I liked having a lot of time (.) to myself / 'cause I like reading and erm / and I learnt French and erm / yeah just had / you know / it was massively chilled erm/ and it was good money / 'cause I wasn't paying any rent / so I was saving a bit of money / and so I quite liked all that / I didn't particularly enjoy the travelling / erm and then I just / but seeing how some people live was an incredibly interesting experience [S: hmm L: I bet] / in terms of waste and erm attitudes / erm (.) so it was something that made me very determined that / that if I wanted to go back to London / then I'd do something that I wanted to do / rather than be a servant / because I did / I massively felt like a servant / it would be / she'd say / you know / I'll meet you at 9 tomorrow / and I'd go into the hotel reception / or wherever I was supposed to be / nothing 'til maybe 11.30 / then I might get a text saying oh I had to have a meeting / so I spent like most of the 6 months just waiting / erm and getting really angry and / at how kind of useless my life was at the time / and I (inaudible) didn't want it to be like that / erm but then there was nice bits you know

J: hmm and did you like her as a person or

P: hmm I don't know really / not / I got on with her fine / we didn't have anything in common / she / she didn't seem to take any interest in me or my life / and so / but it was hard work having to teach somebody one to one that intensively / what do you talk about / so I'd just make her do loads of exercises / so it didn't have ANY professional satisfaction / because I didn't think that

```
my teaching was good / that her learning was good / she
wasn't really learning / erm I / now when I do one to one
I really can't stand it / I (find) it really hard [S: I
can't] / it's my kind of nightmare that one day I'll have
to [S: I can't stand it] go back to doing all that just
to make money
```

In similar vein to Liz's small stories, Peter's presents his EFL experience as unpleasant ('weird' and 'bizarre') and one that made him feel 'angry' and socially inferior ('I massively felt like a servant') – again a mirroring of Liz's experience, who recounted being made to feel as though she were a 'service provider' and 'serving' the future careers of rich students. Peter's small story is thus a kind of antiphonal response to Liz's – repeating and modifying the themes she established, which in turn were triggered by Susan's initial small story. Both these teachers may be said to have found EFL to be a proletarianising experience and both reported that their teaching of elite students was bad. In line with Liz's verdict on the poor quality of her own teaching (despite her DELTA distinction), Peter assesses his teaching as poor with a concomitant lack of student learning. Interestingly, Liz's choice of the term 'useful' to describe how she felt when she shifted from EFL to ESOL is mirrored by Peter's description of his EFL job as causing him to feel that his life was 'useless'. Where Peter's small story is different is in the way close contact with the aristocratic student was perceived as a politically educational experience, much like that of witnessing the Argentinean economic collapse at first hand. The experience made him decide to do something that he wanted to do – rather than continue to work as a 'servant', a role which he admits brought financial rewards but little in the way of job satisfaction. As was the case with Susan and Liz, the implication is that job satisfaction would come about only when work could be made to harmonise with his political outlook.

What, then, does this tell us about these teachers' social class and political identity construction? The interaction, as reported so far, gives a very clear indication of their class position and their political outlook. In fact, class position, as understood by Poulantzas, implies perforce a political stance which we see clearly here. That these three teachers who are closely associated with Action for ESOL – which significantly has a *manifesto* (and not a *mission statement*, more typical of organisations in the neoliberal era) – position themselves as they do is hardly surprising. What is interesting is the way in which the EFL sector is deployed by all of them in their stance taking and the overall management of intersubjectivity. But what of their own class location and, by extension, their views of the class *location* of ESOL teachers more generally?

TALKING ABOUT CLASS LOCATION

As Sayer (2002) has pointed out, sociologists commonly encounter evasiveness and unease when informants are asked to talk about themselves in terms of class location – although he does not frame this in Poulantzas's terms, speaking rather simply of class. Social class can be difficult to talk about in relation to the self, he suggests, as it can trigger feelings of shame regarding its hidden (and not so hidden) injuries

(Sennett and Cobb 1972) and one's perceived moral worth, or embarrassment about sense of (undeserved) status; it can also, he argues, trigger the need to self-justify or to deny that social class has any meaning, or that it even exists. While there is no evidence of evasiveness in the focus group data, it is noteworthy how class location is addressed.

In response to a question from John about the training of teachers in Freirean pedagogy, Peter says that Action for ESOL's raison d'être is addressing the 'systemic unfairness' characterising the lives of migrants, particularly those who speak English as a second language, by providing them with 'linguistic strategies' for combating this. At this point John asks if social class 'comes up' as a topic in training sessions or in ESOL classes. Susan says it does, but that it tends not to be framed explicitly in those terms – rather, it appears in talk about poverty, which is more likely to resonate with students' lived experience. Explicit reference to social class, she suggests, sounds more like a 'teacher-led' topic and therefore less in line with her understanding of the bottom-up pedagogy she espouses. In talking about poverty as a theme, Susan stated that she had on occasion told students that she herself had come from a 'poor back-ground' – although she recognised that never having been unemployed, never having had to negotiate difficult situations at a job centre, or deal with local government as a social housing tenant (common experiences for her own students), meant that she could not over-claim shared experience with many of her students, whose lives were often very precarious. At the mention of precarity, John asks the group about their views on the class location of ESOL teachers in general, given that many have fractional contracts and endure insecure working conditions. In doing so, he turns the conversation away from students and on to the group itself, positioning them to an extent as representatives of the sector. The response, initially from Susan and Liz, suggests their sense of distance – at least in terms of lived experience – from many of their ESOL colleagues (it will be recalled that Liz is an academic and that Susan, in addition to continuing to work as a teacher, is also a teacher educator).

Extract 7.6: 'But the jobs are more and more scarce now'

```
S: I think it's a really good point / but I think you've
got maybe the wrong people in the room to talk about that
/ because we're all (.) / well (.) I don't know / I guess
(.) pretty established / and salaried / and [L: yeah]
have reaped the benefits [L: you'd be better off talking
to casualised people] of the professionalisation of the
sector (inaudible)=
L: =it's massively casualised though
   [some lines omitted in which the background to
casualisation is discussed]
L: and then some people campaigned very actively in the
union about this / about fractionalising (.) [P: hmm]
that / so there's like the / the status of FE within
education which is very Cinderella (.) / and then there's
```

```
the status of teachers [P: hmm] that have different kind
of erm [P: hmm S: hmm] / privileges within (.) an
institution / and that's to do with (.) [P: hmm] / well=
S: =but the jobs are more and more scarce now=
L: =more and more so / so more and more there's [S: so]
casualised labour=
S: =yeah / I think at the moment it's pretty bad [J: hmm]
/ I mean I / yeah we all went / I went through that route
as well of being hourly paid for years and then / but you
kind of then / I don't know=
L: =there was usually a job to be had / [S: inaudible] it
was your route in=
S: =whereas now / and also there's the hourly salaries
now are just / you know / some people are working for
like twelve pounds an hour / fifteen pounds an hour=
L: =that / that's true as well / it's REALLY low pay=
S: =I just / yeah=
L: =and when you consider that / that if you're hourly
paid / that's not counting your preparation (.) [P: hmm]
/ and your travel and your marking and all of that / so
it's actually below the minimum wage I'd say
```

Susan's initial description of the three of them as 'maybe the wrong people' is significant as it indicates her perceived distance of *the group* from other teachers in the sector (as does her choice of the first person plural pronoun: 'we're all ... pretty established'). What makes them wrong appears to be their job security, their salaries and the professionalisation of the sector which they benefited from and which occurred under the New Labour governments (1997–2010). This entailed a move in the FE sector towards greater certification of teachers and qualification at a higher level, which was designed to put them on a par with state-school colleagues. The series of latched utterances between Susan and Liz about casualisation and the way things are 'now' indicate a rapidly constructed alignment on their assessment of the current situation for their colleagues – which is at odds with their own. Liz's comment about the Cinderella status of FE (where government cuts in education funding are often made first) and different kinds of privilege within institutions can be interpreted as referring to teachers (like themselves) who are not hourly paid – and therefore relatively privileged. At this stage Peter intervenes with a comment which can be seen as an attempted summing up of the exchange and an answer to John's original question:

```
P: but if / I mean / teaching is a grey area for class /
and people sometimes say that it is / some teachers will
self-identify as working class and some as middle class
based on their occupation [S: hmm] / erm then presumably
ESOL teaching has got to be (.) on the working class end
of the spectrum
```

Peter recognises that teaching is a liminal area in terms of class location ('teaching is a grey area for class'), and that different teachers will self-identify differently 'based on their occupation' (a possible reference to the status of different sectors and the degree of security teachers might have: for example, hourly paid ESOL teachers in the FE sector versus salaried secondary teachers in the state-school sector). However, he proposes – in light of the picture just painted by his colleagues – that ESOL teachers are *located* (as his use of the spectrum metaphor suggests) closer to the working class. Both Susan and Liz agree with this overall assessment and Liz follows it up with a final small story about the FE sector being a traditional destination for teachers from working-class backgrounds on account of its largely vocational nature.

CONCLUSION

It is clear, then, that for these three teachers their understanding of social class and their political identification are salient aspects of their professional identities. Despite their agreement on the liminality of teachers' class location, it is clear that for these teachers social class is understood in terms of 'systemic unfairness' and the struggle against it, in terms of job security versus precarity, and overwhelmingly (echoing Poulantzas and Harris) in terms of the particular class interests they serve through the work they do. In their discussion of the three pieces of pedagogical materials on the topic of work, their class position emerges through the accumulation of the small stories they tell in which the EFL sector is repeatedly used as a negatively evaluated stance object. Paradoxically (in light of the more recent casualisation), the ESOL sector – which they all entered long before the 2008 financial crisis – allowed Peter and Liz to escape the proletarianisation they endured as EFL teachers. ESOL provided all three of them with the chance to engage in a form of teaching that resonated with their political views and gave them the opportunity to do work they believed to be socially useful. Notwithstanding that, the class location of ESOL teachers – however grey an area teaching might be – is ultimately judged to be closer to that of the working class than to that of the middle class.

In Chapter 2 we argued that we were sticking with the concept of identity despite the charges levelled against it by scholars such as Brubaker and Cooper (2000), on the basis that it has the potential to provide teachers with a resource for becoming more agentive in strategising for change. Following Maclure (1993: 311), we also suggested that identity could usefully be understood as an 'organising principle in teachers' jobs and lives', and as a form of argument allowing them to claim certain identities and disavow others. On the basis of the data presented in this chapter, we can say that for these teachers, all of whom are associated with Action for ESOL, identity can be seen as constituting a powerful argument for a view of English language teaching to migrants as a political intervention; as a means of addressing systemic unfairness and providing migrant students with the linguistic strategies for combating this; and for ESOL teaching itself being seen a way of claiming an identity of social usefulness and social transformation wholly at odds with the narrowly defined remit of teachers more generally at the current moment.

8

QUEERING THE RESEARCH INTERVIEW: HUMOUR, PLAY FRAMES AND FRAME BREAKING

INTRODUCTION

This final data chapter has much in common with the approach we adopted in earlier chapters. Here again we focus on artefacts which are frequently problematic for teachers in many settings – in this case, English language teaching materials – and on a topic which has been the object of much recent scholarly attention – lesbian, gay, bisexual and transgender (LGBT) representation and erasure (Bollas 2016; Dunton 2016; Gray 2013a; Merse 2015). This focus on materials is in addition to the bur-geoning literature on LGBT issues generally in second language teaching (Curran 2006; King 2008; Liddicoat 2009; Macdonald 2014; Nelson 1999, 2004, 2006, 2009, 2010; Yoshihara 2013), as well as the literature dealing with LGBT issues in main-stream education (Moita Lopes 2006; Pinar 1998a, 1998b; Rodriguez et al. 2016). In common with our approach in Chapter 5, we take the research interview – in this case, a single interview involving a gay researcher (John, one of the authors of this book) and a gay teacher (Mark, a pseudonym) – as an instance of interactional data. As has been pointed out elsewhere (Wortham et al. 2011), in addition to *denotational text* produced by interviewees (that is, 'coherent propositional description of nar-rated events' (41) in response to questions), the interviewer and the interviewee also produce *interactional text* – 'a recognizable event in which they adopt interactional positions and engage in social action with respect to each other and the larger social world' (42). Similar to our approach in Chapter 7, we show how the participants' positioning of themselves and one another, and the small stories they tell provide multiple opportunities for their respective identities as gay men to emerge as salient aspects of the interview. In doing this, we draw principally on Erving Goffman's (1974) concept of *framing* and pay particular attention to the participants' frame breaking (Briggs 1986; Fernqvist 2010) and their use of laughter (Jefferson et al. 1978; Coates 2007) as part of their interactional identity work.

By way of introduction, the chapter begins with a necessarily detailed account of the cultural and political background to the literature referred to above, before moving on to a consideration of the main issues related to LGBT representation and erasure in ELT materials. Then after an account of the methodological approach we move on to the interactional data, before concluding with a short consideration of the matters arising.

THE EVOLVING CULTURAL AND POLITICAL BACKGROUND

Writing in the early days of the British gay liberation movement, the sociologist and left-wing gay activist Jeffrey Weeks (1975: 3) stated:

> The last few years or so have shown that many of the original aims of gay libera-tion can be achieved this side of socialism, through the conscious intervention of gay people themselves, pushing at the slackening bar of, (sic) nineteenth century bourgeois morality.

This was indeed prescient for 1975 – a time in which consensual sex between men was legal only if those involved were twenty-one or older and their activities took place in private (which was very narrowly defined). But not even Weeks could have anticipated the changes in the cultural and political landscape that were to follow. If we look at the case of the UK (where Mark and John both work), the recent wave of legal reform has been noteworthy. The twenty-first century began with the repeal of the Sexual Offences Act, which equalised the age of consent (previously set higher for gay men than for heterosexuals). This was followed in 2003 by the repeal of the noto-rious Thatcher era Section 28 of the Local Government Act, which forbade the teach-ing of 'the acceptability of homosexuality as a pretended family relationship' (Local Government Act 1988: 27). The ensuing Gender Recognition Act of 2004 allowed transgender people to acquire legally a new birth certificate recording their sex in accordance with their gender, as well as allowing them to marry. The same year also saw the introduction of the Civil Partnership Act, which gave homosexual couples virtually the same rights as heterosexual couples – but fell short of labelling their unions marriage. In 2010 the Equality Act identified nine protected characteristics – age; disability; gender reassignment; marriage and civil partnership; pregnancy and maternity; race; religion or belief; sex; and sexual orientation – as the basis for a wide-ranging anti-discrimination law which was focused on the workplace and the provision of public services, including education. Most recently, following a cam-paign for full equality, the Marriage (Same Sex Couples) Act was introduced in 2013.

Paradoxically however, this kind of hard-won social change – which Weeks (2007) rightly argues has been transformative for many in the Global North and to an extent for sexual minorities in the Global South – has given rise to unfore-seen consequences which queer scholars have begun to highlight. Terms such as homonormativity (Duggan 2002), homocapitalism (Rao 2015), homonationalism and pink-washing (Franke 2012; Puar 2007; Schulman 2012; Milani and Levon 2016) seek to draw attention to the ways in which increased LGBT visibility in some coun-tries is articulated in the media (and elsewhere) with discourses of contemporary neoliberal citizenship (Richardson 2004, 2005). At the same time, they highlight the ways in which powerful global organisations such as the International Monetary Fund (IMF), the World Bank and a range of nation states (or elements within them) seek to advance their political and economic goals through the strategic deployment of LGBT-friendly discourse in ways which might seem superficially progressive, but which are ultimately judged to be questionable. In short, the winning of LGBT rights 'this side of socialism' means that the role of neoliberal government and the needs of capital – neither of which are uniform across global settings and markets – cannot be ignored in any assessment of what Weeks (2007) refers to as 'the world we have won'.

Duggan (2002) can be credited with coining the term homonormativity – itself a deliberate echo of heteronormativity. The latter has been described as 'those structures, institutions, relations and actions that promote and produce heterosexuality as natural, self-evident, desirable, privileged, and necessary' (Cameron and Kulick 2003: 55). Duggan (179) describes the former as the 'new neoliberal sexual politics', which is understood as:

> a politics that does not contest dominant heteronormative assumptions and institutions but upholds and sustains them while promising the possibility of a demobilized gay constituency and a privatized, depoliticized gay culture anchored in domesticity and consumption.

Although Duggan is careful not to claim that homonormativity is an established order (in the Bourdieusian sense of a doxa), endowed with the same structuring power as heteronormativity, what she identified resonated with queer scholars across a range of disciplines. What they saw was the emergence of a sexual politics based on the quest for equality *within existing social structures* and the winning of rights – which crucially were conceded largely by governments espousing the values of so-called 'progressive neoliberalism' (Fraser 2017) – as all too often entailing the co-opting of LGBT people into the neoliberal project more generally. And indeed, from the 1990s onwards, right-wing gay commentators in the US (Bawer 1993, 2012; Rauch 2004; Sullivan 1995) were assiduous in making the case for moving beyond the oppositional and counter-cultural politics of post-1968 gay liberation in favour of one that embraced 'the fundamental virtues of the American system … the institutions of the free market … and limited government' (IGF CultureWatch website).

From this perspective, 'the world we have won' is more complex than might at first be understood and clearly presents educators who wish to support their LGBT students, while at the same time questioning prevailing normativities (whether hetero or homo), with a set of challenges. This is particularly pressing in a country such as the UK, where the government inspectorate of educational institutions – the Office for Standards in Education, Children's Services and Skills (Ofsted) – revised its inspection framework for colleges of further education (where most adult ESOL provision takes places) in light of the 2010 Equality Act. The revised framework states that LGBT learners comprise a group whose 'needs, dispositions, aptitudes or circumstances' may mean that they 'require particularly perceptive and expert teaching and, in some cases, additional support' (Ofsted 2012: 42). A seminar series funded by the Economic and Social Research Council (ESRC) – *Queering ESOL: Towards a Cultural Politics of LGBT Issues in the ESOL Classroom* (https://queeringesol. wordpress.com) – led by one of the authors this book (John), along with colleagues Melanie Cooke and Mike Baynham, explored these issues over two years from 2013 to 2015. Publications by seminar series participants (Cooke and Gray forthcoming; Merse 2015; Nelson 2015, 2016) suggest that ELT materials and the ways in which they are used have a role to play in supporting LGBT students and teachers (as well as their heterosexual allies), in addition to providing content which allows for the troubling of normative regimes of gender and sexuality. In the following section we turn our attention to the treatment of heteronormativity and erasure in ELT materials by queer scholars.

QUEER THEORY AND LGBT REPRESENTATION AND ERASURE IN ELT MATERIALS

The word queer has been mentioned several times in this chapter in implicit relation to the phenomenon of queer theory, which requires a brief gloss before we continue. Queer theory can best be understood as an assemblage of theoretical positions, all broadly poststructuralist in orientation, which coalesce around the critique of essentialised views of gender, heterosexuality as an institution and the mechanisms by which it is privileged, naturalised and reproduced (Gray 2013a), as well as the more recent critiques of homonormativity referred to above. Its origins, which lie in the US, were spurred on in large part by the ways in which the spiralling AIDS crisis in the 1990s exposed gender, class and race divisions within the so-called LGBT community – a situation in which 'those living in poverty, in low paid jobs, with no medical insurance or without appropriate residency documentation found themselves less able to access health care than white, middle-class gay men' (Gray 2016: 231). This also led to a wider reclaiming of the term, previously a pejorative eschewed by LGBT speakers. As Pinar (1998b: 3) explained at the time, '[q]ueer has become the chosen term for many who have come to be dissatisfied with what they perceive to be the assimilationist politics associated with the terms *gay* and *lesbian*' – no doubt also on account of their perceived essentialism (however strategically this might have been invoked). But terms such as lesbian and gay did not disappear, and today queer is used alongside these labels, often as a way of signalling a non-assimilationist stance or by way of laying claim to an avowedly unstable identity category – a paradoxical reminder of what Judith Butler (1993: 174) refers to as 'the necessary error of identity'.

The concept of a necessary error is also relevant when it comes to issues of representation and erasure in ELT materials. Representation here refers to the way in which language and images are used to construct the world of the target language for the student and, as has been argued elsewhere (Gray and Block 2014), this process of construction is overwhelmingly politically, ideologically and commercially motivated. The representational practices of publishing companies also presuppose practices of erasure (that is, the systematic editing out of certain categories of person and topics deemed unworthy of representation) – practices which have been the subject of a considerable amount of scrutiny over many years in our own field and in education more generally (for example, Anyon 1985; Azimova and Johnson 2012; Block and Gray 2017; Gray 2013b; Sleeter and Grant 2011). As marginalised groups made the case for greater representational inclusivity, some publishers have adopted a strategy of 'mentioning' (Apple and Christian-Smith 1991), essentially a tokenistic exercise in which the struggle to be represented is entirely written out. A similar phenomenon is the greater non-sexist representation of women in contemporary ELT materials, a policy which – however much of an improvement on earlier stereotypical representations it is judged to be – entails no concomitant discussion of feminism and women's struggle to be represented in terms decided by themselves (or at least in terms decided by some women). Writing about how to tackle reform of the (heteronormative) curriculum in ways which might be transformative for students and teachers alike, Britzman (1998: 227) argues in favour of a curriculum that facilitates a proliferation of identifications (see Chapter 2, this volume) in which 'the imagining of a sociality unhinged from the dominant conceptual order' is the goal. In outlining her argument for such a queering of the curriculum, she makes a scathing attack on the case for enhanced LGBT representation as envisioned by some liberal educationalists:

> The normal view on techniques of attitudinal change via provisions of information is that one should attempt to recover authentic images of gays and lesbians and stick them into the curriculum with the hope that representations – in the form of tidy role models – can serve as a double remedy: on the one hand for hostility towards social difference for those who cannot imagine difference, and on the other, for the lack of self esteem in those who are imagined as having no self. (Britzman 1998: 219)

Britzman's choice of the verb *to stick in*, in this case with its connotation of tokenistic insertion, is a clear indication of her position on the 'mentioning' approach adopted by some publishers. She sees such an approach as not simply superficial, but also potentially dangerous:

> Pedagogies of inclusion [. . .] do not facilitate the proliferation of identifications necessary to rethinking and refashioning identity [. . .]. In an odd turn of events, curricula that proport (sic) to be inclusive may actually work to produce new forms of exclusivity if the only subject positions offered are the tolerant normal and the tolerated subaltern. (221)

But even in a curriculum (or textbook) which allows for a proliferation of identifications one has to have something to identify with and it is here we would suggest that LGBT representation becomes unavoidable. Even so, representations will invariably be partial as reality always exceeds that which is selected for inclusion. It will still be necessary, we would argue, to go beyond the words or the images on the page if students are to come to grips with the social processes which produce particular representations and not others. It is not simply a matter of content, but what is done with that content in classrooms (something Britzman would accept). Indeed, it could be argued that LGBT representation is even more pressing today, given that representations of an increasingly normative homosexuality proliferate in the media and in public life generally in ways that Britzman could not have anticipated in the 1990s. From this perspective there is also more to interrogate and deconstruct than in the last decade of the twentieth century. That said, so much of this discussion is hypothetical as LGBT representations in ELT materials (however necessary and erroneous they might be) are in fact very rare. One relatively recent study of ten contemporary textbooks produced in the UK for global consumption concluded that there were no references to same-sex sexual orientation in any of them, and that

> [i]n the treatment of the family, in content on ideal partners, Internet dating and relationships, socialising, travelling and meeting new people, there is a blanket avoidance of any representation of clearly identified LGBT characters. [. . .] There are no reading or listening activities that suggest the existence of sexual diversity and in no activities that students are asked to do is their being LGBT or knowing anyone who is LGBT in any way implied. Rather what we see is the construction of a completely 'monosexual community of interlocutors' (Nelson 2006: 1) for the contextualisation and practice of the language being taught. (Gray 2013a: 49)

Why this type of erasure should be the case, given the co-opting of LGBT rights discourse by capitalist enterprises referred to above, is linked to the specifics of ELT publishing aimed at the global market, in which the UK is a major player. Conservative countries – many of which are numbered among the seventy-two states currently criminalising homosexuality (Carroll and Mendos 2017) – are important markets for UK-produced ELT materials. Unlike the tactics of the World Bank and the IMF (whose LGBT-friendly discourse is often aimed at critics in the Global North who disapprove of the structural readjustment programmes imposed on countries in the Global South), British ELT sees itself as having much to lose from any apparent endorsement of LGBT rights and, it could be argued, is clearly prepared to abnegate any educational responsibility it might have to the LGBT students and teachers who use its materials. In the light of such a situation, as Nelson (2016: 362) has argued, 'language learning materials urgently need updating.' Having thus sketched out the cultural and political background and the key issues regarding LGBT representation and erasure in the materials literature, we now turn to the research on which this chapter is based and in which many of these issues are explored in interaction.

METHODOLOGY AND INFORMANT

The interview with Mark was part of a set of interviews conducted with six English language teachers (three women and three men), all of whom self-identified as lesbian or gay and all of whom had worked in a variety of local and global settings (Gray 2013a). The teachers were all experienced, having between a minimum of thirteen years' and a maximum of thirty years' teaching experience. The aim of the interviews was to explore lesbian and gay teacher thinking on LGBT invisibility and heteronormativity in ELT materials and to elicit their views on what they considered to be the key issues with regard to materials design for the future. Two of the interviewees were already known to John, and through them a further four were recruited. All interviewees were informed by email of the topic of the interview and it was made clear that they were being consulted because of their experience and because they self-identified as lesbian or gay. It was also made clear that John too self-identified as gay. The interviews, which were audio-recorded, revolved around the following questions (Gray 2013a: 62):

1. Do you agree with the assessment of some commentators that, although ELT materials aimed at the global market are less sexist than previously, they continue to marginalise those who identify as LGBT – in terms of who gets to be included?
2. Do you think it is important that there is LGBT representation in ELT material?
3. What do you think of these pieces of material [extracts from *Framework/Level 2* (Goldstein 2003) and *Choice Readings* (Clarke et al. 1996)]?
4. Do you see any problems with regard to incorporating LGBT representation in ELT materials?
5. What do you think is the effect of LGBT invisibility in ELT materials on LGBT teachers/teacher educators – and on those who are not LGBT?
6. What do you think is the effect of LGBT invisibility in ELT materials on LGBT students – and on those who are not LGBT?
7. Can you think of a moment/incident/experience from your own teaching when an LGBT issue became important – and if so, can you tell me what it was, and how you dealt with it?
8. What is the way forward – given the commercial nature of ELT publishing and the diversity of contexts in which English is taught?

As can be seen from Question 3, interviewees were also shown two of the few pieces of ELT material which incorporate LGBT representation and were asked to respond to them. The *Framework/Level 2* (Goldstein 2003) material, aimed at the southern European and South American markets, comprised short gap-fill activities accompanied by photographs in which four couples told how they met. One of the couples consisted of two clearly identifiable men – Ricardo and Simon. The *Choice Readings* (Clarke et al. 1996) activity, aimed at migrants in the US, consisted of an extended reading about a middle-class North American gay couple – Dmitri and Tom – and their adopted child, Elliott.

At the time of the interview Mark, who was previously unknown to John, was 40 and had taken a year out from teaching to study for a postgraduate degree – although he was still teaching an ESOL group one evening a week. He had been a teacher for thirteen years and worked in a variety of settings in the UK and abroad as a teacher and teacher trainer.

In this chapter the focus is on the interview with Mark as an example of interactional text. If the focus is switched in this way (from denotational text to interactional text), the role of the participants is reconceptualised and attention shifts from *what* is said to *how* and *when* it is said and *why* – and what this tells us about the kind of identity work that is going on within the interaction. As was the case with all the interviews, interactional positioning and stance taking vis-à-vis the materials were a feature. However, the interview with Mark was unique in that it was typified by a high degree of humour and laughter, as well as a breakdown of the usual question-and-answer format characterising research interviews. It is for that reason that we focus on it here, given that this breakdown can be seen as an example of what might be called a queering (that is, a troubling or disturbing) of the normative research interview. In exploring these features, as stated earlier, in terms of framing and eventual frame breaking, along with a view of laughter (and humorous talk more generally) as interactionally meaningful, we will suggest that these two phenomena are directly linked and integral to the identity work being done by the participants.

Goffman (1974: 8), who borrowed the concept of frame from the anthropologist Gregory Bateson (who was also seriously interested in the interactional function of laughter), argues that when individuals encounter a novel situation, they attempt to answer the question: 'What is it that is going on here?' In answering this question, individuals are said to draw on their knowledge of what Goffman calls *primary frameworks*, which are akin to schemata (21), and then frame the situation they are in accordingly. Framing an event is thus a matter of interpretation and a decision about how to act for the individual who encounters the novel situation. In addition, thinking about a researcher conducting a research interview, it is a way of attempting to establish how the primary framework of the interview is understood by the researcher and how she or he wishes it to be understood by the interviewee. Commenting on research interviews in terms of framing, the anthropologist Charles Briggs (1986: 46) writes:

> [T]he use of interview techniques presupposes a model of social interaction. The interviewer specifies the issues to be covered, while the respondent supplies the information. The focus of the participants is on conveying the needed information as efficiently, explicitly, completely, and accurately as possible.

That said, he adds, informants may depart from this model and break frame. They do this for a variety of reasons – examples might be that they may wish to change the line of questioning because they feel uncomfortable or they believe it to be irrelevant. One way in which this can take place is through key change, where key refers to the Hymesian notion of 'tone, manner, or spirit in which an act is done' (Hymes 1972: 62). We will suggest that key change can be used by participants in an interaction not only to signal a complete frame break, but also to signal how they want a frame to be understood or that they wish to modify the way in which a frame has been understood up until that point.

Goffman (1974: 45) states that a key change constitutes a temporary transformation in the activity, the discourse or the interaction in question and that '[c]ues will be available for establishing when the transformation is to begin and when it is to end, namely, brackets in time, within which and to which the transformation is to be restricted' (cf. Gumperz's [1982] contextualisation cues). Some ways in which transformations in tone, manner and spirit can be conveyed are through the use of smiling and laughing, which may be accompanied by speech (for example, 'smiling voice' and 'laughing voice' [Pickering et al. 2009]), as well as through conversational humour. Smiling in interaction serves a variety of social functions ranging from the expression of pleasure to deference and appeasement (Cameron 2000). Within the context of a research interview, smiling can be used to help put an informant at ease and to establish and maintain what might be called a frame of conviviality. It allows the interviewer to be seen to defer to the interviewee's insider knowledge (often the reason for the interview), while at the same time enabling the interviewee to signal ongoing deference to the interviewer's questioning. Smiling is also a frequent response or accompaniment to humour, which in turn can trigger laughter. Drawing on foundational work by Jefferson, Sacks and Schegloff (1978: 156), who argue that 'laughter may be distinguished from other non-speech sounds in that it has, for participants, the status of an official conversational activity', Coates (2007) shows that laughter in informal conversation among friends is used to establish 'play frames' as a means of establishing and reinforcing intimacy. Play frames are essentially laughter-inducing, seemingly non-serious forms of talk characterised by punning, extended and repeated use of metaphors, exaggeration, mimicry and so on. From this perspective she argues that laugher is not simply 'an accompaniment to talk: it *is* talk' (44). Not all theorists have taken this view of smiling and laugher in human interaction. Bourdieu (1977: 178) has argued for the need to 'extend economic calculation to all the goods, material and symbolic, without distinction, that present themselves as rare or worthy of being sought after in a particular formation – which may be 'fair words' or smiles, handshakes or shrugs, complements or attention'. From this perspective, smiling and laughter are calculated behaviours designed to bring about personal advantage. In line with Graeber (2001), we take the view that this assessment is unduly limited – while recognising that John wants interview data from Mark, and (as we shall see) Mark also wants something from John. However, in this chapter we will argue that laughter is also used by interactants such as John and Mark, who are not friends, to achieve affiliation – in the Jefferson et al. (1978) terminology – on the basis of their known shared sexual orientation and concern about LGBT issues in educational settings.

In focusing on this aspect of the interview we were influenced by experimental work by Zacher and Niemitz (2003: 93), who argue that smiling voices are easily recognised aurally:

> When speaking on the telephone a smiling face can be detected with some certainty by listening to the partner. [. . .] Everyday experience shows that it is, at least sometimes, possible to identify aurally the emotional state of a speaker, solely by listening to his or her voice, for example in a phone call.

In terms of the analysis of our data samples below, we did not subject the interview recording to acoustic analysis, as Zacher and Niemitz did in their study of hearing smiles. Rather, following Jaspers (2006), we simply listened to the recording several times and coded the transcription for clearly identifiable instances of smiling and laughing while talking.

THE INTERVIEW

The interview began with a number of introductory questions about Mark's background in teaching, his qualifications and the different countries he worked in. At the mention of having worked in China, the following exchange took place:

Extract 8.1 'it was in the middle of nowhere ... but it was an amazing place'

```
J: when were you in China↑ / just as a matter of interest
M: it was 99 to 2001
J: right ok / [M: with VSO*] that must have been really
interesting
M: YEAH /it was amazing [J: yeah] / yeah
J: and were you in some sort of (.) [M: yeah] godforsaken
place / or
M: well it was in the middle of nowhere [J: yeah] / erm
but it was an amazing place [J: yeah] / it was a small
town on the edge of the Gobi desert / so I had (.) / I
could leave my house and go for a walk in the desert [J:
hmm] / the Great Wall of China went through our town
(smiling voice)
J: right (laughing voice)
M: erm so it was in the middle of nowhere / but it was
amazing [J: yeah] / yeah
J: ok
M: didn't teach much about LGBT issues (smiling voice) /
it was / that was quite a big taboo there (smiling voice)
J: I can imagine (smiling voice)
M: erm (.) BUT (.) I mean another teacher / another VSO /
who was one of my best friends / students came out to her
(.) there / I think just knowing that [J: really] / you
know / it / as a westerner [J: yeah] that might be ok
```

[*VSO refers to Voluntary Service Overseas, a charity which sends professionals in various fields to developing world countries]

Here we see the interview getting off to an informal start with John showing interest in Mark's experience in China, which he pre-evaluates as 'interesting' – an assessment which Mark confirms ('it was amazing'), followed by a listing of what the remote destination had to offer. John's initial use of the pejorative 'godforsaken' is noteworthy, as this is a term he would undoubtedly not have used with a Chinese informant. His use of it with Mark shows his awareness that a VSO posting might entail being sent to a remote region; but there is also the implication that, although 'interesting', the destination might have other drawbacks (possibly for Western gay men). Mark's comment about LGBT issues being a 'big taboo' is taken by John as though this were to be expected ('I can imagine') – possibly as a result of Mark's previous two mentions of the town being 'in the middle of nowhere' and John's assumptions about supposedly godforsaken places. However, Mark's ensuing use of 'but', spoken with emphasis, clarifies that even in such a remote place there were LGBT students. His assessment that his friend's status as 'a westerner', taken by the students to imply probable acceptance of being LGBT, is a reminder of how teachers from the Global North (whether LGBT or not) can be seen by students from other parts of the world. The exchange is also characterised by a considerable amount of smiling and laughing voice on the part of both participants, which suggests they are jointly engaged in establishing a frame of conviviality and informality for the interview.

In the following extract we see John bringing this preamble to an end with a downwardly inflected 'right', followed by a pause, which can be interpreted as keying that the interview proper is about to begin. In turning to the first question on the interview schedule, he begins with a summary of a comment by writer and teacher educator Scott Thornbury (1999) on how ELT materials, despite an improvement in the non-sexist representation of women, continue to be blind to the existence of gay people. The way in which this is done suggests that John is at pains for the interview to continue in the way in which it has already been framed as informal by both participants– and in no way academic, despite his deliberate reference to the materials literature. The summary begins as follows:

```
J ok / right / erm right↓ (.) / let's move on then to
talk about erm materials sort of proper / erm there's a
guy called Scott Thornbury / erm who wrote something
about materials round about 10 or 12 years ago / and he
suggested in that little thing that he wrote / that in
terms of the representation of gender [M: hmm] in general
/ that ELT materials had improved hugely
```

In referring to Thornbury in this way ('there's a guy called Scott Thornbury' who 'wrote something') John is clearly proceeding on the basis that Mark might not have heard of him or been familiar with his work. By referring to the article in question, which appeared in the specialist MATSDA (Materials Development Association) journal *Folio*, as 'that little thing that he wrote', he could be seen to be downplaying its significance and thereby avoiding the implication that it was something with which all gay teachers would necessarily be familiar. Such a move can be interpreted as a form of pre-emptive face-work (Goffman 1967), designed to ensure that Mark remains comfortable and is not made to feel less knowledgeable in any way about the topic.

And indeed, the interview continued very much along the lines established in the preamble, with playful sections typified by smiling and laughing alternating with sections of serious talk. Mark was forthcoming in his answer to the first question and agreed that LGBT people were marginalised, saying that they should be represented in materials. In talking about how LGBT representation was approached in the college of further education where he worked on a part-time basis, he highlighted the importance of events such as LGBT history month. In the UK this takes the form of a range of activities in public libraries, bookshops, universities, colleges of further education and some schools which celebrate what was referred to earlier as 'the world we have won'. This led to Mark's first small story about a lesson plan he designed for teachers in his college who wanted to do something to celebrate LGBT history. In telling the story, Mark invokes a play frame in which he positions himself as open to a charge of manipulation of the students, which both interviewer and interviewee align in finding humorous.

Extract 8.2: Mark's first small story – LGBT history lesson plan

```
M: shall I describe it↑
J: yeah / yeah yeah yeah
M: and I did it with a straight colleague as well [J:
hmm] / so (.) erm we and then / it got sent to every
teacher / but / the lesson was erm / it sort of started
off have you ever been /have you ever been stereotyped
[J: hmm] / and then people said yeah they had and bla bla
bla and talked about that a bit / I think that was the
first thing / but anyway / then we put up all the lists
of the different weeks that we have (.) at college / so
we have black history week / erm (2) international
women's day / LGBT history and we put / put those up on a
list and then / so people could remember the dates of
these things /and then said why do we have those things /
and then put a list on the board / like (.) make people
aware / like refugee week / break down stereotypes /
blady bla bla [J: hmm] / and so we had a list of why /
why (laughing) it was important / but sort of like
getting people to buy into it (smiling voice) [J: hmm] /
and then like oh↑ and do you know what it is next week↑
[J: hmm smiling voice] / and then you can see the dates /
ah yes LGBT history / so do you think / kind of / so it
is important isn't it↑ / (.) erm so they've almost said
that they think it's important
J: (laughing)
M: before you tell them (laughing louder) what they're
supporting (laughing voice)
J: laughing loudly (accompanied by slapping sound)
M: so maybe (.) it wasn't sort of as devious as that but
I think it was that / I think one way of making people
understand [J: hmm] / it's just empathy and seeing things
from your own perspective / oh yeah I've been
marginalised [J: hmm] / and I've been left out / and I've
been / experienced prejudice and stuff
```

The small story is significant for a number of reasons. As Mark recounts the stages of the lesson, he triggers a play frame by laughing at the mention of the list of reasons already on the board *before* reminding the students that LGBT history month begins the following week. The IRF (initiate, response, feedback) sequence of teacher to class question ('oh and do you know what it is next week'), the class response ('ah yes LGBT history') and the teacher feedback ('so it is important isn't it') is ventriloquised dramatically by Mark. The addition of 'oh' to his open class question suggests (disingenuous) surprise – as though it had just occurred to him that LGBT history month was about to begin. The 'ah yes' as part of the students' reply is related to the carefully planned board work ('and then you can see the dates') and results in laughter from John. This is followed by louder laughter from Mark and yet louder laughter from John who also appears to slap the table, thereby emphasising his appreciation of Mark's lesson plan. The joke is that the students have been encouraged to 'support' the idea of breaking down stereotypes and raising awareness about various minorities before discovering that they have been positioned as supporters of LGBT rights. Cooke (private communication, April 2017) points out that this is in fact 'the sort of thing all teachers do to ensure collaboration and buy-in from students about particular things' and is integral to the teacher-led IRF sequence. As such, Mark's joke can also be seen as one about the manipulation implicit in all IRF routines. However, the play frame is brought to an end with Mark's 'so maybe' in his resumed non-smiling voice, which is followed by a pause, and an ensuing explanation of what might be called the true rationale underpinning the lesson plan. This is in fact very much along the lines discussed above of 'the proliferation of identifications necessary to rethinking and refashioning identity', suggested by Britzman (1998: 221). Such a perspective seeks to move beyond the limited dichotomy of the 'tolerant normal' versus the 'tolerated subaltern' which she lambasted. Rather, in Mark's approach, the students are initially asked to consider themselves as the victims of discrimination (and in an ESOL class consisting of migrants the chances of this are high) as a way of drawing on their empathy for those who may be different from themselves but with whom they share the common experience of discrimination – thereby (theoretically) paving the way for identification.

In terms of the interaction, Coates (2007: 33) comments on such switches between serious and playful ways of talking as follows: '[w]hen talk occurs in a formal context, interactants may switch to a play frame from time to time to defuse tension or to provide light relief.' We would also suggest that between strangers – who in this case are both gay and both educators – the triggering of and participation in play frames is a way of establishing and maintaining rapport. Humour of this kind, Bateson (1952: 14) argues, also gives those involved in it 'an indirect clue to what sort of view of life they share or might share' and is a way for Mark and John to do being gay teachers together.

One noticeable effect of the play frame is that both participants became more open with one another about themselves as gay men and as gay teachers. Mark went on to explain that he was the only gay teacher – of several gay teachers in the college – to do the LGBT history lesson. All the other teachers who did it self-identified as heterosexual. John asked if this was because the other gay teachers felt that doing such a lesson amounted to coming out to their students – which Mark saw as a possible reason. John then pursued further the issue of coming out to students:

Extract 8.3: 'I've done that'

```
J: erm (.) I mean I / I don't want to intrude in anything
personal / but [M: yeah] would / would you normally come
out in a class / or is that just something if it happens
it happens and if it doesn't / I mean
M: erm (2) no / I mean I've come out to students [J: hmm]
/ so like last
J: {inaudible} I've done that / I mean
M: yeah / last year
```

In terms of an interview in which the aim was to explore Mark's views and to produce denotational text, John's 'I've done that' is completely unnecessary. However, interactionally, it serves to allow him to claim common ground with Mark as someone who has also come out to students on an individual basis. In aligning himself thus, he is orienting to his own identity as a gay man and momentarily away from his identity as a researcher conducting an interview in which the views of the interviewee are assumed to be prioritised. A similar alignment takes place again a few minutes later when John moves on to Question 5 on the interview schedule. Mark explains that despite the absence of LGBT representation in published materials and the annual LGBT history event, he does not regularly produce such material himself.

Extract 8.4: 'I don't want to jeopardise that by me finding out that they're homophobic'

```
M: no and I /I'm annoyed with my- / there is a sense of
fear around it [J: hmm↑] / and I am really confident / I
mean well / everyone knows I'm out and I do put
(laughing) you know some people are gay get over it
posters up (both laughing) / and don't / I'm not scared /
but I am a bit worried that I'll be / one thing/ I think
the thing for me is / you know when you've built up a
really strong relationship with students [J: hmm] / and
you're / maybe this is how I am with my relationships
anyway / but I don't want to jeopardise that by me
finding out that they're homophobic / and then I can't
cope with it
J: yeah
M: so sometimes I avoid it / because I just think / I (.)
/ I don't know where I would go from there
J: yeah / yeah / no I understand that [M: {inaudible}] / and
I think / I think maybe that's common for a lot of us
M: yeah
```

It can be seen from this extract that both participants repeatedly signal affiliation with one another and that Mark, in particular, is prepared to speak quite openly about his fears vis-à-vis relationships generally. The laughter surrounding his putting up posters produced by the campaigning group Stonewall which state 'some people are gay get over it' is triggered by there being one on the wall in John's office, where the interview was taking place. This is a reminder of Mann's (2016) point that the location of the interview has consequences for what is said and also neatly illustrates Bateson's (1952: 15) view that laughter during talk allows participants to reassure one another of their fellow feeling, such that it 'becomes almost a part of the vocabulary' of the interaction. In responding to Mark's admission that fear of jeopardising what is good about his relationships with students is an element in his decision not to produce pedagogic material with LGBT representation, John expresses understanding. His choice of the pronoun 'us' ('I think maybe that's common for a lot of us') is an indication that he wishes to align with Mark and include himself among those who might on occasion prefer avoidance.

As the interview continued, punctuated by frequent key-changing laughter, Mark told a number of small stories related to incidents from his teaching in which an LGBT issue became important. Two of these concerned heterosexist comments by heterosexual male students, which Mark sought to challenge. In the lead-in to these small stories Mark refers to the overwhelmingly heteronormative nature of published materials as meaning that the heterosexism of some male students always needs to be confronted whenever it appears. In the second of these small stories he explains how he decided to speak to the student separately after two young women complained to him that the student in question had referred to them pejoratively as lesbians. Mark ventriloquises his own voice and that of the student being reprimanded. Again, he triggers a play frame in telling the story, which results in affiliative laughter with John.

Extract 8.5: Mark's second small story – reprimanding a student

```
M: I spoke to him on his own and said why did you say
that /and he said I was just making a joke /and I said do
you think they are lesbians / and he said no / and I said
do you think there is anyone who might be lesbian in the
class who didn't like that [J: hmm] / and he said NO NO
and / and I said well / you know I could be gay (2) / you
know/ and he said oh yeah you could be or something / and
I said and anyway I don't like it / do you see why people
might / I always try and do that sort of (smiling voice)
[J: hmm] / make them feel really guilty (smiling voice)
[J: laughing] / and then (both laughing) / and they'll
never do it again [J: yeah] yeah [J: yeah] yeah [J:
laughing] / like when they're really naughty (smiling
voice) that / you know / I used to like teaching before
you were in my class kind of thing [J: hmm] / yeah make
```

```
them feel really guilty
J: ok (smiling voice) / erm before we move to these other
questions / I'll just quickly ask you what / you've sort
of told me in a way what you think /
```

In this small story Mark begins with a dramatisation of the exchange between himself and the student which shows him trying to get the student to consider the impact of his 'joke' on another student who might actually be a lesbian – or on a teacher such as himself who might possibly be gay. In addition to this approach, there is a second one in which Mark invokes his role as a teacher who is responsible for what goes on in his class ('anyway I don't like it'). His 'do you see why some people might' is left unfinished, but the implication is an elipted 'be upset by your behaviour?'. He then triggers a play frame by smiling and suggesting that the rationale for his approach is to make the student feel 'really guilty', which leads to a final quip in which he dramatically articulates the illocutionary force of his reprimand ('I used to like teaching before you were in my class kind of thing'). Although John does not speak much he is an active participant in Mark's telling of the story. The play frame is triggered by Mark's smiling voice which John responds to with a phatic sound of assent, followed by laughter at the suggestion that Mark attempts to make such students feel 'really guilty', which is then followed by them both laughing at this together and echoing each other's 'yeahs'. As Coates (2007: 44) points out:

> Laughter allows participants in playful talk to signal their continued involvement in what is being said, and their continued presence in the collaborative floor. If we assume that a collaborative floor is at all times open to all speakers, then clearly speakers need strategies to signal that they are participating, even when they do not actually produce an utterance. Laughter fits this requirement perfectly.

Interestingly, on this occasion, the play frame invoked by Mark is brought to an end by John. The latter begins his utterance with an 'ok' delivered with smiling voice, thereby maintaining continuity with the play frame established by his interlocutor before slowly resuming his non-smiling voice to continue with his questions. In this way it could be suggested that the participants are orienting to the interview in an increasingly collaborative way – a feature which will become more pronounced as the interview draws to a conclusion. Related to this is another noticeable aspect of the interaction – namely, John's increasingly personal involvement in the topic under discussion – which is captured in the following exchange about erasure:

Extract 8.6: 'do you think it's got an impact on us'

```
J: And then {inaudible} the related question is / what's
the effect on gay and lesbian teachers / because you've
talked a bit about that [M: hmm] / I mean do you think
there is an impact on us as / as / as gays and lesbians /
w- / that very often when we're teaching English (.) /
```

```
you know / w- / we're not in there / in that / do you
think it's got an impact on us
M: (3) I mean I don't / yeah / I mean I just sort of
don't want to use material that doesn't (2) / that
doesn't re- / that I can't relate / or doesn't (3)
acknowledge (2) me [J: hmm]
```

John's question begins as one about the impact of LGBT erasure in materials on 'gay and lesbian teachers', but he almost immediately shifts his focus to 'we' and 'us' – thereby including both himself and Mark as gay men potentially affected by publishers' invisibilising practices. In fact, Mark does not answer this question, although he responds personally by saying *he* does not want to use material which denies *him* recognition. However, the issue of erasure having been raised triggers a lengthy small story from Mark which results in both participants breaking frame in different ways. The small story begins as an answer to the final question on the interview schedule. Mark begins his answer with an inclusive use of 'we', which echoes John's earlier use of first person plural subject and object pronouns.

Extract 8.7: Mark's final small story – (1) preamble

```
J: what do you think is the way forward for / for / for
this issue in / in language teaching
M: I think we have to be braver [J: hmm] / and that means
probably taking some more risks / and I think like on
lots of levels / like teachers (.) do (.) have to be
braver / and generally my experience is that it's always
been ok [J: hmm] / any time something's come up / and (.)
erm / I actually haven't kind of erm / felt attacked by a
student / or felt that my relationship with them has
changed as a result of (.) something / so I think I have
to be braver / and I think maybe coursebooks and
publishers have to be braver / (sharp intake of breath)
as a sort of / I don't know / it's a kind of aside again
/ but / I and I'm not sure if I would want it to / can I
just sort of tell you something that maybe [J: hmm] / we
/ you / we can sort of / we can talk about it afterwards
about how you would include it
J: yeah yeah / you tell me anything you want
M: (2) but I'm just kind of worried it / on the sort of
confidential (.) side
J: what you / you and me [ye-] / this conversation↑ /
[yeah] oh yeah
```

Mark's initial 'we' appears to include all LGBT teachers, as his explanation of his own past experience refers back to comments he made earlier about how hypothetical classroom manifestations of homophobia could negatively impact on his, and by implication any LGBT teacher's, relationship with students. But in fact the kind of imagined attack had not transpired. He then shifts to the first person singular ('I have to be braver') before listing other bodies which also need to be braver in terms of explicitly including LGBT content. Having answered the question, he now raises the issue of something he wants to tell John, but which has implications regarding confidentiality. John's reference to the interview as 'this conversation' is an indication of how the interaction is currently being framed by him. At this stage (not included in the extract), John reminded Mark that all informants were guaranteed anonymity and that no informant or institution would be mentioned by name in any written-up account.

In the following extract Mark embarks on the small story in which he is emotionally very invested. His story leads to a second statement by John, this time on ownership of the interview data, and is followed by a frame break in which Mark assumes the role of the interviewer and poses a direct question to John – in effect queering the genre completely.

Extract 8.8: Mark's final small story – (2) erasure in item writing

```
M: cause I work for ((named provider of ELT tests))
J: right / ok
M: as an item writer [J: yeah yeah] / and (2) their
guidelines say [J: hmm] that you can't mention sexuality
J: really
M: in texts
J: for ESOL
M: yeah / for any / for any / for like mainstream erm
((named provider)) tests [J: hmm] / and I remember
reading this and sort of reading the / the guidelines
J: for the material writing
M: for the yeah / so they / they call it item writing
J: item writing
M: yeah so it's like you / you get a text / you know /
you find a / like if you're writing for reading for
((named test)) for example [J: yeah yeah] / but I wrote
the ((named test)) initially (3) / and then I do remember
kind of thinking is that / can they say that / now what /
what they're saying / I think they would cover themselves
by saying you can't mention any reference to / like any
sort of sexual relation [J: hmm] maybe / but that isn't
clear to me whether that is / (3) so I've always wanted
to write a / a text about two / about a / a gay couple /
or have some reference to that / and just see what
happens
J: in their / in their item stuff
```

M: yeah

[some lines omitted]

M: so [J: hmm] the only time it was ever really (4) /
'cause I WAS thinking about / what to / how I would react
to that / and then I kind of thought well if it's saying
/ if it's more to do with sex [J: hmm] / then I can cope
with that / but I haven't questioned it [J: hmm] / but
one time it did come up was when we were (2) / dealing
with / we were writing / erm so what happens is they
commission writers / and say you've got seven people
working on ((named test)) writing / and then you all send
in your stuff by the commission date / and they pre-edit
it / send it back to you / and you make any amendments /
and then you all go to a meeting together / and you sit
round and read each other's / and stuff like that / and
it all gets standardised / and then it gets pre-tested
and stuff / at the: / at one of those meeting where the
writers came together (2) / this is actually another
colleague of mine who does work for them / had written a
text where a woman had a child / but she had a boyfriend
[J: hmm] / and then they were talking about the fact
that she wasn't married [J: hmm] / and the / the person
from ((named provider)) said / you know / let's just make
her married to be on the safe side / but the / the writer
was a single mother herself and said well NO / let's NOT
(.) do that / why would we / why would we have to do that
/ and she was like but it might offend people from
certain countries / you know / and if that had an impact
on them taking the test / then we would want to avoid
that / and then I remember saying so what about / you
know / if we had a gay character / and then there was / I
can't remember exactly what happened / but I remember
saying that thing but what about the / the impact on
people who aren't / who are single mothers / and then
every time they read it / its (2) erm / erm they're never
represented / I mean that could have an impact on their /
their learning or their testing or whatever / I felt VERY
VERY uneasy about it / but I've sort of let it (.) [J:
yeah] / go in a sort of hypocritical way somehow / but
that's the only thing I was going to say on / 'cause I /
you have to sign confidentiality stuff with ((named
provider)) / about you using that / if you ever did
J: well what I can do (.) is if I / you know I can / I'd
write that / I mean everybody / I've said this to
everybody / I'll write the chapter and send it to

```
everybody / and you can comment on it / and say take that
out↑
M: ok
J: yeah↑ / I mean there's no question of / of / of / you
know you OWN this / erm it's not a question of [M: yeah]
you've given it to me and now it's mine / so I would erm
/ everybody's anonymised [M: yeah] / all institutions are
anonymised / and testing bodies are anonymised / I'm not
going to mention ((named provider)) [M: yeah] / so that
won't be mentioned [M: yeah] / as there are lots of
people who provide tests / erm so I wouldn't mention that
[M: yeah] / but you can / you can / you can comment on it
/ yeah↑
M: what do you think about that↑ / is that↑
```

There are three main points to make about this exchange. In the first place there is the small story itself, which deals with the issue of erasure and is told within the context of Mark's statement that teachers, publishers and materials writers have to be braver in their approach to inclusivity. Mark begins with his suspicions about the ELT test provider's use of the term 'sexuality' as a topic which cannot be mentioned in an examination text. He clearly suspects that it is short-hand for non-normative sexuality (given that 'sexuality' in the sense of sexual orientation is a feature of most human beings). His use of the term 'cover themselves', deployed in the sense of protecting themselves from a charge of discrimination, is indicative of this. But he notes that his suspicions could be tested only by writing material which explicitly referred to a gay couple – something he has not done. There is also an implication here of self-accusation, given his exhortation to himself in the preamble to the story ('I have to be braver') and his categorisation of his decision to let his unease about the matter slip as 'sort of hypocritical'. The argument that reference to certain categories of human being – in this case an unmarried mother with a boyfriend – is deemed to be problematic in some settings where the tests are taken is seen by Mark to miss the point that such erasure is potentially disadvantageous to those test takers (such as unmarried mothers and LGBT students) who are 'never represented'.

John's response to Mark's concerns about confidentiality is a rehearsal of his previous points about anonymity – but with the added clarification that Mark is the owner of the data (although this proviso is standard ethical practice in interview-based research). It could be argued that the previous conviviality of the interview, the sharing of information by *both* parties and its recent framing by John as a conversation, is here reinforced by the manner in which he tells Mark that he has final say on what happens to his words ('you know you own this'). It is this which provides the immediate context for Mark to break frame. With regard to breaking frame, Goffman (1974: 349) states:

> When an individual participates in a definition of the situation, circumstances can cause him suddenly to let go of the grasp the frame has upon him, even though the activity itself may continue.

In this chapter we follow Fernqvist (2010) in understanding breaking frame in research interviews as an agentive act in which the interviewee assumes control of the interaction – often as a way of avoiding a difficult topic. However, in the case of Mark's breaking frame there is no attempt at avoidance – rather his intervention can best be understood as an attempt to elicit denotational text from John. In doing this, he reverses their roles and repositions John as the interviewee. The exchange immediately following this is also significant in terms of breaking frame.

Extract 8.9: 'Sorry'

```
J: well (.) I'll tell you in a minute what I think about
that / but it leads into
M: sorry
J: this here / (audibly rustling paper) erm
```

Initially, John's response could be seen as an attempt to resist the frame break. This is a research interview after all, and as Briggs (1986: 56) explains:

> Playing by the rules prompts the subordination of other components of the inter-action to the mutual goal of the conscious transmission of interesting, accurate, and abundant information. When the system is working properly, the participants accept the roles assigned to them by the structure of the interview. Interviewers provide clear and interesting questions that enable respondents to exhibit their knowledge.

Certainly, Mark's immediate production of 'sorry' is an indication that he feels he may have spoken literally out of turn. However, things may be a little fuzzier in this interview. John defers his answer (which admittedly would be unusual in most conversations) but then continues with no break in his delivery to tell an inappropriately (in terms of general understanding of a research interview) lengthy small story of his own. This too is a serious frame break and amounts to a further queering of the normative research interview. John's small story is an account of how the publishers of the Ricardo and Simon text, which Mark had commented on favourably earlier, had been changed to a heterosexual couple – Ricardo and Simone – by the publishers when a second edition was launched with a more global audience in mind. As John brings his small story to a conclusion, he says:

```
J: and I just wondered / why / why do you think / because
it's very related to what / the story that you've just
told me / why are they doing that / why are these
publishers or / the industry if you like / because the
```

```
testing industry is an industry as well / I mean why are
they / why do you think they did that ↑ (.) / I mean I'll
tell you why I think [M: yeah] they did that
```

We can interpret this question-as-answer as the researcher attempting to have his cake and eat it. He is on record twice as being willing to answer Mark's question, but is clearly holding out for an answer to his own before saying explicitly what he thinks. In effect he accepts that the interview has been queered (something he has contributed to throughout) – but is unwilling to let go of the possibility of eliciting some denotational text from his interlocutor. In the question-as-answer he is also implying that the answer to the question he has just posed to Mark is the same one as the answer to the question Mark put to him. Mark's answer is revealing:

```
M: I think it all comes down to FEAR [J: yeah] / and /
and MONEY / and sales / and (.) erm (2) / I mean again
it/ it is really weird because / I mean it is a bit more
/ you get your sort of at ((named provider)) / the sort
of like Telegraph* crowd / but you get a lot of really
lovely leftie [J: hmm] right-on nice people [J: hmm] /
erm (sharp intake of breath) why wouldn't I (.) question
it (.) more / a sort of fear↑ / I don't know [J: hmm ] /
or not having kind of thought it through on my own [J:
hmm] / or sort of thinking well it's a big business /
that's [J: hmm] / I mean I think it does come down to
money / and (.) / yeah (exhaling) / I mean it's such a
big industry {inaudible}
```

[*The Daily Telegraph* is a conservative British newspaper.]

Although answering John's question ('fear', 'money', 'sales'), Mark returns to his own small story and (by implication) his own failure to write a text for the test providers which included LGBT representation. His question ('why wouldn't I question it more') is essentially addressed to himself – he provides his own answers: fear of challenging the test providers, despite the implied presence of item writers with whom he could identify ('lovely leftie right-on nice people') and who presumably might support him; not having thought it through; and a recognition that the financial implications of LGBT representation might not be good for ELT business. The fear that Mark refers to appears to be twofold – there is his own personal fear of confronting a powerful testing industry he is employed by, and by implication the fear of the industry itself regarding potential loss of sales. As his answer trails off, John chips in and finally answers Mark's original question. He begins with a weary-sounding downwardly inflected 'I know' at the mention of 'a big industry' before becoming more animated in his response.

Extract 8.10: 'you asked me a question so I'm giving you my answer'

```
J: I know↓ / that's what / that's what bugged me about it
/ because you know what / it seems to me / you asked me a
question so I'm giving you my answer
[some lines omitted]
J: what annoyed me about this (hitting the Ricardo and
Simon material with a pen) / this (hitting again) / this
editing out of the gay people was / why don't they just
niche market a bit more↑ / if / if it works in Spain [M:
inhaling deeply] why don't you do two editions↑ / do like
/ you know / [M: {inaudible word}] and it / you know / it
seemed / and the same thing you could do for TESTING↑
M: DEFO
J: you could have your item writing / you could have your
((named test)) for / you know / Saudi Arabia or wherever
M: TOTALLY
J: and [M: really good] / and another one for / you know
/ other people
M: well it would cost a bit more (smiling voice)
J: EXACTLY
```

In this extract John clearly becomes more emotionally involved with the subject, stating he was both 'bugged' and 'annoyed' by the erasure of the LGBT characters from *Framework/Level 2* (Goldstein 2003). His comments are accompanied by physical gestures (hitting the material), rhetorical questions ('why don't you do two editions') and repeatedly raised voice. This is echoed by Mark's equally loud interjections and his evaluation ('really good') of John's suggestion – itself an echo of John's earlier positive evaluation of Mark's lesson plan and other contributions. His comment on the cost of different versions of textbooks and tests for different markets, which is accompanied by a resumption of smiling voice, is met by John's raised voice agreement. This is clearly no longer a traditional research interview. From this point on, both participants continue chatting and sharing anecdotes (yet more small stories) for several more minutes about the issues raised, with Mark returning again to the item-writing meeting in which the unmarried mother reference was removed from the test material and by which he continues to be 'annoyed'.

CONCLUSION

What, then, are we to make of all of this? We see the interview between John and Mark as raising three interrelated issues with regard to (1) qualitative interviews; (2) English language teacher identity; and (3) 'the world we have won' as it relates to the world of education.

With regard to the first of these, De Fina and Perrino (2011: 1) argue that in discussions in the social sciences about the status of interview data in which the interview is often seen as a problem to be overcome, 'the interview as a real communicative event has been understudied.' Their comment was made in the introduction to a special issue of *Language in Society* on the subject of narratives in interviews and the place of interviews in narrative studies generally. In that volume the authors attempted to redress the balance and make the case for a view of the research interview as a 'legitimate interactional encounter' (1), worthy of study in its own right. This endeavour has been uppermost in our minds in this and other chapters in this volume. Such a stance in no way implies a dismissal of denotational text. Rather, in line with Wortham et al. (2011: 49), we take the view that

> interviewers should follow Freud (1900) in attending both to denotational texts and the interactional texts of their interviews. Whatever the value of the propositional descriptions they offer, interviewees also position themselves interactionally and evaluate aspects of the social world through the same discourse that they use to refer to and predicate about the topic.

To this we would add, the same is also true of interviewers. John is repeatedly shown to position himself interactionally throughout the interview – in relation to comments made by Mark, in relation to the Ricardo and Simon text, in relation to the ELT publishing and testing industry – and (eventually) to produce denotational text in response to a question from his interviewee. To ignore the interactional aspect of the interview would be to ignore a significant amount of what is there. Such a focus on interaction is integral to the identity work being done in the interview by both participants, which leads us to our second point. Mark's and John's identity as gay men is repeatedly made relevant in the interview. This is not unexpected, given the topic of LGBT invisibility and heteronormativity in ELT materials, and the fact that they are both gay. Although their professional identities as educators and as interviewer and interviewee are evidenced throughout, their identities as gay men are shown to be difficult to disambiguate. Through the introduction of play frames triggered by smiling and laughing, Mark and John establish rapport and express solidarity with one another as educators who are simultaneously gay men and who know about the strategies frequently employed by LGBT teachers in negotiating their way through the overwhelmingly heteronormative settings in which they work, and the relentlessly heteronormative tools they are provided with for doing it, such as textbooks and tests. Their sustained affiliative identity work – partly, no doubt, carried out by John as a means of eliciting denotational text – leads ultimately to a transformation of the interview. The breaking frame, when it eventually happens, can be seen as direct result of the identity work preceding it, and in the eventual conflation of the interviewer and the interviewee roles it is their personal involvement as gay men on the topic of LGBT representation and erasure (but also of others such as unmarried mothers) in ELT which emerges as key to their concerns.

This leads us to our third and final point. This chapter was written in 2017, fifty years after the passing of the Sexual Offences Act in 1967 which decriminalised homosexual acts between consenting men over the age of twenty-one in the UK. The interview took place within the context of the long list of early twenty-first-century reforms referred to at the beginning of this chapter. In many ways it is extraordinary that the content of the interview is what it is and that two gay educators talk the way they do, surrounded as they are by so much progressive legislation. The hard truth is that so many educational settings, despite occasional tokenistic acts of inclusion (such as LGBT history celebration), remain, as Ferfolja (2014: 30) puts it, 'overwhelmingly heteronormative organisations where the heterosexual matrix discursively operates to reinforce dominant [cis-]gendered and [hetero]sexual power relations'. At the same time, in the light of the very limited LGBT representation there is in ELT materials – such as the extended reading on Dmitri, Tom and Elliott referred to earlier – there is a risk that essentially conservative white middle-class couples are simply added to the normative representational mix (a criticism made by a lesbian teacher interviewed in Gray [2013a]). In concluding, we take our cue from Mark that we all, regardless of our sexual orientation, need to be braver and begin, as Nelson (2009: 218) suggests – despite the enforced marginalisation required by the 'edu-businesses' (Ball 2012) in whose grasp we are deeply entangled – to design language lessons, write materials and carry out research that does not continue to portray 'strangely monosexual versions of the world'. This will not be easy, but in doing so, all of us – researchers, teacher educators, teachers and students – stand to benefit.

9

ENGLISH LANGUAGE TEACHER IDENTITY AND LANGUAGE AND DISCOURSE AS SOCIAL (INTER)ACTION: IMPLICATIONS AND APPLICATIONS

INTRODUCTION

The pace of research on language teacher identity (LTI) is showing no sign of abating, as the recent special issues of the *TESOL Quarterly* (Varghese et al. 2016) and *Modern Language Journal* (De Costa and Norton 2017), as well as the recent edited volumes by Cheung et al. (2015) and Barkhuizen (2017a), attest. The studies presented in the five empirical chapters in this volume hope to have contributed to this research effort by highlighting the unique insights that can be attained through a sustained and rigorous focus on how identities emerge, are performed, accepted, resisted or are in any way made relevant, in moment-by-moment social interaction. Of course, such an approach on its own cannot hope to answer all the questions about LTI which are stimulated by the wide range of theoretical perspectives taken on the construct (as seen in Chapter 2 of this volume), and the pressing need to incorporate notions of identity in the practical endeavours of educating and developing language teachers and improving outcomes for learners.

However, we argue in this final chapter of the book that *any* of the approaches to identity advocated by current researchers, and the identity-related topics that they recommend should be pursued need to take into account the dynamic and co-constructed nature of the interactional settings in which identity-relevant language and discourses are produced. In fact, not doing so may render language and discourse, which are almost always claimed as central to what identity is, as rather opaque windows on to what is taken to be some 'other' reality, whether buried in the speaker/writer's mind (conscious or unconscious) or inhabiting some wider, external, realm of social, historical, economic or cultural 'forces'. In this chapter, we review some of the key issues relating to LTI that have been the focus of recent work, and discuss them through the prism of our findings as presented in Chapters 4–8. We then go on to illustrate how a focus on social interaction can contribute to the specific topics for future research suggested by current researchers, and in so doing raise some methodological issues. The final part of the chapter, and of the book, turns to how research findings on LTI may have implications and applications for language teacher education and professional development.

SOCIAL INTERACTION AND CURRENT CONCEPTUALISATIONS
OF LTI

As identity is a multifaceted and complex construct, it is not realistic to try to pin it down with a pithy definition. Rather, it may be more advisable, as Barkhuizen (2017a) suggests, to see it as a 'composite conceptualisation', with a number of dimensions, each of which can be the focus of any research study, with no one study attempting to capture or operationalise them all. What researchers, and practitioners, will decide to focus on as they pursue identity-related topics will then depend on their own interests and purposes, as different aspects of identity will come into relief in their own contexts. Barkhuizen's 'composite conceptualisation' is also useful as it provides a helpful at-a-glance overview of what the construct 'language teacher identity' can entail, and how it might be approached. Indeed, Barkhuizen offers the conceptualisation as an instrument for 'relative, situated reflection, interpretation, development, and use by teachers and researchers' (2017a: 3). That is the invitation we take up in this chapter, by using the conceptualisation and its different facets as a prism through which to view the themes which emerged in the empirical chapters in the book, and thus to assess their contribution to the LTI research agenda. Barkhuizen's 'composite conceptualisation' is as follows:

1. Language teacher identities (LTIs) are cognitive, social, emotional, ideological, and historical – they are both inside the teacher and outside in the social, material and technological world. LTIs are being and doing, feeling and imagining, and storying.
2. They are struggle and harmony: they are contested and resisted, by self and others, and they are also accepted, acknowledged and valued, by self and others.
3. They are core and peripheral, personal and professional, they are dynamic, multiple, and hybrid, and they are foregrounded and backgrounded.
4. And LTIs change, short-term and over time – discursively in social interaction with teacher educators, learners, teachers, administrators, and the wider community, and in material interaction with spaces, places and objects in classrooms, institutions and online. (Barkhuizen 2017a: 4)

In his introductory chapter to the edited volume, Barkhuizen uses the conceptualisation as a way to organise the personal reflections on LTI presented by experienced scholars in the individual chapters. Here, we break up the conceptualisation in a rather different way (four chunks instead of seven) and use it as a framework for discussing the issues which emerged in the empirical chapters in this volume.

1. Language teacher identities (LTIs) are cognitive, social, emotional, ideological, and historical – they are both inside the teacher and outside in the social, material and technological world. LTIs are being and doing, feeling and imagining, and storying.

In the five empirical chapters, the analytical focus on social interaction clearly highlights the cognitive, social, emotional, ideological, historical and narrative dimensions of LTI. The cognitive dimension emerges in the way in which a great deal of what the teachers do in their talk is to make available inferences about what they, or others, know, think and believe in the way they build their accounts of experience or perform other social actions, such as getting someone to do something. Thus, in Chapter 4, in the lesson-planning sessions, being positioned as having more or less access to certain types of knowledge has clear consequences for what you can do, or for how others can constrain your actions. Or, in Chapter 5, ESOL teachers' descriptions of practices not only present them in a certain light, but also show how they have access to areas of practical knowledge, including ways to meet individual learners' needs best. Also in this chapter, the way the teachers build up a negative stance towards ILPs (they are 'all codswallop') allows for clear inferences as to 'beliefs' about their utility.

In terms of the 'social' dimension, the analyses show that LTIs are social in two senses. First, they are social in the more micro or localised sense that many of the discursive acts teachers carry out in the interactional settings are social actions with identity implications: for example, in the ways they orient to different membership categories in Chapter 6. LTIs are also 'social' in the broader sense that wider circulating discourses about what it means to be a language teacher are taken up by participants: for example, in Chapter 7 where different political connotations about what it means to be an EFL or an ESOL teacher emerge in the discussion.

The emotional dimension of LTIs can be well handled by a focus on social interaction and discursive construction. Just as 'cognitive' aspects such as knowledge and belief can be a participants' concern in the way they, for example, produce accounts or descriptions of reality, so emotions can be a feature of talk in the ways in which people build into their discourse descriptions of feelings such as joy, sadness, anger or frustration. One example is the 'accent story' in Chapter 6, in which the Spanish teacher builds up her story about having problems in ordering a soft drink to allow for clear inferences about her feelings of frustration and disappointment. The ESOL teachers in Chapter 7 expressed feelings of marginalisation and isolation as EFL teachers teaching 'posh' people, with one describing herself as 'a fish out of water' and 'not fitting in' as an EFL teacher, only to find 'relief' as an ESOL teacher. In Peter's story about teaching a baroness, he talks about his own feelings of being 'massively conflicted' and 'angry the whole time'. In Chapter 8, there are clear emotional overtones in the way the interviewee is 'annoyed' with himself for not producing specifically LGBT materials for use in the classroom. At the same time, he is 'worried' about disclosing information to the interviewer about the testing company he writes for, and 'very, very uneasy' about the company's policy of editing out certain categories of person from examination texts. Interestingly, in terms of the frame breaking which occurs in the interview, the interviewer also admits to being 'annoyed' and 'bugged' by commercial publishers' erasure of LGBT characters from textbooks. Seeing emotions as something participants 'do' in ongoing social interaction, as opposed to something they 'have' and which can be revealed by mining their discursive productions, can make an original contribution to the recent interest in emotion in LTI research (for example, Song 2016; Wolff and De Costa 2017).

LTIs as ideological and historical emerge in all the chapters: that is, the teachers construct identities and position themselves in relation to powerful circulating ideologies (about the nature of what makes a good TESOL teacher, or 'native speakerism', for example) and these are historically situated – in that they may refer to dominant discourses which are pervasive at a certain time, such as in the ways in which ILPs have been promoted as 'key texts' in ESOL. In Chapter 4, the trainee teachers are immersed in a practice which reproduces a powerful ideology in TESOL, that teachers must be trained to produce effective, efficient pre-packaged language lessons, but without access to the knowledge which might be capable of generating these, or other practices, or of providing the means to critique them. The ESOL teachers in Chapter 5, who struggled to accommodate the requirement to use ILPs in their practices, used their 'small stories' to position themselves in relation to these 'key texts', which carried with them a pervasive ideology around performance management culture in adult education. The non-native teachers in Chapter 6, in their categorisations of people and groups, show that the ideology of 'native speakerism' is a powerful influence, especially in the ways in which members of the category 'native speaker' are imbued with attributes relating to authenticity or genuineness, such as having a 'proper accent'. For the ESOL teachers in Chapter 7 there is a pervasive rejection of the ideological undercurrents of commercial EFL, in which teachers may be positioned as 'servants' or 'service providers' to the rich, and an embracing of the more socially useful practices of ESOL, which are more in line with these teachers' political outlook and class position. Thus for the teachers in Chapter 7, ideology comes into play through their repudiation of the marketisation of education which typifies the neoliberal era, but also through their adherence to the values and practices of Action for ESOL, its opposition to government-imposed austerity on the sector generally and its view of education as socially transformative.

In all of the chapters, there is evidence of the importance of 'storying', or narrative, in the ways in which teacher participants construct identities and position themselves and others in relation to identity categories. This is obviously seen more clearly in the chapters in which 'storying' is an explicit focus of analysis, as in the use of 'small stories' in Chapters 5, 7 and 8. While we recognise that 'storying' is a deep way in which all humans engage with experience as a 'mode of thought' (Bruner 1986) – indeed, it is how we make experience comprehensible to ourselves and others – our approach here has not been to analyse teachers' narratives for this deep experiential content, or to claim any privileged access to such content through the narrative texts they produce. To illustrate this point, we can draw on a distinction that Barkhuizen, Benson and Chik (2014) make between two types of focus in narrative inquiry. In one type, the researchers are more concerned with the *content* of narratives: that is, what the narratives tell us about the people who tell them, and the events and situations they relate. This kind of narrative inquiry has been very influential in work on teacher identity in general education, most notably in the work of Clandinin and Connelly (for example, Clandinin 2013; Clandinin and Connelly 2000), and, in second language education, in the work of Johnson and Golombek (for example, Johnson and Golombek 2002, 2011). It can also be seen in Barkhuizen's use of 'short stories' in his 2017 study of home language tutors' language identities. As he points out, 'short stories' can be distinguished from 'small stories' in that the former focus on the stories' content rather than on any performance or linguistic aspects (2017b: 65). The other type of narrative inquiry puts its analytic focus on *how* narratives are constructed and *what social actions* are accomplished in and through their telling. This is the approach to narrative which is taken in the chapters in this book, not only in the 'small stories' analyses, but also anywhere teachers produce accounts of situations and events, which could be seen to have a 'narrative' or 'storying' component. In sum, these two perspectives suggest that LTIs are 'storied' in two main ways: narratives are privileged sites of access to teachers' constructions of their lived experiences, and indeed are a main way in which they make their experiences 'liveable'; but they are also things teachers 'do' in accomplishing a whole range of social actions in moment-by-moment interaction. Thus, in addition, or as an alternative to, asking 'What does this story tell us about this teacher's lived experience?', we can ask 'What is this teacher doing, in terms of identity, by telling this story in this way, right now?'. A clear example of this is the ways in which the ESOL teachers in Chapter 5 use their accounts of their experiences with ILPs to position themselves, their students and administrators in various ways, and also to build a stance and (mis) alignment to ILPs, with all of this having consequences for the types of identities that are made relevant.

One dimension of this first segment of the 'composite conceptualisation' of LTIs which could receive more attention is that of imagining. Imagination is seen as closely linked to identity in frameworks such as Wenger's 'Communities of Practice' (1998) or in Holland, Lachicotte, Skinner and Cain's (1998) sociocultural perspective on 'figured worlds'. It is also, through the concept of 'image', a key concept in Clandinin and Connelly's work on teacher identity and personal practical knowledge. In earlier work on collaborative lesson planning (Morton and Gray 2010), we looked at how Wenger's concept of imagination came into play in the ways in which the trainer and trainees aligned themselves with classroom worlds beyond the immediate setting of the training session. More recently, Kubanyiova (2016, 2017) has drawn on Markus and Nurius's (1986) psychological work on 'possible selves' to provide a greater understanding of how language teachers' desired (and feared) imagined future selves can influence their sense-making practices as they engage (or do not engage) in professional development activities and attempt to support learning in their interactions with students. As Kubanyiova (2017: 101) puts it, 'it is not what teachers know and believe but who they see when they imagine themselves in the future that shapes their sense-making in ways that are consequential to both their own development and their students' learning.' However, novice language teachers' imagined identities may not long survive contact with the realities of early experiences of teaching. Xu (2012), in his study of four female novice English teachers in China, found that, for three of them, their imagined identities fell apart and were replaced, in two cases, by rule-based 'practiced identities' which reflected institutional constraints, rules and regulations. In only one case did a teacher have the resilience to maintain her imagined identity in the face of these pressures.

Barkhuizen (2016), in a study of a pre-service teacher's imagined identities over a period of almost nine years, links the notion of imagined identities to the concept of investment, originally developed in the context of language learning in the work of Norton and colleagues (for example, Darvin and Norton 2015; Norton 2000/2013). De Costa and Norton (2017) give further examples of how the notion of investment is being fruitfully applied in studies of LTI, such as in the work of Reeves (2009), Stranger-Johannessen and Norton (2017) or Waller, Wethers and De Costa (2016). Just as language learners may invest in language learning efforts in order to acquire more symbolic, social or economic capital, language teachers may invest in their own professional development, by acquiring new skills with which to enhance the learning opportunities of their students, and which may involve powerful and deep transformations in how they see themselves as teachers and how they see their students.

However, as Kubanyiova (2017) points out, the strength and direction of these investments will be driven by the kinds of desired, ought-to or feared future selves teachers imagine for themselves. For example, in her own work with a group of teachers in Slovakia, she noted how, for some of them, investing in participating in a professional development activity was driven more by a desire to increase linguistic capital in the form of English proficiency than by any desire to improve language learning outcomes for students. In Chapter 6 of this volume, this notion of investment in a future imagined self can be seen in the retrospective accounts of the Spanish teachers who, most likely at great personal expense and prolonged absence from home and loved ones, invested in their own future linguistic (and possibly cultural and economic) capital by living and working abroad: in the US, for example. These experiences are echoed in the literature reviewed in that chapter, which shows that ideal future selves (such as being a coordinator, conference speaker or trainer) can be powerful drivers of language teachers' investment in their own professional development (Sayer 2012).

In terms of methodological approach, Kubanyiova proposes a 'grounded theory ethnography' approach to investigating language teachers' possible future selves which involves exploring their sense-making and other actions across a range of settings, rather than simply relying on their verbalisations of their visions of themselves in the future. In the chapters in this book, we also did not attempt to elicit teachers' articulations of their vision statements, with the result that there is a relative lack of discursive constructions relating to possible future selves. The approach to social interaction taken in this book would preclude the 'mining' of teachers' statements about their future imagined selves. However, there is ample scope for detailed analysis of how, why, where and when teachers project themselves into the future in any relevant interactional setting, what categories are made relevant in doing so, and what types of actions are accomplished in terms of the activity (whether, for example, professional developmental or in interaction with students) in which they are involved.

2. They are struggle and harmony: they are contested and resisted, by self and others, and they are also accepted, acknowledged and valued, by self and others.

The studies presented in the five chapters show that when LTIs are made relevant in social interactions, they can be portrayed as sites of struggle, conflict and contestation, or can be fairly stable and harmonious. There are aspects of LTIs which are presented as having value: for example, by being more in line with other aspects of one's identity, such as political commitments. There are other LTIs which may be seen as imposed, and which come into conflict with other core values, such as having a genuine concern for the needs and welfare of students. These issues emerge clearly in the two chapters specifically on ESOL teachers, and this is not surprising, as ESOL in the UK is one of the more politically charged contexts for language teaching, as professionals have to deal with an extremely vulnerable section of society. For some ESOL teachers, such as Liz and Peter in Chapter 7, in a previous existence they had struggled with a 'conflicted' EFL identity, in which they saw themselves in the unwanted role of serving the wealthy. By turning to adult ESOL, they portrayed themselves as having achieved a more harmonious identity, one which was aligned with their political interests. For the teachers who talked about ILPs, they clearly oriented to an identity as professionals who genuinely cared for the vulnerable students they taught, but this identity came into conflict with the requirement for accountability which was imposed by the prevalent regime of managerialism under which they had to work. Thus, they assumed a 'false' identity, of 'going through the motions' as they worked with ILPs, and were at pains to ward off any interpretation that they had 'bought into' the system.

In the collaborative lesson-planning sessions, even a trainee teacher who was positioned as having less agency and epistemic access was able, at least temporarily, to shake off this ascribed identity and bring about a change of footing by the discursive act of refusing to accept the terms of the trainer's 'gift' of a pre-packaged activity. Thus, even discursive and situated identities which are well ingrained in practices which have sedimented over years, such as 'expert' trainers advising novice teachers about how to teach, can be contested and resisted by specific interactional moves. Of course, these 'novice' and 'expert' LTIs can be both accepted and contested, by the same participants, over the course of the same interactional event. In this way, close-up micro-analyses, such as the ones exemplified in this book, are well equipped to track how this identity work is done, showing how, over the course of even a short interactional sequence, participants can shift in and out of accepting or contesting an identity-related position.

3. They are core and peripheral, personal and professional, they are dynamic, multiple, and hybrid, and they are foregrounded and backgrounded.

As language teachers engage in social interactions in a variety of settings, they may choose, for different purposes related to the goals of the interaction, to highlight certain LTIs as being of core importance to their professional lives, and others as more peripheral. They may draw upon categorisations that relate to the more personal dimensions of their lives, what Zimmerman (1998) calls 'transportable' identities, or they may highlight more situated, professional identities. In any account of practice or personal narrative, different aspects of their personal and/or professional identities may be brought to the centre-stage or left in the background. In order to understand how identities can be oriented to as multiple, overlapping or hybrid, it is useful to work with the concept of intersectionality, as suggested by Varghese et al. (2016). Intersectionality, as proposed, for example, in the work of Crenshaw (1991), refers to how social identities such as race, gender or class are not mutually exclusive, but interact with each other, especially in the ways in which people may be discriminated against or even become victims of violence. As Crenshaw puts it, there is a 'need to account for multiple grounds of identity when considering how the social world is constructed' (1991: 1245).

Intersectionality provides a principled foundation for seeing the professional lives of language teachers as sites of struggle or possible harmony between multiple, overlapping or possibly hybrid identities, which can be personal and/or professional. An approach which fits with this perspective is Nagatomo's (2012) study of female Japanese university teachers of English, whose gendered identities intersected with their institutional identities and the various positions they took up in discursive events. As Varghese et al. (2016) suggest, intersectionality can highlight how both privileged and marginalised LTIs can coexist in teachers' lives, and how these identities interact with those of their students. And, as Barkhuizen points out, LTIs can be foregrounded or backgrounded. For example, for the ESOL teachers in Chapter 7, when they described their experiences as EFL teachers, they appeared to foreground a somewhat marginalised identity as in-person servers to rich students (members of the aristocracy or business people). However, it could also be said that they were able to benefit from a more privileged LTI, that of native-speaking teacher, who may be highly employable for that reason alone in some circumstances, and this LTI is backgrounded in these accounts. Although such foregrounding and backgrounding are part of all identity work, an intersectionality perspective suggests that there is 'always seepage across [. . .] dimensions' (Block and Corona 2016: 511) and that axes of oppression, differentiation and privilege interlock and co-create one another. This is particularly noticeable in Chapter 8, where both the interviewer's and the interviewee's sense of themselves as teachers cannot in any meaningful way be disambiguated from their sense of themselves as gay men. Following Block and Corona (2016), who argue that all identities are necessarily intersectional, we take the view that an insectionality lens on teacher identity is also politically useful, as it can enable teachers (to echo the point made in Chapter 1) 'to extend their horizons beyond the micro-context of the classroom to the macro-context of the social, political and economic conditions within which the classroom is located' (Block and Gray 2016: 488).

4. And LTIs change, short-term and over time – discursively in social interaction with teacher educators, learners, teachers, administrators, and the wider community, and in material interaction with spaces, places and objects in classrooms, institutions and online.

A focus on social interaction and LTIs can deal with the concept of change in three main ways:

1. Micro-analysis can track shifts in identity position or footing brought about by even the most fleeting of discursive acts, such as aspects of turn design, or at the level of adjacency pairs in the organisation of short sequences.
2. Changes (and their protagonists) can be a category or organising principle in the accounts of their experiences produced by teachers: for example, in the 'small stories' they tell.
3. A focus on social interaction can go beyond individual speech events (Wortham and Reyes 2015) to track how LTIs emerge and are consolidated or transformed over longer periods of time and from one speech event to another.

In the analyses in the five empirical chapters in this book, we have focused on the first two ways of dealing with change, mainly due to the nature of the datasets available to us. Thus, at the 'micro'-level, we saw in the lesson-planning session in Chapter 4 how a small change in discourse identity by a trainee (asking a certain type of question) leads to a change of footing, with the trainer taking on the role of explainer of underlying principles rather than provider of a pre-packaged set of instructions to carry out. In Chapter 5, where ESOL teachers talk about their responses to the requirement to use ILPs, in one interview a subtle shift in positioning, and thus identity-relevant inferences, is brought about in a response to an interviewer's question which seems to suggest that the teacher has 'bought into' the ILP system. Micro-analysis at this level is able to bring out these subtle shifts, providing much-needed empirical evidence of the frequently mentioned dynamic, subtle, fluid and shifting nature of identity.

In terms of tracking change over longer periods of time, the second approach, as in the analysis of 'small stories' has the strength of seeing 'change' as a participants' category. In their accounts and descriptions, participants can explicitly refer to differences between the past and the present or make inferences available in the way they construct events and actions. For example, in Chapter 6, teachers highlight their own agency in effecting a change from rather incompetent English speaker to speaker with enough competence to be an effective teacher. These accounts highlight the teachers' own initiative and agency in, for example, living and working abroad, as a way of developing a competence in English that the poor teaching they received was unable to provide for them. And, at a more general level, across all the accounts, we can infer a wider shift being oriented to by these teachers: from 'traditional' teachers who were barely competent in English and relied on outdated methods such as translation and memorisation, to younger, more communicatively competent teachers who have a wider repertoire of teaching approaches and strategies (see Clarke 2008, on the contrast between 'traditional' and 'new' teachers). Interestingly, though, such a shift is associated with contact with native speakers, whether with 'imported' teachers or assistants, or with ordinary people when living abroad, with the assumption being that non-native-speaking teachers can change (that is, improve). However, for that to happen, their own agency needs to intermingle with that of those who hold the keys to 'real English' – native speakers.

The third approach to tracking change in social interaction, that of looking for patterns across a series of speech events, is not one that features in the five chapters, as the datasets analysed consisted of single speech events. However, the analyses of these speech events show clear potential for extension with the use of a wider lens. The principles underlying the approaches to social interaction taken in all the chapters apply just as much to analyses across different speech events over longer periods of time. For example, even in the relatively short span of time of an intensive CELTA course (normally one month), it would be possible to track changes in identity orientations between, for example, very early, highly scaffolded lesson-planning experiences and those later in the course, when trainees are expected to plan more independently. It could be hypothesised that there would be some (slight) levelling of the 'expert–novice' asymmetry as trainees move from more to less peripheral engagement in the community of practice (Lave and Wenger 1991). In Chapter 6, it was pointed out that many language teachers do not make any reference to concepts such as English as EIL or ELF, mainly because, it could be argued, these have much wider currency in the academic community than in the world of ELT practice. However, critical and practical engagement with these concepts – for example, in sustained continuing professional development or Masters programmes with practica and/ or opportunities for action research – could be expected to lead to shifts in identity positioning – of both teachers themselves and how they see the future possibilities of their students. Collecting data on social interactions across a range of settings (training and development workshops, classroom interactions, reflective dialogues, online contributions) would afford possibilities to track how LTIs shift over time – for example, in the ways teachers may adopt, adapt, mix or resist identities related to native-speaker models and alternatives such as ELF.

LANGUAGE AND DISCOURSE AS SOCIAL (INTER)ACTION AND THE FUTURE RESEARCH AGENDA FOR LTI

In this section, we identify some possible future directions for researching LTIs and argue that a focus on language and discourse as social (inter)action can have a key role to play across a wide range of theoretical and methodological perspectives. We expand upon De Costa and Norton's (2017) discussion of the importance of an ecological perspective which encompasses macro-, meso- and micro-levels and their call for a transdisciplinary approach to LTI research. Within this overarching perspective, we discuss a range of more specific tendencies, foci and topics: the turn from epistemological to axiological concerns in LTI research; the importance of affect; multilingualism and globalisation; social categories (with a specific focus on social class and political economy); identity and (as) pedagogy. In discussing each topic, we suggest ways in which a focus on language and discourse as social (inter) action can contribute to the research effort, arguing that such a focus is compatible with an overall ecological and transdisciplinary approach to investigating LTIs. We end the section by commenting on two methodological trends which we see as gathering pace in the near future: the continued use of narrative as a way of tapping into language teachers' constructions of their experience, and for examining how teacher identity is talked into being. But it is not only 'talked' into being, as more and more researchers are exploring the possibilities of visual narrative techniques. This, in turn, can be seen as related to the other main methodological trend: the widening of the semiotic lens when we want to explore how teachers make meanings that relate to their identities, which requires a focus on multimodality and embodiment, particularly in computer-mediated communication. We argue that seeing identity construction through language and discourse as social (inter)action is eminently compatible with both these trends.

Current research on language teacher cognition and identity is increasingly adopting an overall contextual, or ecological, approach in which language teacher identity, along with related constructs such as belief and agency, is seen as part of interlocking and interrelated complex systems (Kalaja et al. 2015). Within the broader field of language teacher cognition, Kubanyiova and Feryok (2015) call for this type of research to connect with the wider 'social turn' in applied linguistics, by showing how '[t]he micro-perspective of language teachers' inner worlds and individual practices is embedded in the larger ecologies of workplaces, educational systems, national language policies, and global issues' (445). Li (2017) takes a discursive psychological perspective on teacher cognition, seeing it as socially constructed and contextual, but with the main focus on the social interaction that enables psychological phenomena such as belief and knowledge to be analysed as publicly and visibly displayed participants' matters.

In Chapter 3, we argued that an approach to LTIs that put social interaction at its centre needed to address the challenge of incorporating different levels of analysis, of connecting observations at the micro-level of interactional detail with the wider social, political and cultural issues that enable and constrain who and what language teachers can be. We argued that the concept of indexicality and the notions of scale which are used in current sociolinguistics were a means of connecting these layers of analysis. We hope to have shown in the empirical chapters in the book that a rigorous focus on the details of social interaction in no way precludes attention to how meso (institutional) or macro (ideological) issues are treated as significant realities by language teachers. Indeed, as Horner and Bellamy (2016) argue, approaches which emphasise the role of discourse in the construction of identity can allow researchers to dispense with 'macro–micro' formulations. As they put it, 'studies on language and identity that employ discourse analytic and ethnographic methods are an optimal means of linking fine-grained observations of spoken interaction with the functioning of broader social, political and economic structures' (331).

We hope to have demonstrated such an approach by showing, in the five empirical chapters in the book, how teachers, in ongoing social interaction, positioned themselves in identity-relevant ways to a wide range of phenomena that they encountered in both their more proximal (setting of the current interaction, institutional context) and their more distant (social, historical, ideological) environments. As will be developed further below in relation to individual topics, we argue that a focus on language and discourse as social (inter)action can help to circumvent some of the dichotomous conceptualisations relating to notions of social/individual, inner/outer and micro/macro that have been problematic in much social research. It can thus make a strong contribution to a future research agenda that takes an ecological perspective and is open to the complexity inherent in conceptualising identity in relation to phenomena at different scales (both of space and time – see Lemke 2000) and also to possibly overlapping constructs such as belief and agency (Kalaja et al. 2015), and, more recently, intentionality (Kubanyiova and Feryok 2015).

Current conceptualisations of LTI see it as a 'composite' construct (Barkhuizen 2017a) or 'multidimensional' and 'multifaceted' (Cheung 2017; Trent 2015), and, as such, not amenable to being captured and understood within the parameters of a single disciplinary area. Researchers increasingly call for a 'transdisciplinary' (De Costa and Norton 2017) or 'interdisciplinary' (De Costa and Norton 2016; Kubanyiova 2017) approach. While both these terms may be used with similar intentions, they are often defined ambiguously (Choi and Pak 2006), and it can be revelatory and consequential for the future LTI research agenda to distinguish between them. According to Choi and Pak (2006), 'interdisciplinary' refers to reciprocal interaction (thus 'inter') between disciplines, in order to 'generate new common methodologies, perspectives, knowledge, or even new disciplines' (359). On the other hand, 'transdisciplinary' transcends disciplinary boundaries (hence 'trans') to 'look at the dynamics of whole systems in a holistic way' (359). A transdisciplinary approach may be called for to deal with 'wicked problems': that is, those which are difficult to define and resist being solved through existing methods of inquiry (Bernstein 2015). Another distinguishing feature of a transdisciplinary approach is that it involves not only scientists and scholars from different disciplines, but also non-researchers and other stakeholders. It would seem, then, that recent calls for a more ecological view of LTIs which takes into account their complexity, and the need to involve language teachers themselves in identity research, would make it ripe for a transdisciplinary approach. It may be that LTIs are a 'wicked' problem, or 'wicked mess' (McGregor 2015), though such a view may unnecessarily highlight identity as a 'problem' or a negative issue. However, LTIs definitely do share the characteristics of wicked problems outlined by McGregor (2015, citing Carley and Christie 2000), in that they involve

(a) uncertainty; (b) inconsistency of needs, preferences, and values; (c) an unclear sense of all consequences and/or the cumulative impact of collective action; and, (d) fluid, heterogeneous, pluralistic participation in problem definition and solution.

In this sense, future research on LTIs will need to adopt the kind of grounded, ethnographic and ecological approaches proposed by researchers such as Kalaja et al. (2015), De Costa and Norton (2017) and Kubanyiova (2017). This is entirely compatible with recent thinking on transdisciplinarity, which advocates the use of ethnographic methods that encourage the involvement and participation of stakeholders (Bernstein 2015). Within this overall ethnographic orientation, a focus on language and discourse as social (inter)action which maintains a strong 'emic' perspective on the sense-making practices of participants as they engage in the full range of practices relevant to their LTIs can make a key contribution to this effort.

A further key feature of current transdisciplinary approaches to research is their concern with ethical issues. According to Bernstein (2015), transdisciplinarity requires researchers to take into account their own subjectivity and to reflect on the ethics of studies where there is a power differential between researchers and research participants. When this happens, Bernstein claims that the resulting research 'transcends standard interpretive social science and becomes transdisciplinary in that it brings in the subjects of research participating in the research on an equal footing with the investigators' (2015: section 2, para. 2). This concern with ethical issues, within transdisciplinary approaches, is very much in line with the recent turn in LTI research from more epistemological concerns, to axiological concerns related to ethics and values. Morgan and Clarke (2011: 825) describe the turn towards values, morals and ethics as 'perhaps the most significant development in language teacher identity research' in particular as it relates to teachers' decision making around curricula and language policies at the institutional level and their interpersonal relationships with students. Kubanyiova and Feryok (2015) advocate a research agenda that 'explicitly engages with its worthwhile purposes and puts moral values and ethical principles at the centre of our work' (445). Kubanyiova and Crookes (2016) propose that language teachers' identity role should be that of 'moral agent', thus highlighting the purposes and values of language teaching both at the wider political, structural and societal level, and at the level of teachers' own inner orientations, especially their investment in the relations between themselves and students (120). A recent example of such ethics-centred research on LTIs is Miller, Morgan and Medina (2017), which uses Foucault's concept of ethical self-formation to explore the identity formation over nine years of an elementary reading and language arts teacher. As De Costa and Norton point out in their introduction to the *Modern Language Journal* special issue on LTIs, 'in addition to addressing the cognitive dimensions of learning, language teachers also need to attend to the ethical aspects of learning in order to become successful professionals' (2017: 9).

In discussing this 'ethical turn', Clarke (2017: 265) suggests that it 'raises questions of agency and determinism in relation to identity – questions which, in turn, return us to language and discourse'. Once again, then, we see the centrality of language and discourse, whichever perspective on LTIs is taken. Of course, this also raises questions about the definitions of 'language' and 'discourse', and it is clear that the work of researchers such as Clarke (for example, Clarke 2008) and Miller, Morgan and Medina (2017) uses a rather different, Foucauldian, conception of 'discourse' to the one used in the more ethnomethodological approach taken in most chapters in this book. That being said, as Billig (2009) points out, in both a Foucauldian and a conversation-analytic view of discourse, discourses and rhetorical devices, rather than people, are depicted as agents of action. The difference is that, as Billig reminds us, a Foucauldian analysis describes what whole patterns of discourse do, while conversation analysis and discursive psychology explicate what particular interactional moves do or accomplish (2009: para. 36). Billig argues that, ultimately, issues of discourse, agency and subjectivity will not be solved by further theorising, but are in essence a rhetorical problem for researchers: that is, there is a need to write in such a way that people, rather than abstract entities, processes or 'devices', are seen as agents (however constrained) of their own action. As Billig puts it, discourse analysts 'should seek to describe what speakers are doing, when they interact' (2009: para. 53). In this sense, how people orient to values, morals and ethics and associated questions about identity and agency can be seen through the lens of language and discourse as social (inter)action. And this is not just in the ways in which people talk about or make inferences about these things themselves, but in the ways in which we, as discourse analysts, depict them as being more or less agentive.

The 'turn' towards ethics, morals and values, and a focus on the Foucauldian concept of 'care-of-the-self' are also related to a growing awareness of the role of affect and emotion in the constitution of language teacher identity. De Costa and Norton (2017), drawing on and extending the Douglas Fir Group's (2016) transdisciplinary framework for language teaching, identify emotion and affect as a fundamental theme of significance for all levels of language teaching. In discussing the importance of emotion in language teacher identity formation, Varghese et al. (2016) observe that the research provokes us 'to ask how teachers and teacher educators come to view teachers' emotional lives as a source of agency in identity construction' (560). Current work on language teacher emotion draws on poststructuralist and feminist perspectives on emotion and identity formation, in which teacher emotions are seen as 'part of the very fabric constituting the self, but they are also socially organized and managed ... [with] power and resistance ... at the centre of understanding the place of emotion in self-formation' (Zembylas 2005: 24).

In the field of language teaching, Benesch (2012, 2017) uses Hochschild's (1979) seminal notions of *emotion work* or *emotion management* to highlight the emotional labour which English language teachers are expected to do in institutions driven by a neoliberal, free-market ideology in which resources are squeezed and demands for accountability are increased. Song (2016) focuses on the feelings of vulnerability South Korean English language teachers experience, particularly in relation to their work with study abroad returnee students, and how this impacts on their orientations towards their own professional development. Wolff and De Costa (2017) show how one non-native English language teacher (NNEST) overcame the emotional challenges she encountered on a US MA TESOL programme. Within an overall framework which highlights the reflexive relationships between emotion and identity formation, they argue for the necessity to focus on positive emotions, and the need for language teacher education programmes to 'recognize and build on the emotional and identity resources that NNEST bring with them' (2017: 87).

Just as with the other possible foci for research on LTIs, a concern with emotion is also heavily reliant on language and discourse data, very often in the form of narratives. As Zembylas (2005: 23) points out, such narrative research has 'prompted educators to explore teacher identity formation as articulated through talk, social interaction, and self-presentation'. For example, Song's (2016) study was based on interviews with five secondary English teachers, which were analysed for these teachers' emotional experiences of 'vulnerability'. In Wolff and De Costa's (2017) study, the dataset consisted of semi-structured interviews, class observations, stimulated verbal and written reports, and prompted journal entries (80). The data were analysed using procedures from grounded, qualitative research: namely the constant-comparative approach (Corbin and Strauss 2015). These approaches to the analysis of language and discourse data have clearly yielded important findings and shed much light on the relationships between, in this case, emotions and identity formation. However, approaches more like the ones which have been used in the empirical chapters in this volume, which see language and discourse as social (inter) action, can make a further contribution to this effort, by seeing aspects of affect and emotion as discursively constructed by participants in ongoing interactions. Indeed, there is an intense research effort on emotion as a social interactional phenomenon (see the edited volume by Peräkylä and Sorjonen 2012). In this work, studies focus on 'ways in which emotional stances are expressed and responded to in naturally occurring spoken interactions' (Sorjonen and Peräkylä 2012: 3). Even the 'deepest' feelings, such as desires and repressed emotions, can be subjected to such a discursive approach, as can be seen in discursive psychological and conversation-analytic approaches to psychoanalysis.

Billig (2009), in proposing a discursive psychological reworking of essential Freudian concepts such as repression, claims that '[t]he solution involves recasting "the unconscious". Instead of being seen as a hidden mental entity, it is seen as an activity – that of repressing – that itself is at root a discursive activity' (para. 41). This can also be applied to the Lacanian approach to language teacher identity as put forward by Clarke (2017), in which identity is seen as 'extimate' (that is, both interior and exterior). Conversation analysis has been used to examine the talk of psychoanalytic therapy sessions, as seen, for example, in the work of Buchholz and Kächele (2013) and Peräkylä (2013). As Buchholz and Kächele put it, 'CA enriches psychoanalytic conceptions of the unconscious by focusing on other activities (sequences and categories) more than traditional conceptions of the unconscious do' (10). Research on English language teacher identity which wants to take on the challenge raised by Clarke (2017) to take up 'psychoanalytic notions', such as desire and the unconscious, could draw on this existing CA research on psychoanalytic encounters to explore how these issues are taken up in unfolding talk-in-interaction. More broadly, work on emotion and LTIs could build on the studies of emotion and interaction as seen in Peräkylä and Sorjonen's (2012) edited volume, particularly the discursive psychological approach. As Wiggins and Potter (2017: 97) point out, 'Emotions like "anger", for example, can be worked up as physical, uncontrollable events ("boiling over", "burning up with rage") to characterize an event as a brief "lapse" in one's usual demeanour.' Studies on LTIs could focus on how emotions are 'worked up' in teachers' accounts of events, or how emotional stances are expressed, and what particular actions and activities are performed by such 'working up' and constructions of stance.

A key current and future theme in research on LTIs is how language teachers respond to the reality of their increasingly multilingual classrooms in an era of globalisation, and the identity-related implications. De Costa and Norton (2016) identify this as one of the major theoretical developments which will continue to stimulate identity-related research in the future. Kubanyiova and Crookes (2016), in putting forward an argument for increased importance to be given to the moral dimensions in language teacher education and development, highlight the deep changes in the language teacher's role as they meet the challenge of working in increasingly multilingual contexts in an age of globalisation:

> For much of the 20th century, the 'modern language' teacher (in the United States) had the primary role of introducing an unknown 'other' language and culture to the purportedly monolingual mainstream high school or university student. Now, the contribution of the 'additional language' teacher across language learning contexts (e.g., foreign, second, bilingual, heritage, complementary, immersion, etc.) is to promote, maintain, and strengthen the multicultural nature of his or her society, enable students to navigate the complex language learning demands in their multilingual lifeworlds, and in some cases act as an advocate for minority cultures within a dominant culture and country. (119)

Studies on language teacher identity will increasingly attempt to disentangle the complex relationships between language teachers' own multilingual identities and the ways in which they support their students in navigating their 'multilingual lifeworlds'. Examples are the studies by Higgins and Ponte (2017) and Zheng (2017), which show that groups of teachers, although outwardly belonging to an identifiable category such as 'elementary teacher' or 'international teaching assistant' (ITA), far from showing homogeneity in relation to their own multilingual identities and their relationship to how they approach pedagogy for linguistically diverse student groups, in fact draw on different identity resources.

Higgins and Ponte (2017) describe how elementary teachers drew on different sources of identity, including their own ethnolinguistic identities, in the ways in which they participated in a professional development programme designed to introduce pedagogies that responded to the needs of multilingual students in Hawaiian classrooms. They found that there was a possibility that ethnolinguistic identities (that is, whether the teachers had experience of multiple language use, or loss, in their families or communities) impacted on how and whether they developed an identity more open to multilingual pedagogy. However, it may have been the 'affinity' identities (Gee 2000), generated through participating in the professional development activity with colleagues, that had greater impact on their changing views and practices towards multilingual pedagogies. Zheng's (2017) case study of two ITAs teaching College Composition classes in the US shows that while they both became successful teachers, they developed rather different identities with respect to multilingualism. One of the teachers held to a more monolingual perspective on language diversity, while the other more readily adopted a translingual perspective which sees language difference as a meaning-making resource. Zheng concludes that ITAs arrive with different language histories, which may impact on their ability to draw on their multilingual identities, and that they need support to encourage them to reflect on the relationship between their own (multilingual) identity and pedagogy.

We envisage that all studies on language teacher identity will need to position the teacher with regard to these profoundly changing roles, and none will be able to avoid engaging with what May (2014) describes as the 'multilingual turn'. The topic of this volume, *English* language teacher identity, will be particularly sensitive in this respect, as applied linguistics struggles with the tension between the perception of English as an arm of a homogenising neoliberal globalisation destructive of non-English-speaking cultures (Piller and Cho 2013; Rapatahana and Bunce 2012) and the more optimistic scenario that English can take its place in a multilingual world as a translingual practice (Canagarajah 2013). A focus on language and discourse as social (inter)action can make a double contribution in this respect: first, it can provide fine-grained micro-analyses of the multilingual practices, including language alternation (Filipi and Markee forthcoming), in the different settings in which English language teachers work; second, it can examine language teachers' accounts of their, and their students', multilingual practices, thus highlighting how perceptions, opinions, attitudes and emotions relating to linguistic diversity are 'worked up' in the ways in which language teachers talk about them.

Three of the five empirical chapters in this volume focus explicitly on social categories (Chapter 6 on ethnolinguistic identity, Chapter 7 on class and Chapter 8 on LGBT identity). This does not mean that we consider other social category identities, such as race and gender, unimportant. In the general field of language learning and teaching, De Costa and Norton (2016) call for more research on these identities in the era of globalisation. Varghese et al. (2016: 561), while recognising the importance of these social categories in identity research, argue that 'further work is needed in developing a more complex picture of how identities are constructed and employed beyond mere categories and produced within and by other systems of oppression.' We thus expect that interest in these social categories as they impinge on, and intersect with, other aspects of language teachers' identities, will continue to grow. For example, there is growing research interest on race and ethnicity in language learning in general (Anya 2016) and in ELT in particular (Jenks 2017), and this work can be further extended to specific studies on LTIs.

One social category which we expect will attract further attention in LTI research is that of social class. Until relatively recently – for example, in the work of Block (2014a) – class did not receive much attention as an explicit issue in applied linguistics research on identity, though it is implicit in work which draws on Bourdieu's notions of different types of capital and learners' (and teachers') investment (De Costa and Norton 2016). This 'erasure' of social class as an issue in TESOL (Block 2014a) is curious because, as Varghese et al. (2016: 562) point out, '[a]lthough they are often obscured from vision, the themes of social class and poverty inevitably undergird the work of TESOL professionals.' It seems that class is just not talked about much in TESOL, or, when it is, it is done through proxies such as the expressions of social (dis)comfort with certain groups of people, as was seen in Chapter 7. However, as Block (2017) argues, future research on LTIs will be unable to ignore the 'bigger picture' of how the economic regimes teachers live and work in affect who they are seen to be and what they can do. As Block argues, the effects of these regimes include the lowering of teachers' status around the world as they fall out of the middle class and join the 'precariat' (Standing 2011), doing routinised, highly regimented and controlled work under greater surveillance. As Block (2017: 35) puts it, 'LTIs are changing as the political economy that envelops them changes.' Future LTI research will have to take this into account. As Hayes (2017: 58) pointedly asks: 'What is the impact on teachers' sense of identity when their professionalism is denigrated by society at large?'. Future work such as that in Chapter 7, which shows how language teachers position themselves with regard to the political and economic conditions that affect them in ongoing social (inter)action, can make an important contribution to answering questions like this.

A final theme which we see as growing in importance in research on LTIs in the future, and which a focus on language and discourse as social (inter)action can contribute to, is that of identity in connection with pedagogy. There are two main (but intertwined) possible lines of research here, as identified by Morgan (2004). The first is 'teacher identity *and* pedagogy': that is, the relationships between teachers' existing and developing identity orientations (whichever they are) and their practices (and possibly results) in supporting learning. The other is 'teacher identity *as* pedagogy', which Morgan describes as 'the strategic performance of a teacher's identity in ways that counteract stereotypes held by a particular group of students' (2004: 172). Taking a poststructural perspective, Morgan shows that there is potential for opening up new identity spaces in the ways in which the teachers' identity, seen as an 'image-text' (Simon 1995), interacts with the identities of students. Zheng's (2017) study takes up this idea of 'identity-as-pedagogy' in showing how one ITA, Sara, drew on her translingual identity as a pedagogical resource.

Both these perspectives (pedagogy and/as identity) have much to offer in research on LTIs, and indeed for the practices of language teacher education and professional development, as will be discussed below. The identity and pedagogy approach still has enormous unfulfilled potential, as identity has only recently captured attention and has been proposed as central to language teacher education and teacher development – as part of a shift from individual and cognitive to more collective, situated and ecological perspectives (for example, Borg 2017; Kalaja et al. 2015; Kanno and Stuart 2011; Kubanyiova 2017; Kubanyiova and Feryok 2015). However, the identity-as-pedagogy approach offers even more exciting prospects, as a 'conflation or synthesis more in keeping with the continuous interweaving of identity negotiation and language learning' (Morgan 2004: 178). Kamhi-Stein (2013: 113), drawing on English language teachers' autobiographical narratives, shows a range of ways in which teachers 'can draw on their life experiences as a means to identify commonalities with their students that could inform their instructional practices'. We would hope that the arguments and empirical studies presented in this book are ample evidence that a perspective on language and discourse as social (inter)action is uniquely placed to uncover the ways in which the synthesis of identity and pedagogy actually occurs in real-time interactions.

METHODOLOGICAL INNOVATIONS: FOCUS ON (VISUAL) NARRATIVE, MULTIMODALITY, EMBODIMENT AND COMPUTER-MEDIATED COMMUNICATION

As Cheung, Ben Said and Park (2015: xv) point out in the introduction to their edited volume on LTIs, narrative has 'imposed itself as a powerful instrument in providing a clear sense of who teachers are via the stories they narrate'. We envisage that this will continue to be the case, and that different forms of narrative inquiry will continue to be a strong driving force in research on LTIs. Narrative, from a methodological perspective, is a way of pulling together a range of related constructs, such as identity, reflection and investment. It can be used as a tool to access language teachers' ways of knowing, as in Barkhuizen's (2011) concept of 'narrative knowledging', or for promoting and stimulating reflection (Kamhi-Stein 2013). Varghese et al. (2016: 564) see the ways in which reflection, narrative, identity and investment are connected as 'a space that carries much potential for understanding possibilities for agentive and transformative identity work'. Hayes (2017: 59) suggests three rich future directions for narrative research: autoethnographies of individual teachers, in which they explore their personal experience in relation to the wider social meanings of education in general and language teaching in particular; narratives of language teachers who work in conflict zones, specifically how they position themselves, maintain motivation and support students in situations where they, and their students, may be victims of violence; and how language teachers are depicted in the media, and how they react to these (often negative) portrayals. All three of these topics are extremely amenable to an approach in which language and discourse are seen as social (inter) action. This can be seen in De Costa and Norton's (2016) suggestion that, while a range of ways of analysing narratives will certainly continue to be used, a particularly promising approach is one in which there is a focus on the 'positionings adopted by the interlocutor', and, in the case of interviews, 'how identity is performed in this particular speech event' (593).

One particularly promising avenue of inquiry within narrative research is the growing interest in visual methods. Borg, Birello, Civera and Zanatta (2014) make use of both visual and verbal data in their study of the impact of a university teaching methodology course on pre-service primary school teachers' beliefs. Kalaja (2015) reports the use of visual methods (drawings) in a study on student teachers' beliefs on an MA programme in Finland. This study was innovative in that it asked participants to look ahead and envision themselves as foreign language teachers in the near future, rather than looking back on their previous experience. The participants were encouraged to use both the visual mode (drawings) and verbal mode (writing), although the drawings, which depicted classroom events (the 'visual narratives') were treated as the primary data source. De Laurentiis Brandão (2017) uses a visual narrative methodology to trace a Brazilian pre-service English language teacher's identity construction in the context of designing and using materials on a pre-service teacher education course. This study highlights the combination between the visual data and the verbal interactions which 'contextualise' them. In De Laurentiis Brandão's study, these verbal data consisted of the teacher's recorded explanations of the drawings, journal entries, samples of the materials she designed, recorded conversations with the researcher, and online interactions (on Facebook, for example). Thus, the use of visual methods creates rich contexts for the production of spoken, written and online interaction, all of which are amenable to analyses which, taking the approach advocated in this book, highlight their co-constructed and contingent nature.

An exciting future development in LTI research, which is closely linked to the growing interest in visual narrative methods, will be the increasing attention to communication in non-linguistic modes (image, gesture, gaze, movement, artefacts), often in computer-mediated communication (CMC). A multimodal perspective on how identities are produced in interaction takes us beyond what Block (2014b) describes as 'lingualism': that is, an exclusive reliance on spoken or written linguistic data in exploring identity. Block critiques much existing work for this lack of attention to communication in other modes, arguing that what has been missing has been 'an active engagement with embodiment and multimodality as a broadened semiotically based way of looking at what people do when they interact' (Block 2014b: 56). In his work on social class in applied linguistics, Block makes a strong case for such a multimodal approach, claiming that

> class must be understood as embodied, multimodal symbolic behaviour (for example, how one moves one's body, the clothes one wears, the way one speaks, how one eats, the kinds of pastimes one engages in, etc.) and, in part, a matter of style. (Block 2014b: 66)

This can be applied to many aspects of language teacher identity, for, as Alsup (2006: 88) points out, 'In addition to mastering the language of the teacher and having the necessary pedagogical and theoretical knowledge, a new teacher must learn how to physically embody the identity of teacher.' Thus, future LTI studies could fruitfully look at how language teachers use their bodies, dress, movement, ways of speaking and other modes in interactions across the range of settings relevant to their professional lives.

A focus on multimodality is especially relevant for language learning, with the Douglas Fir Group (2016) including as fundamental theme 2 in its transdisciplinary framework for second language acquisition (SLA) research the principle that 'Language learning is semiotic learning,' which requires the use of a wide range of meaning-making resources, including 'the full array of nonverbal signs – gestures, facial expressions, body positioning, accompanying action, head movement, etc.' (27). This is linked to theme 4, which states that 'Language learning is multimodal, embodied and mediated' (29). De Costa and Norton (2017: 11) extend these themes to language teaching, and identify the need for language teachers to 'develop multimodal and embodied teaching repertoires'. Two contributions in the special issue of *The Modern Language Journal*, which De Costa and Norton edited, exemplify this focus on multimodal teaching strategies. Higgins and Ponte (2017) carried out professional development which focused on multiliteracy, which, drawing on the New London Group (1996), highlights the 'proliferation of multimodal ways of making meaning, where communication is increasingly visual, auditory, and spatial' (19). Stranger–Johannessen and Norton (2017) focus on the use of multilingual digital stories to develop children's literacy in a rural Ugandan primary school. One teacher in the study, Monica, made effective use of multimodal strategies with her young learners: for example, by using a story in physical education, *Listen to My Body*, which allowed them to use English in playful and meaningful ways with the language working alongside text, images and body movement.

As Stranger–Johannessen and Norton's study shows, a multimodal approach is conducive to work on understanding communicative practices around digital media. In the wider field of applied linguistics work on language and identity, Domingo (2016) advocates a multimodal ethnographic approach to studying the constraints and affordances of new media in mediating people's social interactions and constructing their identities. However, she points out that, so far, multimodality has not been widely adopted in studies on language and identity, and argues that it is an approach that broadens our notions of what 'content' is in online environments. It could also be said that a combination of multimodality with a focus on computer-mediated communication has not proliferated in studies on teacher identity (though see Nykvist and Mukherjee 2016). A focus on computer-mediated communication, multimodality and embodiment in LTI research would be extremely timely, given recent 're-envisioning' of the roles and tasks of language teachers by Kubanyiova and Crookes (2016), who argue that computers and virtual reality have reinstated the body as being of central importance in language teaching. They mention the importance of gesture, and point out that 'conceptions of literacy that go beyond the spoken word [are] both more obviously part of what we should teach and what technology allows us to research' (123). From a methodological perspective, an approach to language as social (inter)action is eminently suited to the task of bringing the body and other multimodal resources into focus, as seen in recent conversation-analytic perspectives on multimodal interaction in L2 classrooms (Sert 2015) and, in the digital sphere, in L2 chat rooms (Jenks 2014). Bringing together these multimodal and digital perspectives, within what Domingo (2016) advocates as a 'multimodal ethnographic' perspective, but adding a layer of fine-grained interaction analysis, could make a very significant contribution to LTI research.

IMPLICATIONS AND APPLICATIONS FOR ENGLISH LANGUAGE TEACHER EDUCATION AND PROFESSIONAL DEVELOPMENT

In this, the final section of the book, we draw on the analyses presented in the empirical chapters and the wider literature on (language) teacher identity to present a case that identity formation, development and maintenance should be at the heart of English language teacher education and professional development. We argue that, too often, in the initial preparation and continuing professional development of English language teachers, knowledge is separated from identity – with a resulting artificial division between what a language teacher knows or is expected to know and who he or she is. This is not just a problem restricted to second language teacher education, but appears to be the case in teacher education generally. Alsup (2006) wonders why university teacher education programmes do not address professional identity development. As she puts it, 'the role of the university teacher education program seems to be to provide knowledge about learning theories and pedagogical approaches, not help the new teacher develop an identity' (4). Varghese et al. (2016: 557) also comment on this lack of attention to teacher identity in teacher education, both in general and in language teacher education (LTE): 'it is rare if not impossible to actually find a teacher education program, let alone a [sic] LTE program, that makes teacher identity its central organizing principle.' This lack of attention to identity as central to teacher learning is curious in the light of research which clearly shows that identity, or what Day and Gu (2010) call the 'person in the professional', is central to the processes of teacher learning and professional development, and for issues of work–life balance and retention.

In the field of second language (L2) teacher education, Kanno and Stuart (2011) offer an explanation for this state of affairs. They claim that the problem has to do with what is foregrounded and what is left in the background. For Kanno and Stuart, although identity has been 'part of this discussion', it 'rarely takes central stage' (250): that is, it is always the different types of knowledge that are foregrounded. For Kanno and Stuart, this is a misguided approach to language teacher education, for, while what language teachers need to know is highly important, they claim that 'the central project in which novice L2 teachers are involved in their teacher learning is not so much the acquisition of the knowledge of language teaching as it is the development of a teacher identity' (249). Indeed, it can be argued that placing the emphasis on acquiring the different types of knowledge (for example, of SLA, language description or teaching methods) without relating this to the development of a teacher identity may well be counter-productive. Of course, the acquisition of knowledge can contribute to strengthening a professional identity, but without attention to the emotional, ethical and moral dimensions of teaching, which a focus on identity implies, such knowledge may be 'inert', to use Whitehead's (1929) term: that is, it will be difficult to use for the productive purposes of supporting learners to deal with the complex multilingual environments in which they live. There are thus strong arguments for moving identity to the centre of teacher education programmes: the need to strengthen and foster language teachers' future teaching selves; seeing teacher learning as developing an identity as a member of a professional community of practice; supporting teachers to develop the resources to deal with the emotional pressures of learning to teach and sustaining motivation to teach; strengthening teachers' awareness of the moral and ethical dimensions of language teaching; and helping teachers to see the connections between their own identity and agency and the wider contexts of the institutional and social forces that constrain who they are and what they can do.

The analyses in the empirical chapters in this book can shed some light on how identity may be moved closer to the centre in language teacher education and professional development programmes. As seen in Chapter 4, interactional settings such as collaborative lesson planning can be sites where a positive image of teachers' future selves can be built and where they can gradually move from the periphery to the centre of a professional community of practice. Indeed, as Clarke (2008: 198) points out, teacher education can be seen 'as a dynamic process of identity development alongside the development of a community of practice'. This development takes place in and through the interactions which take place in the different settings of teacher education (Singh and Richards 2006), which include events such as collaborative lesson-planning sessions. To make the best use of such events as contexts for student teachers' identity development, teacher educators can develop interactional skills which enable them to avoid the pitfalls of over-emphasising knowledge asymmetry, and instead, use their own identities as experienced practitioners (who also have their doubts and uncertainties) to open up spaces for dialogue, which allow student teachers to envisage rich, complex future teaching selves. Thus, these spaces can be used not only as an opportunity to model effective practices and 'tricks of the trade' (which also have their importance), but also to create spaces where both experienced practitioners and novices can see and enact language teaching as a practice where ethics, judgement, certainty, doubt and all kinds of emotions come into play. It is in these close-up personal encounters, which are an essential part of the everyday tasks of language teaching, that teacher educators can help to support the development of two main aspects of novice teachers' identities, as identified by Xu (2012: 577):

> First, ESOL teacher educators may need to attend more consciously to the forma- tion of imagined identities so that preservice teachers who will become novice teachers can be more aware of and critical about their imagined communities. Second, perseverance and agency should be further emphasized by teacher educa- tors and administrators in novice teachers' development so that the direction of the transformation of their professional identities can be more effectively and positively guided.

The conversations in lesson-planning sessions (and indeed in post-teaching feed- back) need to range beyond the technical aspects of teaching (which are of course important) to take into account novice teachers' imagined present and future worlds of practice too, and to strengthen the resources which will allow them to persevere in the face of inevitable challenges and create spaces for their own agency.

Chapter 5 shows how English language teachers may adopt a critical stance towards a 'tool' (ILPs) which carries with it institutional and wider societal expecta- tions about what their role should be. Given that the teachers who participated in this study were generally experienced professionals, it may be expected that they have developed resilience and a critical stance towards a practice that they see as conflicting with their prime responsibility to support their students – both personally and in their learning. ILPs were a prominent feature in ESOL practices some years ago, but all language teachers (and indeed all teachers) need to know that they will be subjected throughout their careers to waves of initiatives, normally imposed top- down without consultation, which will have powerful impacts on their professional lives. Language teacher education needs not only to equip teachers with the resources to take a critical perspective on such initiatives, but also to foment the strength and resilience to make space for these initiatives in their practices, and, if deemed neces- sary, to resist them. For this to happen, in language teacher education programmes, teachers must not simply be presented with tools, procedures and initiatives as if they were the 'only' or 'best' way to do things, but be supported in examining the assumptions underlying such initiatives, their overt and ulterior purposes, and their possible effects on students. In this way, language teacher education and professional development programmes can work to foment a solid professional identity, in which language teachers' critical faculties and the ethical and moral dimensions of language teaching are brought to the fore.

The focus on language identities in Chapter 6 points to the need for language teacher education and professional development programmes to directly address issues around which varieties of language teachers use, which varieties they (should) teach, and who they are as language users and learners. The findings in the chapter, and the literature reviewed, suggest that explicit discussion of these topics is rare in teacher education and in teachers' professional experiences. Reflection on language identity is equally pertinent for 'native' and 'non-native' teachers of English. For 'native' teachers, we have seen how some may cling to quasi-colonial attitudes about the linguistic abilities and teaching approaches of their 'non-native' counterparts. For 'non-native' teachers, the pernicious ideology of 'native speakerism' endures in many places, and is manifested in their own feelings of insecurity, discrimination in the workplace, and hiring practices. English language teacher education programmes need to tackle these issues head on, with all prospective and practising teachers being supported to develop a solid professional language identity and a critical perspective on the conflicting claims about the benefits or otherwise of language practices and varieties, whether standard or non-standard, 'native' or 'non-native'. This is especially so because the roles and tasks of English language teachers are rapidly changing as they need to adapt to the multilingual realities their students will live in (Kubanyiova and Crookes 2016).

Chapter 7 focuses on an aspect of language teacher identity – social class – that has, to all intents and purposes, been 'erased' from discussions of language teaching (Block 2014a). Given that this is the case, we would not expect to find much attention to social class in existing language teacher education programmes. Indeed, Block (2014a), in his book on social class in applied linguistics, recognises that language teacher education is an area that is missing from his discussion. As he puts it,

in language teacher education on the whole, there seems to be little space for conversations about the eventual class position in society of second language teachers or how teachers might incorporate into their teaching the raising of class consciousness among their students. (p. 166)

The second option is one that he understandably sees as unlikely to be taken up, as it would be seen as 'too subversive'. However, there is evidence in the ESOL teachers' talk in Chapter 7 that there is a willingness to use materials which do raise issues of class consciousness for students: for example, in their positive stance towards the textbook *Problem-posing at Work* (Auerbach and Wallerstein 2004), which adopts a critical pedagogy perspective.

Block sees the first option, that of conversations about teachers' own eventual class position in society, as being 'tame enough' to be included in teacher education programmes. Such discussions need not be 'tame' if they involve critical engagement with the proposition that, for example, EFL teachers do not have 'careers' (Johnston 1997). This question is even more pertinent in the twenty-first century with the increasing precaritisation of teachers' work (as Block [2017] himself points out). Language teacher education programmes should take necessary steps to equip teachers with what Kubanyiova and Crookes (2016) call 'teacher-level or teacher-specific knowledge', which is an understanding of the administrative structures of their institutions and how they are affected by networks of power and control. Of close relevance to issues of social class, they argue that this should include knowing 'how to work with other teachers and how to build networks, preferably knowing of the existence of teacher unions, and if necessary lawyers, to defend their interests and protect them when and if they are under attack' (122). The findings discussed in this book, and work such as Block's on social class, suggest that it is time that this crucial aspect of language teacher (and student) identity be no longer erased from the conversation in language teacher education and professional development programmes.

Finally, Chapter 8 addresses the all-important issue of teachers' non-normative sexual orientation and the ways in which, despite massive change in social attitudes across much of the Global North, all of which has been accompanied by legislative reform, commercial publishers and test providers whose business is focused on the global market refuse to move with the times. Rather, they continue to adhere to retrograde and discriminatory practices of erasure which are entirely determined by financial interests. Textbook publishers and test providers already stand accused in the burgeoning literature on LGBT issues in educational settings, yet they remain impervious to this critique. It is only when LGBT teachers, teacher educators and their allies *as a collective* actively challenge these practices that change can begin to occur. In the short term, we see teacher education programmes as the best avenue for addressing this institutional intransigence. If novices are inducted into teaching in such a way that they are sensitised to the issues faced by LGBT teachers and students, if they are reminded of the legitimacy of LGBT identities and of the possible consequences of the denial of recognition, and if they are shown ways in which heteronormativity (and homonormativity) can be challenged, materials, however socially conservative and discriminatory they may be, can be interrogated and used productively in the classroom. However, until such times, LGBT teachers (such as those in Chapter 8), in whatever sector they work, are likely to find themselves frustrated by the constraints in which they find themselves, making it up as they go along and acting largely on their own.

In bringing this chapter and the volume overall to a conclusion, we return to a point we made in the first two chapters: namely, that identity – despite the problems associated with it – is a potentially useful concept in the working lives of ELT professionals. While the dominant neoliberal order may be fracturing (Davies 2014; Fraser 2017; Hall et al. 2015), it is unlikely that teachers' lives are to become any easier in the short term. Undoing the damage done since the imposition of neoliberalism on the profession – the marketisation of education at all levels, the introduction and use of league tables, the individualisation of work, excessive accountability to regimes of inspection and a narrowing knowledge base inter alia – will be a lengthy and doubtlessly painful process. But such a fracturing is also an opportunity, one which has the potential to allow teachers to lay claim to being the kinds of professionals they want to be – and in that endeavour, the conceptual affordances of identity may prove to be particularly useful.

APPENDIX: TRANSCRIPTION SYMBOLS

(Selected and adapted from Jefferson 2004)

wo::rd	colons indicate an elongated or stretched sound
(.)	short silence (less than 0.5 seconds)
(2.5)	duration of silence in seconds and tenths of seconds
(word)	unclear or uncertain transcription
( )	unintelligible utterance
((laughter))	transcriber's comments in double brackets
<u>word</u>	emphasised talk
<u>WORD</u>	spoken in louder voice
<word>	spoken at slower pace than surrounding talk
>word<	spoken at faster pace than surrounding talk
wo-	cut-off
[ ]	overlapping talk
=	no break or gap between utterances
↑ ↓	significant rise or fall in pitch height
.	final, falling tone
,	'continuing' tone
/	marks a chunk of talk (not used in Jefferson's conventions)

REFERENCES

Aboshiha, P. (2008), 'Identity and dilemma: the "native speaker" English language teacher in a globalizing world', unpublished doctoral thesis, Canterbury Christ Church University, Canterbury, UK.

Action for ESOL (2012), *The ESOL Manifesto: A Statement of Our Beliefs and Values*, available at <http://actionforesol.org/wp-content/uploads/2012/02/ESOL-manifesto-leaflet-v4b-online.pdf> (last accessed 25 July 2017).

Agha, A. (2006), *Language and Social Relations*, Cambridge: Cambridge University Press.

Akbari, R. (2008), 'Postmethod discourse and practice', *TESOL Quarterly*, 42 (4): 641–52.

Alsup, J. (2006), *Teacher Identity Discourses: Negotiating Personal and Professional Spaces*, Mahwah, NJ: Lawrence Erlbaum Associates.

Andreasson, A. (1994), 'Norm as a pedagogical paradigm', *World Englishes*, 13 (3): 395–409.

Andrews, S. (2007), *Teacher Language Awareness*, Cambridge: Cambridge University Press.

Antaki, C., and G. Widdicombe (eds) (1998), *Identities in Talk*, London: Sage.

Anya, U. (2016), *Racialized Identities in Second Language Learning: Speaking Blackness in Brazil*, New York/Abingdon: Routledge.

Anyon, J. (1985), 'Workers, labor and economic history, and textbook content', in M. W. Apple and L. Weis (eds), *Ideology and Practice in Schooling*, Philadelphia: Temple University Press, pp. 37–60.

Apple, M. W., and L. K. Christian-Smith (eds) (1991), *The Politics of the Textbook*, London: Routledge.

Auerbach, E., and N. Wallerstein (2004), *Problem-posing at Work: English for Action*, Edmonton: Grass Roots Press.

Azimova, N., and B. Johnson (2012), 'Invisibility and ownership of language: Problems of representation in Russian language textbooks', *The Modern Language Journal*, 96 (3): 337–49.

Baker, W. (2015), *Culture and Identity through English as a Lingua Franca: Rethinking Concepts and Goals in Intercultural Communication*, Berlin/Boston: De Gruyter Mouton.

Ball, D. L., M. H. Thames and G. C. Phelps (2008), 'Content knowledge for teaching: What makes it special?' *Journal of Teacher Education*, 59 (5): 389–407.

Ball, S. J. (2003), *Class Strategies and the Education Market: The Middle Classes and Social Advantage*, London: Routledge Falmer.

Ball, S. J. (2012), *Global Education, Inc.: New Policy Networks and the Neo-liberal Imaginary*, London: Routledge.

Bamberg, M. (1997), 'Positioning between structure and performance', *Journal of Narrative and Life History*, 7 (1–4): 335–42.

Bamberg, M. (2004), 'Positioning with Davie Hogan: Stories, tellings, and identities', in C. Daiute and C. Lightfoot (eds), *Narrative Analysis: Studying the Development of Individuals in Society*, London: Sage, pp. 135–57.

Bamberg, M. (2007), 'Stories: big or small – why do we care?', in M. Bamberg (ed.), *Narrative – State of the Art*, Amsterdam: John Benjamins, pp. 165–74.

Bamberg, M., and A. Georgakopolou (2008), 'Small stories as a new perspective in narrative and identity analysis', *Text & Talk*, 28 (3): 377–96.

Barkhuizen, G. (2010), 'An extended positioning analysis of a pre-service teacher's better life small story', *Applied Linguistics*, 31 (2): 282–300.

Barkhuizen, G. (2011), 'Narrative knowledging in TESOL', *TESOL Quarterly*, 45 (3): 391–414.

Barkhuizen, G. (2016), 'A short story approach to analyzing teacher (imagined) identities over time', *TESOL Quarterly*, 50 (3): 655–83.

Barkhuizen, G. (ed.) (2017a), *Reflections on Language Teacher Identity Research*, London: Routledge.

Barkhuizen, G. (2017b), 'Investigating language tutor social inclusion identities', *The Modern Language Journal*, 101–S1: 61–75.

Barkhuizen, G., P. Benson and A. Chik (2014), *Narrative Inquiry in Language Teaching and Learning Research*, New York: Routledge.

Baroni, R. (2014), 'Tellability', *The Living Handbook of Narratology*, available at <http://www.lhn.uni-hamburg.de/article/tellability> (last accessed 26 July 2017).

Bartels, N. (ed.) (2005), *Applied Linguistics and Language Teacher Education*, New York: Springer.

Bateson, G. (1952), 'The Position of Humour in Human Communication', Macy Conferences 1952, available at <https://www.yumpu.com/en/document/view/38125482/the-position-of-humor-in-human-communication> (last accessed 27 July 2017).

Bawer, B. (1993), *A Place at the Table: The Gay Individual in American Society*, New York: Touchstone.

Bawer, B. (2012), *The Victims' Revolution: The Rise of Identity Studies and the Closing of the Liberal Mind*, New York: HarperCollins.

Baynham, M. J. (2011), 'Stance, positioning and alignment in narratives of professional experience', *Language in Society*, 40 (1): 63–74.

Baynham, M. (2014), 'Identity: Brought about or brought along? Narrative as a privileged site for researching intercultural identities', in F. Dervin and K. Risager (eds), *Researching Identity and Interculturality*, Abingdon: Routledge, pp. 67–85.

Baynham, M., C. Roberts, M. Cooke, J. Simpson, K. Ananiadou, J. Callaghan, J. McGoldrick and C. Wallace (2007), *Effective Teaching and Learning ESOL*, London: National Research and Development Centre for Literacy and Numeracy.

Beijaard, D., P. C. Meijer and N. Verloop (2004), 'Reconsidering research on teachers' professional identity', *Teaching and Teacher Education*, 20 (2): 107–28.

Bendle, M. F. (2002), 'The crisis of "identity" in high modernity', *The British Journal of Psychology*, 53 (1): 1–18.

Benesch, S. (2012), *Considering Emotions in Critical English Language Teaching: Theories and Praxis*, New York: Routledge.

Benesch, S. (2017), *Emotions and English Language Teaching: Exploring Teachers' Emotion Labor*, New York: Routledge.

Benwell, B., and E. Stokoe (2006), *Discourse and Identity*, Edinburgh: Edinburgh University Press.

Benwell, B., and E. Stokoe (2010), 'Analysing identity in interaction: Contrasting discourse, genealogical, narrative and conversation analysis', in M. Wetherell and C. T. Mohanty (eds), *The Sage Handbook of Identities*, London: Sage, pp. 56–77.

Bernstein, J. H. (2015), 'Transdisciplinarity: A review of its origins, development, and current issues', *Journal of Research Practice*, 11 (1), Article R1, available at <http://jrp.icaap.org/index.php/jrp/article/view/510/412> (last accessed 26 July 2017).

Billig, M. (2009), 'Discursive psychology, rhetoric and the issue of agency', *Semen*, 27, available at <http://semen.revues.org/8930> (last accessed 26 July 2017).

Block, D. (2005), 'Convergence and resistance in the construction of personal and professional identities: Four French modern language teachers in London', in S. A. Canagarajah (ed.), *Reclaiming the Local in Language Policy and Practice*, Mahwah, NJ: Lawrence Erlbaum Associates, pp. 167–96.

Block, D. (2006), 'Identity in applied linguistics: where are we?', in T. Omoniyi and G. White (eds), *The Sociolinguistics of Identity*, London: Continuum, pp. 34–49.

Block, D. (2007), *Second Language Identities*, London: Continuum.

Block, D. (2014a), *Social Class in Applied Linguistics*, London: Routledge.

Block, D. (2014b), 'Moving beyond "lingualism": multilingual embodiment and multimodality in SLA', in S. May (ed.), *The Multilingual Turn: Implications for SLA, TESOL and Bilingual Education*, London: Routledge, pp. 54–77.

Block, D. (2015), 'Becoming a language teacher: Constraints and negotiation in the emergence of new identities', *Bellaterra Journal of Teaching & Learning Language & Literature*, 8 (3): 9–26.

Block, D. (2017), 'Journey to the center of language teacher identity', in G. Barkhuizen (ed.), *Reflections on Language Teacher Identity*, New York: Routledge, pp. 31–6.

Block, D., and V. Corona (2016), 'Intersectionality in language and identity research', in S. Preece (ed.), *The Routledge Handbook of Language and Identity*, London: Routledge, pp. 507–22.

Block, D., and J. Gray (2016), '"Just go away and do it and you get marks": The degradation of language teaching in neoliberal times', *Journal of Multilingual and Multicultural Development*, 37 (5): 481–94.

Block, D., and J. Gray (2017) 'French language textbooks as ideologically imbued cultural artefacts: Political economy, neoliberalism and (self) branding', in S. Coffey and U. Wingate (eds), *New Directions for Research in Foreign Language Education*, Abingdon: Routledge.

Block, D, J. Gray and M. Holborow (2012), *Neoliberalism and Applied Linguistics*, London: Routledge.

Blommaert, J. (2005), *Discourse: A Critical Introduction*, Cambridge: Cambridge University Press.

Bolin, G. (2012), 'The forms of value: Problems of convertibility in field theory', *tripleC*, 10 (1): 33–41.

Bollas, A. (2016), *Heteronormativity and the Ideal Self in ELT Published Materials*, unpublished MA dissertation, Leeds Beckett University, UK.

Borg, S. (2006), *Teacher Cognition and Language Education: Research and Practice*, London: Continuum.

Borg, S. (2017), 'Identity and teacher research', in G. Barkhuizen (ed.), *Reflections on Language Teacher Identity*, New York/Abingdon: Routledge, pp. 126–32.

Borg, S., M. Birello, I. Civera and T. Zanatta (2014), *The Impact of Teacher Education on Pre-service Primary English Language Teachers*, London: British Council.

Bourdieu, P. (1977), *Outline of a Theory of Practice* (Vol. 16), Cambridge: Cambridge University Press.

Bourdieu, P. (1984), *Distinction: A Social Critique of the Judgement of Taste*, London: Routledge.

Bourdieu, P. (1985), 'The social space and the genesis of groups', *Theory and Society*, 14 (6): 723–44.

Bourdieu, P. (1991), 'The production and reproduction of legitimate language', in J. B. Thompson (ed.), *Language and Symbolic Power*, Cambridge: Polity Press, pp. 43–65.

Bourdieu, P. (1993), *The Field of Cultural Production*, Cambridge: Polity Press.

Braine, G. (2010), *Nonnative Speaker English Teachers: Research, Pedagogy, and Professional Growth*, New York: Routledge.

Braverman, H. (1974), *Labor and Monopoly Capital*, New York: Monthly Review Press.

Breman, J. (2013), 'Reviews', *New Left Review*, 84: 130–8.

Briggs, C. (1986), *Learning How to Ask: A Sociolinguistic Appraisal of the Role of the Interview in Social Science Research*, Cambridge: Cambridge University Press.

Britzman, D. (1994), 'The terrible problem of knowing thyself: Toward a poststructural account of teacher identity', *Journal of Curriculum Theorizing*, 9 (3): 23–46.

Britzman, D. (1998), 'Is there a queer pedagogy? Or, stop reading straight', in W. Pinar (ed.), *Curriculum: Toward New Identities*, New York: Garland Publishing, pp. 211–31.

Brubaker, R., and F. Cooper (2000), 'Beyond "identity"', *Theory and Society*, 29 (1): 1–47.

Bruner, J. (1986), *Actual Minds, Possible Worlds*, Cambridge, MA: Harvard University Press.

Buchholz, M. B., and H. Kächele (2013), 'Conversation analysis – A powerful tool for psychoanalytic practice and research', *Language and Psychoanalysis*, 2 (2): 228–43.

Bucholtz, M., and K. Hall (2005), 'Identity and interaction: A sociocultural linguistic approach', *Discourse Studies*, 7 (4–5): 585–614.

Burgess, A. (2008), 'The literacy practices of recording achievement: How a text mediates between the local and the global', *Journal of Education Policy*, 23 (1): 49–62.

Butler, J. (1990), *Gender Trouble*, New York: Routledge.

Butler, J. (1993), *Bodies That Matter: On the Discursive Limits of 'Sex'*, Abingdon: Routledge.

Byrne, B. (2012), 'Qualitative interviewing', in C. Seale (ed.), *Researching Society and Culture* (3rd edn), London: Sage, pp. 206–26.

Callaghan, J. (2006), *Methodological Reflections on a Study of how ESOL Teachers Construct Professional Identities at the Juncture of Multiple, Ill-defined and Conflicting Agendas*, unpublished MA dissertation, University of Leeds, UK.

Cameron, D. (2000), 'Styling the worker: Gender and the commodification of language in the globalized service economy', *Journal of Sociolinguistics*, 4 (3): 323–74.

Cameron, D., and D. Kulick (2003), *Language and Sexuality*, Cambridge: Cambridge University Press.

Canagarajah, S. (2013), *Translingual Practice: Global Englishes and Cosmopolitan Relations*, New York/Abingdon: Routledge.

Canagarajah, S. (2017), 'Multilingual identity in teaching multilingual writing', in G. Barkhuizen (ed.), *Reflections on Language Teacher Identity Research*, London: Routledge, pp. 67–73.

Carley, M., and I. Christie (2000), *Managing Sustainable Development*, London: Earthscan.

Carroll, A., and L. M. Mendos (2017), *State-sponsored Homophobia – A World Survey of Sexual Orientation Laws: Criminalisation, Protection and Recognition*, ILGA, available at <http://ilga.org/downloads/2017/ILGA_State_Sponsored_Homophobia_2017_WEB.p df> (last accessed 27 July 2017).

Charlesworth, S. (2000), *A Phenomenology of Working Class Experience*, Cambridge: Cambridge University Press.

Cheung, Y. L. (2017), 'Writing teacher identity: Current knowledge and future research', in G. Barkhuizen (ed.), *Reflections on Language Teacher Identity*, New York: Routledge, pp. 246–51.

Cheung, Y. L., S. Ben Said and K. Park (2015), *Advances and Current Trends in Language Teacher Identity Research*, London: Routledge.

Choi, B. C. K., and A. W. P. Pak (2006), 'Multidisciplinarity, interdisciplinarity, and transdisciplinarity in health research, services, education and policy. 1. Definitions, objectives, and evidence of effectiveness', *Clinical and Investigative Medicine*, 29 (6): 351–64.

Choi, T.-H. (2013), *Curriculum Innovation through Teacher Certification: Evaluation of a Government Intervention and its Effects on Teacher Development and English Language Pedagogy in South Korea*, unpublished PhD thesis, King's College London, UK.

Clandinin, D. J. (2013), *Engaging in Narrative Inquiry*, Walnut Creek, CA: Left Coast Press.

Clandinin, D. J., and F. M. Connelly (2000), *Narrative Inquiry: Experience and Story in Qualitative Research*, San Francisco: Jossey-Bass.

Clarke, M. (2008), *Language Teacher Identities: Co-constructing Discourse and Community*, Bristol: Multilingual Matters.

Clarke, M. (2009), 'The ethico-politics of teacher identity', *Educational Philosophy and Theory*, 41 (2): 185–200.

Clarke, M. (2017), 'The intimate alterity of identity', in G. Barkhuizen (ed.), *Reflections on Language Teacher Identity*, New York: Routledge, pp. 264–9.

Clarke, M. A., B. K. Dobson and S. Silberstein (1996), *Choice Readings*, Ann Arbor, MI: University of Michigan Press.

Coates, J. (2007), 'Talk in a play frame: More on laughter and intimacy', *Journal of Pragmatics*, 39 (1): 29–49.

Cook, V. (1992), 'Evidence for multicompetence', *Language Learning*, 42 (4): 557–91.

Cook, V. (1999), 'Going beyond the native speaker in language teaching', *TESOL Quarterly*, 33 (2): 185–209.

Cooke, M., and J. Gray (forthcoming), 'Queering ESOL: Sexual citizenship and intersectionality in ESOL classrooms', in M. Cooke and R. Peutrell (eds), *Brokering Britain, Educating Citizens*, Bristol: Multilingual Matters.

Cooke, M., and J. Simpson (2008), *ESOL: A Critical Guide*, Oxford: Oxford University Press.

Corbin, J., and A. Strauss (2015), *Basics of Qualitative Research: Techniques and Procedures for Developing Grounded Theory* (4th edn), Oakwood, CA: Sage.

Coté, J. (2006), 'Identity studies: How close are we to developing a social science of identity? – An appraisal of the field', *Identity: An International Journal of Theory and Research*, 6 (1): 3–25.

Cowen, B. (1995), 'The state and control of teacher education: The knowledge fit for teachers', in R. Gardner (ed.), *Contemporary Crises in Teacher Education*, Birmingham: British Association of Teachers and Researchers in Overseas Education, pp. 18–34.

Creese, A. (2005), 'Mediating allegations of racism in a multiethnic London school: What speech communities and communities of practice can tell us about discourse and power', in D. Barton and K. Tusting (eds), *Beyond Communities of Practice*, Cambridge: Cambridge University Press, pp. 55–76.

Crenshaw, K. (1991), 'Mapping the margins: Intersectionality, identity politics, and violence against women of color', *Stanford Law Review*, 43 (6): 1241–99.

Curran, G. (2006), 'Responding to students' normative questions about gays: Putting queer theory into practice in an Australian ESL class', *Journal of Language, Identity, and Education*, 5 (1): 85–95.

Danielewicz, J. (2001), *Teaching Selves: Identity, Pedagogy, and Teacher Education*, New York: State University of New York Press.

Darvin, R., and B. Norton (2015), 'Identity and a model of investment in applied linguistics', *Annual Review of Applied Linguistics*, 35: 36–56.

Davies, A. (2004), 'The native speaker in applied linguistics', in A. Davies and C. Elder (eds), *The Handbook of Applied Linguistics*, Oxford: Blackwell, pp. 430–51.

Davies, W. (2014), *The Limits of Neoliberalism: Authority, Sovereignty and the Logic of Competition*, London: Sage.

Day, C., and Q. Gu (2010), *The New Lives of Teachers*, Abingdon: Routledge.

De Costa, P. I., and B. Norton (2016), 'Future directions in identity research on language learning and teaching', in S. Preece (ed.), *The Routledge Handbook of Language and Identity*, Abingdon: Routledge, pp. 586–601.

De Costa, P., and B. Norton (2017), 'Introduction: Identity, transdisciplinarity, and the good language teacher', *The Modern Language Journal*, 101: 3–14.

De Fina, A. (2011), '"We are not there. In fact now we will go to the garden to take the rain": Researcher's identity and the Observer's Paradox', in J. Angouri and M. Marra (eds), *Constructing Identities at Work*, Basingstoke: Palgrave, pp. 223–45.

De Fina, A., and S. Perrino (2011), 'Introduction: Interviews vs. "natural" contexts: a false dilemma', *Language in Society*, 40 (1): 1–11.

De Laurentiis Brandão, A. C. (2017), 'Visualizing EFL teacher identity (re)construction in materials design and implementation', *Applied Linguistics Review*, <https://doi.org/10.1515/applirev-2016-1060> (last accessed 26 July 2017).

Dewey, M. (2015), 'ELF, teacher knowledge, and professional development', in H. Bowles and A. Cogo (eds), *International Perspectives on English as a Lingua Franca*, Basingstoke: Palgrave Macmillan, pp. 176–93.

Domingo, M. (2016), 'Language and identity research in online environments: A multimodal ethnographic perspective', in S. Preece (ed.), *Routledge Handbook of Language and Identity*, Abingdon: Routledge, pp. 541–57.

Dorling, D. (2014), *Inequality and the 1%*, London: Verso.

Douglas Fir Group (2016), 'A transdisciplinary framework for SLA in a multilingual world', *The Modern Language Journal*, 100: 19–47.

Du Bois, J. W. (2007), 'The Stance Triangle', in R. Englebretson (ed.), *Stancetaking in Discourse: Subjectivity, Evaluation, Interaction*, Amsterdam: John Benjamins, pp. 139–82.

Duff, P., and Y. Uchida (1997), 'The negotiation of teachers' sociocultural identities and practices in postsecondary EFL classrooms', *TESOL Quarterly*, 31 (3): 451–86.

Du Gay, P. (2007), *Organizing Identity Persons and Organizations 'After Theory'*, London: Sage.

Duggan, L. (2002), 'The new homonormativity: The sexual politics of neoliberalism', in D. Nelson (ed.), *Materializing Democracy: Toward a Revitalized Cultural Politics*, Durham, NC, and London: Duke University Press, pp. 175–94.

Dunton, S. (2016), *Stirring the Hornet's Nest: Teacher Attitudes Towards Pre-made LGBT-themed EFL Materials*, unpublished MA dissertation, Birkbeck College, London, UK.

Durkheim, E. (1984 [1893]), *The Division of Labor in Society*, New York: Free Press.

Edwards, J. (2009), *Language and Identity: An Introduction. Key Topics in Sociolinguistics*, Cambridge: Cambridge University Press.

Engels, F. (2009 [1845]), *The Condition of the Working Class in England*, Oxford: Oxford University Press.

Erikson, R., and J. Goldthorpe (1992), *The Constant Flux: A Study of Class Mobility in Industrial Societies*, Oxford: Oxford University Press.

Ferfolja, T. (2014), 'Reframing queer teacher subjects: Neither in nor out but present', in A. Harris and E. M. Gray (eds), *Queer Teachers, Identity and Performativity*, Basingstoke: Palgrave Macmillan, pp. 29–44.

Fernqvist, S. (2010), '(Inter)active interviewing in childhood research: On children's identity work in interviews', *The Qualitative Report*, 15 (6): 1309–27, available at <http://nsuworks.nova.edu/tqr/vol15/iss6/1> (last accessed 26 July 2017).

Filipi, A., and N. Markee (eds) (forthcoming), *Capturing Transitions in the Second Language Classroom: A Focus on Language Alternation Practices*, Amsterdam: John Benjamins.

Filson, G. (1988), 'Ontario teachers' deprofessionalization and proletarianization', *Comparative Education Review*, 32 (3): 298–317.

Foucault, M. (1982), 'The subject and power', in H. Dreyfus and P. Rabinow (eds), *Beyond Structuralism and Hermeneutics*, London: Harvester Wheatsheaf.

Foucault, M. (2003), *Society Must Be Defended: Lectures at the Collège de France, 1975–76*, translated by D. Macey, New York: Picador.

Franke, K. (2012), 'Dating the state: The moral hazards of winning gay rights', *Columbia Human Rights Law Review*, 49 (1): 1–46.

Fraser, N. (2017), 'The end of progressive neoliberalism', *Dissent*, available at <https://www.dissentmagazine.org/online_articles/progressive-neoliberalism-reactionary-populism-nancy-fraser> (last accessed 27 July 2017).

Freeman, M. (2007), 'Life "on holiday"? In defense of big stories', in M. Bamberg (ed.), *Narrative – State of the Art*, Amsterdam: John Benjamins, pp. 155–63.

Freud, S. (1900), *The Interpretation of Dreams*, trans. by J. Strachey, New York: Avon Books.

Gee, J. P. (1999), *An Introduction to Discourse Analysis: Theory and Method*, Abingdon: Routledge.

Gee, J. P. (2000), 'Identity as an analytic lens for research in education', *Review of Research in Education*, 25: 99–125.

Georgakopoulou, A. (2007), *Small Stories, Interaction and Identities*, Amsterdam: John Benjamins.

Giddens, A. (1973), *The Class Structure of the Advanced Societies*, London: Hutchinson.

Giroux, H. (1985), 'Teachers as transformative intellectuals', *Social Education*, 49 (5): 376–9.

Glenn, P., and C. LeBaron (2011), 'Epistemic authority in employment interviews: Glancing, pointing, touching', *Discourse and Communication*, 5 (1): 3–22.

Goffman, E. (1963), *Stigma: Notes on the Management of Spoiled Identity*, Upper Saddle River, NJ: Prentice Hall.

Goffman, E. (1967), *Interaction Ritual: Essays on Face-to-face Behaviour*, Harmondsworth: Penguin Books.

Goffman, E. (1974), *Frame Analysis: An Essay on the Organization of Experience*, Cambridge, MA: Harvard University Press.

Goldstein, B. (2003), *Framework/Level 2*, London: Richmond Publishing.

Golombek, P. (2017), 'Grappling with language teacher identity', in G. Barkhuizen (ed.), *Reflections on Language Teacher Identity Research*, London: Routledge, pp. 151–7.

Golombek, P., and S. R. Jordan (2005), 'Becoming "black lambs" not "parrots": A poststructuralist orientation to intelligibility and identity', *TESOL Quarterly*, 39 (3): 513–33.

Gorz, A. (1982), *Farewell to the Working Class: An Essay on Post-industrial Socialism*, London: Pluto Press.

Gove, M. (2010), Speech to the National College for Teaching and Leadership, available at <https://www.gov.uk/government/speeches/michael-gove-to-the-national-college-annual-conference-birmingham> (last accessed 7 July 2014).

Gove, M. (2013), 'I refuse to surrender to the Marxist teachers hell-bent on destroying our schools: Education Secretary berates "the new enemies of promise" for opposing his plans', *Mail Online*, available at <http://www.dailymail.co.uk/debate/article2298146/> (last accessed 7 August 2014).

Graeber, D. (2001), *Toward an Anthropological Theory of Value: The False Coin of Our Own Dreams*, Basingstoke: Palgrave Macmillan.

Gray, J. (2010), *The Construction of English: Culture, Consumerism and Promotion in the ELT Global Coursebook*, Basingstoke: Palgrave Macmillan.

Gray, J. (2013a), 'LGBT invisibility and heteronormativity in ELT materials', in J. Gray (ed.), *Critical Perspectives on Language Teaching Materials*, Basingstoke: Palgrave Macmillan, pp. 40–63.

Gray, J. (2013b), 'Introduction', in J. Gray (ed.), *Critical Perspectives on Language Teaching Materials*, Basingstoke: Palgrave Macmillan, pp. 1–16.

Gray, J. (2016), 'Language and non-normative sexual identities', in S. Preece (ed.), *The Routledge Handbook of Language and Identity*, Abingdon: Routledge, pp. 225–40.

Gray, J., and D. Block (2012), 'The marketization of language teacher education and neoliberalism: Characteristics, consequences and future prospects', in D. Block, J. Gray and M. Holborow, *Neoliberalism and Applied Linguistics*, London: Routledge, pp. 114–43.

Gray, J., and D. Block (2014), 'All middle class now? Evolving representations of the working class in the neoliberal era: the case of ELT textbooks', in N. Harwood (ed.), *English Language Teaching Textbooks: Content, Consumption, Production*, Basingstoke: Palgrave Macmillan.

Gregson, M., and Nixon, L. (2011), 'Unlocking the potential of Skills for Life (SfL) tutors and learners: A critical evaluation of the implementation of SfL policy in England', *Teaching in Lifelong Learning*, 3 (1): 52–66.

Gumperz, J. (1982), *Discourse Strategies*, Cambridge: Cambridge University Press.

Hall, C. (1805), *The Effects of Civilization on the People in European States*, referred to in R. Williams (1976), *Keywords: A Vocabulary of Culture and Society*, London: Fontana Press, p. 67.

Hall, S. (1992a), 'The question of cultural identity', in S. Hall, D. Held and T. McGrew (eds), *Modernity and its Futures*, Cambridge: Polity Press/Blackwell/The Open University, pp. 274–316.

Hall, S. (1992b), 'The west and the rest: Discourse and power', in S. Hall and B. Gieben (eds), *Formations of Modernity*, Cambridge: Polity Press/Blackwell/The Open University, pp. 275–320.

Hall, S. (1992c), 'Introduction', in S. Hall and B. Gieben (eds), *Formations of Modernity*, Cambridge: Polity Press/Blackwell/The Open University, pp. 1–16.

Hall, S. (1996), 'Introduction: Who needs "identity"?', in S. Hall and P. du Gay (eds), *Questions of Cultural Identity*, London: Sage, pp. 1–17.

Hall, S., and P. du Gay (eds) (1996), *Questions of Cultural Identity*, London: Sage.

Hall, S., D. Massey and M. Rustin (eds) (2015), *After Neoliberalism?: The Kilburn Manifesto*, London: Lawrence and Wishart.

Hallman, H. L. (2015), 'Teacher identity as dialogic response: A Bakhtinian perspective', in Y. L. Cheung, S. Ben Said and K. Park (eds), *Advances and Current Trends in Language Teacher Identity Research*, London: Routledge, pp. 3–15.

Hamilton, M. (2009), 'Putting words in their mouths: The alignment of identities with system goals through the use of individual learning plans', *British Educational Research Journal*, 35 (2): 221–42.

Hammersley, M. (1997), 'On the foundations of critical discourse analysis', *Language and Communication*, 17 (3): 237–48.

Hanks, W. F. (2005), 'Pierre Bourdieu and the practices of language', *Annual Review of Anthropology*, 34: 67–83.

Harp, J., and G. Betcherman (1980), 'Contradictory class locations and class action: The case of school teachers' organizations in Ontario and Quebec', *The Canadian Journal of Sociology/Cahiers canadiens de sociologie*, 5 (2): 145–62.

Harré, R., and L. van Langenhove (1999), *Positioning Theory*, Oxford: Blackwell.

Harré, R., T. Pilkerton-Cairnie, F. M. Moghaddam, D. Rothbart and S. R. Sabat (2009), 'Recent advances in positioning theory', *Theory and Psychology*, 19 (1): 5–31.

Harris, K. (1982), *Teachers and Classes: A Marxist Analysis*, London: Routledge and Kegan Paul.

Harvey, D. (2014), *Seventeen Contradictions and the End of Capitalism*, Oxford: Oxford University Press.

Hayes, D. (2017), 'Narratives of identity: Reflections on English language teachers, teaching and educational opportunity', in G. Barkhuizen (ed.), *Reflections on Language Teacher Identity*, New York: Routledge, pp. 54–60.

Heritage, J. (2012a), 'The epistemic engine: Sequence organization and territories of knowledge', *Research on Language and Social Interaction*, 45 (1): 30–52.

Heritage, J. (2012b), 'Epistemics in action: Action formation and territories of knowledge', *Research on Language and Social Interaction*, 45 (1): 1–29.

Heritage, J. (2013), 'Epistemics in conversation', in J. Sidnell and T. Stivers (eds), *Handbook of Conversation Analysis*, Boston: Wiley–Blackwell, pp. 370–94.

Heritage, J., and G. Raymond (2005), 'The terms of agreement: Indexing epistemic authority and subordination in talk-in-interaction', *Social Psychology Quarterly*, 68 (1): 15–38.

Hester, S., and P. Eglin (1997), 'Membership categorization analysis: An introduction', in S. Hester and P. Eglin (eds), *Culture in Action: Studies in Membership Categorization Analysis*, Washington, D.C.: University Press of America, pp. 1–24.

Higgins, C. (2017), 'Towards sociolinguistically informed language teacher identities', in G. Barkhuizen (ed.), *Reflections on Language Teacher Identity Research*, London: Routledge, pp. 37–42.

Higgins, C., and E. Ponte (2017), 'Legitimating multilingual teacher identities in the mainstream classroom', *The Modern Language Journal*, 101: 15–28.

Hochschild, A. R. (1979), 'Emotion work, feeling rules, and social structure', *The American Journal of Sociology*, 85 (3): 551–75.

Holborow, M. (2015), *Language and Neoliberalism*, Abingdon: Routledge.

Holland, D. C., W. S. Lachicotte, D. G. Skinner and W. C. Cain (1998), *Identity and Agency in Cultural Worlds*, Cambridge, MA: Harvard University Press.

Holliday, A. (2015), 'Native-speakerism: Taking the concept forward and achieving cultural belief', in A. Swan, P. J. Aboshiha and A. Holliday (eds), *(En)countering Native-speakerism: Global Perspectives*, Basingstoke: Palgrave, pp. 11–25.

Holliday, A., and P. Aboshiha (2009), 'The denial of ideology in perceptions of "non-native speaker" teachers', *TESOL Quarterly*, 43 (4): 669–89.

Horner, K., and J. Bellamy (2016), 'Beyond the micro–macro interface in language and identity research', in S. Preece (ed.), *Routledge Handbook of Language and Identity*, Abingdon: Routledge, pp. 320–34.

Hymes, D. H. (1972), 'Models of the interaction of language and social life', in J. J. Gumperz and D. H. Hymes (eds), *Directions in Sociolinguistics: The Ethnography of Communication*, New York: Holt, Rinehart and Winston, pp. 35–71.

IGF CultureWatch, available at <https://igfculturewatch.com/> (last accessed 1 December 2017).

Jaspers, J. (2006), 'Stylizing standard Dutch by Moroccan boys in Antwerp', *Linguistics and Education*, 17 (2): 131–56.

Jefferson, G. (2004), 'Glossary of transcript symbols with an introduction', in G. H. Lerner (ed.), *Conversation Analysis: Studies from the First Generation*, Amsterdam/Philadelphia: John Benjamins, pp. 13–31.

Jefferson, G., H. Sacks and E. Schegloff (1978), 'Notes on laughter in pursuit of intimacy', in

G. Button and J. R. E. Lee (eds), *Talk and Social Organisation*, Bristol: Multilingual Matters, pp. 152–205.

Jenkins, J. (2007), *English as a Lingua Franca: Attitude and Identity*, Oxford: Oxford University Press.

Jenkins, R. (2008), *Social Identity*, London: Routledge.

Jenks, C. (2013a), '"Your pronunciation and your accent is very excellent": Orientations of identity during compliment sequences in English as a Lingua Franca encounters', *Language and Intercultural Communication*, 13 (2): 165–81.

Jenks, C. (2013b), 'Are you an ELF? The relevance of ELF as an equitable social category in online intercultural communication', *Language and Intercultural Communication*, 13 (1): 95–108.

Jenks, C. J. (2014), *Social Interaction in Second Language Chat Rooms*, Edinburgh: Edinburgh University Press.

Jenks, C. J. (2017), *Race and Ethnicity in English Language Teaching: Korea in Focus*, Bristol: Multilingual Matters.

Johnson, K. E., and P. R. Golombek (eds) (2002), *Teachers' Narrative Inquiry as Professional Development*, New York: Cambridge University Press.

Johnson, K. E., and P. R. Golombek (2011), 'The transformative power of narrative in second language teacher education', *TESOL Quarterly*, 45 (3): 486–509.

Johnston, B. (1997), 'Do EFL teachers have careers?', *TESOL Quarterly*, 31 (4): 681–712.

Joseph, J. (2004), *Language and Identity: National, Ethnic, Religious*, Basingstoke: Palgrave Macmillan.

Kachru, B. B. (1985), 'Standards, codification and sociolinguistic realism: The English language in the outer circle', in R. Quirk and H. G. Widdowson (eds), *English in the World: Teaching and Learning the Language and Literatures*, Cambridge: Cambridge University Press, pp. 11–30.

Kalaja, P. (2015), '"Dreaming is believing": The teaching of foreign languages as envisioned by student teachers', in P. Kalaja, A. M. F. Barcelos, M. Aro and M. Ruohotie-Lyhty (eds), *Beliefs, Agency and Identity in Foreign Language Learning and Teaching*, Basingstoke: Palgrave, pp. 124–46.

Kalaja, P., A. M. F. Barcelos, M. Aro and M. Ruohotie-Lyhty (2015), *Beliefs, Agency and Identity in Foreign Language Learning and Teaching*, Basingstoke: Palgrave Macmillan.

Kamhi-Stein, L. D. (ed.) (2013a), *Narrating Their Lives: Examining English Language Teachers' Professional Identities within the Classroom*, Ann Arbor, MI: University of Michigan Press.

Kanno, Y., and C. Stuart (2011), 'Learning to become a second language teacher: Identities-in-practice', *The Modern Language Journal*, 95 (2): 236–52.

Kasper, G. (2009), 'Locating cognition in second language interaction and learning: Inside the skull or in public view?', *International Review of Applied Linguistics*, 47 (1): 11–36.

Kay, J. (1993), *Other Lovers*, Hexham: Bloodaxe Books.

Keucheyan, R. (2013), *The Left Hemisphere: Mapping Critical Theory Today*, London: Verso.

King, B. (2008), '"Being gay guy, that is the advantage": Queer Korean language learning and identity construction', *Journal of Language, Identity, and Education*, 7 (3/4): 230–52.

Korobov, N. (2010), 'A discursive psychological approach to positioning', *Qualitative Research in Psychology*, 7 (3): 263–77.

Korobov, N., and M. Bamberg (2007), '"Strip poker! They don't show nothing": Positioning identities in adolescent male talk about a television game show', in M. Bamberg, A. De Fina and D. Schiffrin (eds), *Selves and Identities in Narrative*, Amsterdam: John Benjamins, pp. 253–72.

Kubanyiova, M. (2009), 'Possible selves in language teacher development', in Z. Dörnyei and E. Ushioda (eds), *Motivation, Language Identity and the L2 Self*, Bristol: Multilingual Matters, pp. 314–32.

Kubanyiova, M. (2016), *Teacher Development in Action: Understanding Language Teachers' Conceptual Change*, Basingstoke: Palgrave.

Kubanyiova, M. (2017), 'Understanding language teachers' sense making in action through the prism of future self guides', in G. Barkhuizen (ed.), *Reflections on Language Teacher Identity Research*, New York: Routledge, pp. 100–6.

Kubanyiova, M., and G. Crookes (2016), 'Re-envisioning the roles, tasks, and contributions of language teachers in the multilingual era of language education research and practice', *The Modern Language Journal*, 100: 117–32.

Kubanyiova, M., and A. Feryok (2015), 'Language teacher cognition in applied linguistics research: Revisiting the territory, redrawing the boundaries, reclaiming the relevance', *The Modern Language Journal*, 99 (3): 435–49.

Kuhn, A. (1995), *Family Secrets: Acts of Memory and Imagination*, London: Verso.

Kumaravadivelu, B. (2016), 'The decolonial option in English teaching: Can the subaltern act?', *TESOL Quarterly*, 50 (1): 66–85.

Laplanche, J., and J. Pontalis (1988), *The Language of Psychoanalysis*, London: Karnac Books.

Larsen, M. S. (1980), 'Proletarianization and educated labour', *Theory and Society*, 9 (1): 131–75.

Latour, B. (2004), 'Why has critique run out of steam? From matters of fact to matters of concern', *Critical Inquiry*, 30 (2): 225–48.

Latour, B. (2005), *Reassembling the Social: An Introduction to Actor-Network Theory*, Oxford: Oxford University Press.

Lave, J., and E. Wenger (1991), *Situated Learning: Legitimate Peripheral Participation*, Cambridge: Cambridge University Press

Lawn, M., and J. Ozga (1988), 'The educational worker? A reassessment of teachers', in J. Ozga (ed.), *Schoolwork: Approaches to the Labour Process of Teaching*, Maidenhead: Open University Press, pp. 81–98.

Lemke, J. L. (2000), 'Across the scales of time: Artifacts, activities, and meanings in ecosocial systems', *Mind, Culture, and Activity*, 7(4): 273–90.

Lenin, V. (1982 [1919]), 'The abolition of classes [section from 'A great beginning']', in A. Giddens and D. Held (eds), *Classes, Power and Conflict: Classical and Contemporary Debates*, Berkeley: University of California Press, pp. 57–9.

Leung, C., R. Harris and B. Rampton (1997), 'The idealised native speaker, reified ethnicities, and classroom realities', *TESOL Quarterly*, 31 (3): 543–60.

Lévi-Strauss, C. (1971), *L'Homme nu*, Paris: Plon.

Lévi-Strauss, C. (1978), *Myth and Meaning*, London: Routledge and Kegan Paul.

Li, L. (2017), *Social Interaction and Teacher Cognition*, Edinburgh: Edinburgh University Press.

Liddicoat, A. (2009), 'Sexual identity as linguistic failure: Trajectories of interaction in the heteronormative language classroom', *Journal of Language, Identity, and Education*, 8 (2–3): 191–202.

Local Government Act (1988), London: HMSO, available at <http://www.legislation.gov.uk/ukpga/1988/9> (last accessed 27 July 2017).

Luk, J. C. M., and A. M. Y. Lin (2008), *Classroom Interactions as Cross-cultural Encounters: Native Speakers in EFL Lessons*, Mahwah, NJ: Lawrence Erlbaum Associates.

Macdonald, S. (2014), *Exploring LGBT Lives and Issues in Adult ESOL*, London: British Council.

McGregor, S. L. T. (2015), 'Integral dispositions and transdisciplinary knowledge creation',

Integral Leadership Review, 15 (1), available at <http://integralleadershipreview.com/12548–115–integral-dispositions-transdisciplinary-knowledge-creation/> (last accessed 15 July 2017).

Maclure, M. (1993), 'Arguing for your self: Identity as an organising principle in teachers' jobs and lives', *British Educational Research Journal*, 19 (4): 311–22.

Maguire, M. (2005), 'Textures of class in the context of schooling: The perceptions of a "class-crossing" teacher', *Sociology*, 39 (3): 427–43.

Mann, S. (2011), 'A critical review of qualitative interviews in applied linguistics', *Applied Linguistics*, 32 (1): 6–24.

Mann, S. (2016), *The Research Interview*, Basingstoke: Palgrave Macmillan.

Markus, H. R., and P. Nurius (1986), 'Possible selves', *American Psychologist*, 41 (9): 954–69.

Marx, K. (1966 [1865]), *Capital: A Critique of Political Economy, Volume 3*, Moscow: Progress Publishers.

Marx, K. (1976 [1867]), *Capital: A Critique of Political Economy, Volume 1*, London: Penguin.

Marx, K. (1978a [1852]), 'The Eighteenth Brumaire of Louis Bonaparte', in R. C. Tucker (ed.), *The Marx–Engels Reader*, New York: W. W. Norton, pp. 594–617.

Marx, K. (1978b [1847]), 'The coming upheaval', in R. C. Tucker (ed.), *The Marx–Engels Reader*, New York: W. W. Norton, pp. 218–19.

May, S. (2014), *The Multilingual Turn: Implications for SLA, TESOL and Bilingual Education*, New York/Abingdon: Routledge.

Mayer, D. (1999), 'Building teaching identities: Implications for pre-service teacher education', paper presented to the Australian Association for Research in Education, Melbourne, Available at <http://www.aare.edu.au/data/publications/1999/may99385.pdf> (last accessed 19 June 2017).

Merse, T. (2015), 'Queer-informed approaches and sexual literacy in ELT: Theoretical foundations and teaching principles', *Language Issues*, 26 (1): 13–20.

Milani, T., and E. Levon (2016), 'Sexing diversity: Linguistic landscapes of homonationalism', *Language and Communication*, 51: 69–86.

Miller, E. R., B. Morgan and A. L. Medina (2017), 'Exploring language teacher identity work as ethical self-formation', *Modern Language Journal*, 101: 91–105.

Miller, J. (2009), 'Teacher identity', in A. Burns and J. C. Richards (eds), *The Cambridge Guide to Second Language Teacher Education*, Cambridge: Cambridge University Press, pp. 172–81.

Moita Lopes, L. P. (2006), 'Queering literacy teaching: Analyzing gay-themed discourses in a fifth-grade class in Brazil', *Journal of Language, Identity, and Education*, 5 (1): 31–50.

Morgan, B. (2004), 'Teacher identity as pedagogy: Towards a field-internal conceptualisation in bilingual and second language education', *International Journal of Bilingual Education and Bilingualism*, 7 (2–3): 172–88.

Morgan, B., and M. Clarke (2011), 'Identity in second language teaching and learning', in E. Hinkel (ed.), *Handbook of Research in Second Language Teaching and Learning* (Vol. 2), New York: Routledge, pp. 817–36.

Morton, T., and J. Gray (2010), 'Personal practical knowledge and identity in lesson planning conferences on a pre-service TESOL course', *Language Teaching Research*, 14 (3): 1–21.

Morton, T., T. McGuire and M. Baynham (2006), *Literature Review on Research in Teacher Education in Adult Literacy, Numeracy and ESOL*, London: National Research and Development Centre for Literacy and Numeracy.

Motha, S. (2006), 'Racializing ESOL teacher identities in U.S. K-2 public schools', *TESOL Quarterly*, 40 (3): 495–518.

Moussu, L., and E. Llurda (2008), 'Non-native English-speaking English language teachers: History and research', *Language Teaching*, 41 (3): 315–48.

Nagatomo, D. H. (2012), *Exploring Japanese University English Teachers' Professional Identity*, Bristol: Multilingual Matters.

National Institute of Adult Continuing Education (2010), 'Citizenship Materials for ESOL Learners', available at <http://www.esoluk.co.uk/NIACE_pack/Citizenship_materials.pdf> (last accessed 26 July 2017).

Nelson, C. (1999), 'Sexual identities in ESL: Queer theory and classroom inquiry', *TESOL Quarterly*, 33 (3): 371–91.

Nelson, C. (2004), 'A queer chaos of meanings: Coming out conundrums in globalised classrooms', *Journal of Gay and Lesbian Issues in Education*, 2 (1): 27–46.

Nelson, C. (2006), 'Queer inquiry in language education', *Journal of Language, Identity, and Education*, 5 (1): 1–9.

Nelson, C. (2009), *Sexual Identities in English Language Education*, Abingdon: Routledge.

Nelson, C. (2010), 'A gay immigrant student's perspective: Unspeakable acts in the language class', *TESOL Quarterly*, 44 (3): 441–64.

Nelson, C. (2015), 'LGBT content: Why teachers fear it, why learners like it', *Language Issues*, 26 (1): 6–12.

Nelson, C. (2016), 'The significance of sexual identity to language learning and teaching', in S. Preece (ed.), *The Routledge Handbook of Language and Identity*, Abingdon: Routledge, pp. 351–65.

New London Group (1996), 'A pedagogy of multiliteracies: Designing social futures', *Harvard Educational Review*, 66 (1): 60–93.

Norton, B. (1997), 'Language, identity, and the ownership of English', *TESOL Quarterly*, 31 (3): 409–29.

Norton, B. (2000/2103), *Identity and Language Learning: Extending the Conversation*, Bristol: Multilingual Matters.

Norton, B. (2010), 'Identity, literacy, and English-language teaching', *TESL Canada Journal*, 28 (1): 1–13.

Norton Pierce, B. (1995), 'Social identity, investment, and language learning', *TESOL Quarterly*, 29 (1): 9–31.

Nykvist, S., and M. Mukherjee (2016), 'Who am I? Developing pre-service teacher identity in a digital world', *Procedia – Social and Behavioral Sciences*, 217: 851–7.

Ochs, E., and C. Taylor (1995), 'The "father knows best dynamic" in dinnertime narratives', in K. Hall and M. Bucholtz (eds), *Gender Articulated: Language and the Socially Constructed Self*, New York: Routledge, pp. 97–120.

Ofsted (2012), 'Handbook for the inspection of further education and skills', available at <http://www.ofsted.gov.uk/resources/handbook-for-inspection-of-further-education-and-skills-september-2012> (last accessed 27 July 2017).

Ozga, J., and M. Lawn (1981), *Teachers, Professionalism and Class: A Study of Organized Teachers*, Lewes: Falmer Press.

Pajares, M. F. (1992), 'Teachers' beliefs and educational research: Cleaning up a messy construct', *Review of Educational Research*, 62 (3): 307–22.

Park, G. (2012), '"I am never afraid of being recognized as an NNES": One teacher's journey in claiming and embracing her nonnative-speaker identity', *TESOL Quarterly*, 46 (1): 127–51.

Pavlenko, A. (2003), '"I never knew I was a bilingual": Reimagining teacher identities in TESOL', *Journal of Language, Identity, and Education*, 2 (4), 251–68.

Pavlenko, A. (2007), 'Autobiographic narratives as data in applied linguistics', *Applied Linguistics*, 28 (2): 163–88.

Pedrazzini, L., and A. Nava (2011), 'Researching ELF identity: A study with non-native English teachers', in A. Archibald, A. Cogo and J. Jenkins (eds), *Latest Trends in ELF Research*, Newcastle: Cambridge Scholars Publishing, pp. 269–84.

Pennington, M., and J. C. Richards (2016), 'Teacher identity in language teaching: Integrating personal, contextual, and professional factors', *RELC Journal*, 47 (1): 5–23.

Peräkylä, A. (2013), 'Conversation analysis in psychotherapy', in J. Sidnell and T. Stivers (eds), *The Handbook of Conversation Analysis*, Oxford: Wiley–Blackwell, pp. 551–74.

Peräkylä, A., and M.-L. Sorjonen (2012), *Emotion in Interaction*, Oxford: Oxford University Press.

Phillipson, R. (1992), *Linguistic Imperialism*, Oxford: Oxford University Press.

Pickering, L., M. Corduas, J. Eisterhold, B. Seifried, A. Eggleston and S. Attardo (2009), 'Prosodic markers of saliency in humorous narratives', *Discourse Processes*, 46 (6): 517–40.

Piller, I., and J. Cho (2013), 'Neoliberalism as language policy', *Language in Society*, 42 (1): 23–44.

Pinar, W. (ed.) (1998a), *Curriculum: Toward New Identities*, New York: Garland Publishing.

Pinar, W. (ed.) (1998b), *Queer Theory in Education*, Mahwah, NJ: Lawrence Erlbaum Associates.

Pomerantz, A. (1984), 'Agreeing and disagreeing with assessments: Some features of preferred and dispreferred turn shapes', in J. M. Atkinson and J. Heritage (eds), *Structures of Social Action: Studies in Conversation Analysis*, Cambridge: Cambridge University Press, pp. 57–101.

Potter, J. (1996), *Representing Reality: Discourse, Rhetoric and Social Construction*, London: Sage.

Potter, J., and A. Hepburn (2005), 'Qualitative interviews in psychology: Problems and possibilities', *Qualitative Research in Psychology*, 2 (4): 281–307.

Poulantzas, N. (1973), 'On social classes', *New Left Review*, 1 (78): 27–54.

Poulantzas, N. (1975), *Classes in Contemporary Capitalism*, London: Verso.

Puar, J. (2007), *Terrorist Assemblages: Homonationalism in Queer Times*, Durham, NC, and London: Duke University Press.

Rampton, B. (2006), *Language in Late Modernity: Interaction in an Urban School*, Cambridge: Cambridge University Press.

Rampton, M. B. H. (1990), 'Displacing the "native speaker": Expertise, affiliation and inheritance', *ELT Journal*, 44 (2): 97–101.

Rao, R. (2015), 'Global homocapitalism', *Radical Philosophy*, 194: 38–49.

Rapatahana, V., and P. Bunce (eds) (2012), *English Language as Hydra (Its Impacts on Non-English Language Cultures)*, Clevedon, Bristol: Multilingual Matters.

Rauch, J. (2004), *Gay Marriage: Why It Is Good for Gays, Good for Straights, and Good for America*, New York: Henry Holt and Company

Raymond, G., and J. Heritage (2006), 'The epistemics of social relations: Owning grandchildren', *Language in Society*, 35 (5): 677–705.

Reeves, J. (2009), 'Teacher investment in learner identity', *Teaching and Teacher Education*, 25 (1): 34–41.

Richards, K. (2006), '"Being the teacher": identity and classroom conversation', *Applied Linguistics*, 27 (2): 51–77.

Richards, K. (2011), 'Engaging identities: Personal disclosure and professional responsibility', in J. Angouri and M. Marra (eds), *Constructing Identities at Work*, Basingstoke: Palgrave Macmillan, pp. 204–26.

Richardson, D. (2004), 'Locating sexualities: From here to normality', *Sexualities*, 7 (4): 391–411.

Richardson, D. (2005), 'Desiring sameness? The rise of a neoliberal politics of normalisation', *Antipode*, 37 (3): 515–35.

Rodriguez, N. M., W. J. Martino, J. C. Ingrey and E. Brockenbrough (eds) (2016), *Critical Concepts in Queer Studies and Education: An International Guide for the Twenty-first Century*, New York: Springer.

Sacks, H. (1974), 'On the analysability of stories by children', in R. Turner (ed.), *Ethnomethodology: Selected Readings*, Harmondsworth: Penguin Books, pp. 216–32.

Sacks, H. (1992a), *Lectures on Conversation*, Volume I, G. Jefferson (ed.), with introduction by E. A. Schegloff, Oxford: Blackwell.

Sacks, H. (1992b), *Lectures on Conversation*, Volume II, G. Jefferson (ed.), with introduction by E. A. Schegloff, Oxford: Blackwell.

Sacks, H., E. A. Schegloff and G. Jefferson (1974), 'A simplest systematics for the organization of turn-taking for conversation', *Language*, 50 (4): 696–735.

Savage, M., F. Devine, N. Cunningham, M. Taylor, Y. Li, J. Hjellbrekke, B. Le Roux, S. Friedman and A. Miles (2013), 'A new model of social class? Findings from the BBC's Great British Class Survey Experiment', *Sociology*, 47 (2): 219–50.

Sayer, A. (2000), *Realism and Social Science*, London: Sage.

Sayer, A. (2002), '"What are you worth?": Why class is an embarrassing subject', *Sociological Research Online*, 7 (3), available at <http://www.socresonline.org.uk/7/3/sayer.html> (last accessed 26 July 2017).

Sayer, A. (2005a), 'Class, moral worth and recognition', *Sociology*, 39 (5): 947–63.

Sayer, A. (2005b), *The Moral Significance of Class*, Cambridge: Cambridge University Press.

Sayer, P. (2012), *Ambiguities and Tensions in English Language Teaching: Portraits of EFL Teachers as Legitimate Speakers*, New York: Routledge.

Schatzki, T. (1996), *Social Practices: A Wittgensteinian Approach to Human Activity and the Social*, Cambridge: Cambridge University Press.

Schegloff, E. A. (2007), 'A tutorial on membership categorization', *Journal of Pragmatics*, 39 (3): 462–82.

Schulman, S. (2012), *Israel/Palestine and the Queer International*, Durham, NC, and London: Duke University Press.

Seddon, T. (1997), 'Education: deprofessionalised? Or reregulated, reorganised and reauthor-ised?', *Australian Journal of Education*, 41 (3): 247–61.

Seidlhofer, B. (2015), 'ELF-informed pedagogy: From code-fixation towards communicative awareness', in P. Vettorel (ed.), *New Frontiers in Teaching and Learning English*, Newcastle upon Tyne: Cambridge Scholars Publishing, pp. 19–30.

Sennett, R., and J. Cobb (1972), *The Hidden Injuries of Class*, New York: W. W. Norton.

Sert, O. (2015), *Social Interaction and L2 Classroom Discourse*, Edinburgh: Edinburgh University Press.

Seymour, R. (2012), 'We are all precarious – on the concept of the "precariat" and its minuses', New Left Project, available at <http://www.newleftproject.org/index.php/site/article_com-ments/we_are_all_prec   arious_on_the_concept_of_the_precariat_and_its_misuses> (last accessed 26 July 2017).

Shain, F., and D. Gleeson (1999), 'Under new management: Changing conceptions of teacher professionalism and policy in the further education sector', *Journal of Education Policy*, 14 (4): 445–62.

Shulman, L. (1987), 'Knowledge and teaching: Foundations of the new reform', *Harvard Educational Review*, 57 (1): 1–22.

Silverstein, M. (2003), 'Indexical order and the dialectics of sociolinguistic life', *Language & Communication*, 23 (3–4): 193–229.

Simon, R. I. (1995), 'Face to face with alterity: Postmodern Jewish identity and the eros of pedagogy', in J. Gallop (ed.), *Pedagogy: The Question of Impersonation*, Bloomington: University of Indiana Press, pp. 90–105.

Simpson, J. (2015), 'English language learning for adult migrants in superdiverse Britain', in J. Simpson and A. Whiteside (eds), *Adult Language Education and Migration: Challenging Agendas in Policy and Practice*, Abingdon: Routledge, pp. 200–13.

Simpson, J. (2016), 'English for speakers of other languages: Language education and migration', in G. Hall (ed.), *The Routledge Handbook of English Language Teaching*, Abingdon: Routledge, pp. 177–90.

Singh, G., and J. C. Richards (2006), 'Teaching and learning in the language teacher education course room: A critical sociocultural perspective', *RELC Journal*, 37 (2): 149–75.

Skeggs, B. (2004), *Class, Self, Culture*, Abingdon: Routledge.

Sleeter, C., and C. Grant (2011), 'Race, class, gender, and disability in current textbooks', in E. F. Provenzo, Jr, A. N. Shaver and M. Bello (eds), *The Textbook as Discourse: Sociocultural Dimensions of American Schoolbooks*, London: Routledge, pp. 183–215.

Soars, L., and J. Soars (2011), *New Headway Elementary*, Oxford: Oxford University Press.

Song, J. (2016), 'Emotions and language teacher identity: Conflicts, vulnerability, and transformation', *TESOL Quarterly*, 50 (3): 631–54.

Sorjonen, M.-L., and A. Peräkylä (2012), 'Introduction', in A. Peräkylä and M.-L. Sorjonen (eds), *Emotion in Interaction*, Oxford, Oxford University Press, pp. 3–15.

Spivak, G. C. (1999), *A Critique of Postcolonial Reason*, Cambridge, MA: Harvard University Press.

Standing, G. (2011), *The Precariat: The New Dangerous Class*, London: Bloomsbury Academic.

Stevanovic, M., and A. Peräkylä (2012), 'Deontic authority in interaction: The right to announce, propose, and decide', *Research on Language and Social Interaction*, 45 (3): 297–321.

Stivers, T., L. Mondada and J. Steensig (2011), 'Knowledge, morality and affiliation in social interaction', in T. Stivers, L. Mondada and J. Steensig (eds), *The Morality of Knowledge in Conversation*, Cambridge: Cambridge University Press, pp. 3–24.

Stokoe, E. (2003), 'Mothers, single women and sluts: Gender, morality and membership categorization in neighbour disputes', *Feminism & Psychology*, 13 (3): 317–44.

Stokoe, E. (2009), 'Doing actions with identity categories: Complaints and denials in neighbour disputes', *Text and Talk*, 29 (1): 75–97.

Stokoe, E. (2012), 'Moving forward with membership categorization analysis: Methods for systematic analysis', *Discourse Studies*, 14 (3): 277–303.

Stranger-Johannessen, E., and B. Norton (2017), 'The African storybook and language teacher identity in digital times', *The Modern Language Journal*, 101: 45–60.

Streeck, W. (2011), 'The crises of democratic capitalism', *New Left Review*, 71: 5–29.

Sullivan, A. (1995), *Virtually Normal: An Argument about Homosexuality*, New York: Vintage.

Swan, A. (2015), 'Redefining English language teacher identity', in A. Swan, P. J. Aboshiha and A. Holliday (eds), *(En)Countering Native Speakerism: Global Perspectives*, Basingstoke: Palgrave MacMillan, pp. 59–74.

Tajfel, H., and J. C. Turner (1986), 'The social identity theory of intergroup behaviour', in S. Worchel and W. G. Austin (eds), *Psychology of Intergroup Relations* (2nd edn), Chicago: Nelson-Hall, pp. 7–24.

Thompson, E. P. (1963), *The Making of the English Working Class*, London: Penguin.

Thornbury, S. (1999), 'Window-dressing or cross-dressing in the EFL sub-culture', *Folio*, 5 (2): 15–17.

Tracy, K., and J. S. Robles (2013), *Everyday Talk: Building and Reflecting Identities* (2nd edn), New York: Guilford.

Trent, J. (2012), 'The discursive construction of teacher identity: The experience of NETs in Hong Kong schools', *TESOL Quarterly*, 46 (1): 104–26.

Trent, J. (2015), 'Towards a multifaceted, multidimensional framework for understanding teacher identity', in Y. L. Cheung, S. B. Said and K. Park (eds), *Advances and Current Trends in Language Teacher Identity Research*, New York: Routledge, pp. 44–58.

Tsui, A. B. M. (2003), *Understanding Expertise in Teaching: Case Studies of Second Language Teachers*, Cambridge: Cambridge University Press.

Tsui, A. B. M. (2007), 'Complexities of identity formation: A narrative inquiry of an EFL teacher', *TESOL Quarterly*, 41 (4): 657–80.

Valmori, L., and P. I. De Costa (2016), 'How do foreign language teachers maintain their proficiency? A grounded theory investigation', *System*, 57: 98–108.

Varghese, M. M., and B. Johnston (2007), 'Evangelical Christians and English language teaching', *TESOL Quarterly*, 41 (1): 5–31.

Varghese, M., M. Morgan, B. Johnston and K. A. Johnson (2005), 'Theorizing language teacher identity: Three perspectives and beyond', *Journal of Language, Identity, and Education*, 4 (1): 21–44.

Varghese, M. M., S. Motha, G. Park, J. Reeves and J. Trent (2016), 'In this issue', *TESOL Quarterly*, 50 (3): 545–71.

Vásquez, C. (2011), 'TESOL, teacher identity, and the need for "small story" research', *TESOL Quarterly*, 45 (3): 535–45.

Veblen, T. (2007 [1899]), *The Theory of the Leisure Class*, Oxford: Oxford University Press.

Verloop, N., J. van Driel and P. Meijer (2001), 'Teacher knowledge and the knowledge base of teaching', *International Journal of Educational Research*, 35(5): 441–61.

Waller, L., K. Wethers and P. I. De Costa (2016), 'A critical praxis: Narrowing the gap between identity, theory, and practice', *TESOL Journal*, 8 (1): 4–27.

Watson Todd, R., and P. Pojanapunya (2009), 'Implicit attitudes towards native and non-native speaker teachers', *System*, 37 (1): 23–33.

Weber, M. (1968 [1922]), *Economy and Society, Volumes 1 & 2*, Berkeley: University of California Press.

Weeks, J. (1975), 'Where Engels Feared to Tread', *Gay Left*, 1: 3–5.

Weeks, J. (2007), *The World We Have Won: The Remaking of Erotic and Intimate Life*, Abingdon: Routledge.

Wenger, E. (1998), *Communities of Practice: Learning, Meaning, and Identity*, Cambridge: Cambridge University Press.

West, C., and D. H. Zimmerman (1983), 'Small insults: A study of interruptions in cross-sex conversations between unacquainted persons', in B. Thorne, C. Kramarae and N. Hendey (eds), *Language, Gender and Society*, Rowley, MA: Newbury House, pp. 102–17.

Wetherall, M. (2010), 'The field of identity studies', in M. Wetherall and C. T. Mohanty (eds), *The Sage Handbook of Identities*, London: Sage, pp. 3–26.

Whitehead, A. N. (1929), *The Aims of Education and Other Essays*, New York: Free Press.

Widdicombe, S. (1998a), '"But you don't class yourself": The interactional management of category membership and non-membership', in C. Antaki and S. Widdicombe (eds), *Identities in Talk*, London: Sage, pp. 52–70.

Widdicombe, S. (1998b), 'Epilogue: Identity as an analysts' and a participants' resource', in C. Antaki and S. Widdicombe (eds), *Identities in Talk*, London: Sage, pp. 191–206.

Widdowson, H. (1995), 'Review of Fairclough's Discourse and Social Change', *Applied Linguistics*, 16 (4): 510–16.

Widdowson, H. (1998), 'The theory and practice of critical discourse analysis', *Applied Linguistics*, 19 (1): 136–51.

Wiggins, S., and J. Potter (2003), 'Attitudes and evaluative practices: Category vs. item and subjective vs. objective constructions in everyday food assessments', *British Journal of Social Psychology*, 42 (4): 513–31.

Wiggins, S., and J. Potter (2017), 'Discursive psychology', in C. Willig and W. Stainton- Rogers (eds), *The SAGE Handbook of Qualitative Research in Psychology* (2nd edn), London: Sage, pp. 93–109.

Williams, R. (1976), *Keywords: A Vocabulary of Culture and Society*, London: Fontana Press.

Williams, R. (2001 [1961]), 'Individuals and societies', in J. Higgins (ed.), *The Raymond Williams Reader*, Oxford: Blackwell, pp. 65–83.

Wodak, R. (1997), 'Critical discourse analysis and the study of doctor–patient interaction', in B. L. Gunnarsson, P. Linell and B. Nordberg (eds), *The Construction of Professional Discourse*, London: Longman, pp. 173–200.

Wodak, R. (2006), 'Medical discourse: Doctor–patient communication', in K. Brown (ed.), *Encyclopaedia of Language and Linguistics*, Amsterdam: Elsevier, pp. 681–8.

Wolff, D., and P. I. De Costa (2017), 'Expanding the language teacher identity landscape: An investigation of the emotions and strategies of a NNEST', *Modern Language Journal*, 101–S: 76–90.

Woods, D. (1996), *Teacher Cognition in Language Teaching: Beliefs, Decision Making and Classroom Practice*, Cambridge: Cambridge University Press.

Woods, D., and H. Çakır (2011), 'Two dimensions of teacher knowledge: The case of communicative language teaching', *System*, 39 (3): 381–90.

Wortham, S., K. Mortimer, K. Lee, E. Allard and K. D. White (2011), 'Interviews as interactional data', *Language in Society*, 40 (1): 39–50.

Wortham, S., and A. Reyes (2015), *Discourse Analysis Beyond the Speech Event*, Abingdon/New York: Routledge.

Wright, E. O. (2005), *Approaches to Class Analysis*, Cambridge: Cambridge University Press.

Wyatt, M. (2009), 'Practical knowledge growth in communicative language teaching', *TESL-EJ*, 13 (2): 1–23.

Xu, H. (2012), 'Imagined community falling apart: A case study on the transformation of professional identities of novice ESOL teachers in China', *TESOL Quarterly*, 46 (3): 568–78.

Yoshihara, R. (2013), 'Learning and teaching gender and sexuality issues in the EFL classroom: Where students and teachers stand', *The Language Teacher Online*, 37 (5): 8–11, available at <www.jalt-publications.org/tlt> (last accessed 27 July 2017).

Young, T. J., and S. Walsh (2010), 'Which English? Whose English? An investigation of "non-native" teachers' beliefs about target varieties', *Language, Culture and Curriculum*, 23 (2): 123–37.

Zacher, V., and C. Niemitz (2003), 'Why can a smile be heard? A new hypothesis on the evolution of sexual behaviour and voice', *Anthropologie*, XL1 (1–2): 93–8.

Zembylas, M. (2005), *Teaching with Emotion: A Postmodern Enactment*, Greenwich, CT: Information Age Publishing.

Zheng, X. (2017), 'Translingual identity as pedagogy: International teaching assistants of English in college composition classrooms', *The Modern Language Journal*, 101: 29–44.

Zhu, H., and W. Li (2016), '"Where are you really from?": Nationality and ethnicity talk (NET) in everyday interactions', *Applied Linguistics Review*, 7 (4): 449–70.

Zimmerman, D. H. (1998), 'Identity, context and interaction', in C. Antaki and S. Widdicombe (eds), *Identities in Talk*, London: Sage, pp. 87–107.

INDEX

Aboshiha, P., 79, 93
accent (native), 74
accountability
  conversation analysis, 59
  managerial, 69
  moral, 59–60
Action for ESOL, 103, 106, 107, 113, 114,
  116, 145
affinity identity (Gee), 157
agency, 9, 10, 11, 24, 26, 29, 30, 37, 39, 42,
  44, 46, 48, 51, 63, 64, 65, 66, 67, 69, 76,
  91, 110, 148, 150, 152, 153, 154, 155,
  163, 164
Agha, A., 12, 25, 52
Akbari, R., 16
alignment, 6, 54, 83, 96, 104, 105, 106, 107,
  110, 115, 130, 146
Alsup, J., 161, 162
American English, 77, 86–7, 91
Andrews, S., 38
Antaki, C., 26
Arabic, 89
assessments (in conversation analysis), 45,
  47, 48, 49, 50, 51
audit culture, 57
Auerbach, E., 104, 165
Australian teacher of English, 90
authenticity (and native and non-native
  speakers), 73, 74, 75, 76, 80, 84, 93
autobiographical narratives, 159
autoethnography, 160
axiological concerns in identity research,
  151, 154

BAK (Beliefs, Assumptions, Knowledge), 38
Baker, W., 81
Bamberg, M., 18, 33, 57, 58, 59, 60, 61, 62

Barkhuizen, G., 2, 3, 5, 32–3, 57, 58, 60, 142,
  143, 145, 146, 147, 149, 153, 160
Bartels, N., 38
Bateson, G., 124, 129, 131
Baynham, M., viii, 18, 19, 53, 54, 56, 58, 60,
  63, 65, 69, 96, 119
Bellamy, J., 152
Bendle, M. F. 14, 15, 16
Benesch, S., 155
Ben Said, S., 3, 159
Benson, P., 33, 145
Benwell, B., 12, 25
Bernstein, J. H., 153, 154
big stories, 57–8
Billig, M., 154, 156
Block, D., viii, 2, 4, 8, 10, 12, 15, 16, 17, 20,
  21, 95, 96, 98, 102, 120, 149, 158, 160–1,
  165, 166
Blommaert, J., 1, 12, 13, 28–9, 31, 32
Borg, S., 37, 57, 159, 160
Bourdieu, P., 6, 15, 18, 28–9, 73, 95, 98, 99,
  110, 125, 158
  Bourdieusian capital(s), 101, 110
  Bourdieusian doxa, 119
Braine, G., 72, 73, 74
Briggs, C., 117, 124, 137
British English, 77, 91
Britzman, D., 19, 20, 121, 129
Brubaker, R., 14, 15, 17, 18, 19, 116
Bruner, J., 57, 145
Buchholz, M. B., 156
Bucholtz, M., 30–1
Butler, J., 18, 120

Cain, W. C., 146
Callaghan, J., 53, 55, 56
Canagarajah, S., 5, 158